THE DIARIES OF THOMAS WILSON, D.D.

Also by C. L. S. Linnell

With A. F. Kersting: ENGLISH CATHEDRALS (Batsford)
With W. Harrod: SHELL GUIDE TO NORFOLK (Faber)
With S. J. Wearing: NORFOLK CHURCH MONUMENTS (Norman Adlard, Ipswich)
MONUMENTS OF ELY CATHEDRAL (Norman Adlard, Ipswich)
MONUMENTS OF SUFFOLK (Suffolk Institute of Archaeology)
SOME EAST ANGLIAN CLERGY (Faith Press)

DR THOMAS WILSON

From the print by T. Lawrence after the portrait by Wright of Derby

The Diaries of
THOMAS WILSON, D.D.
1731-37 and 1750

Son of Bishop Wilson of Sodor & Man

EDITED BY
C. L. S. LINNELL

LONDON
S·P·C·K
1964

First published in 1964
by S.P.C.K.
Holy Trinity Church
Marylebone Road
London N.W.1

Printed in Great Britain by
The Camelot Press Ltd., London and Southampton

Contents

Illustrations

Extract from the Pedigrees of Wilson and Patten [1]

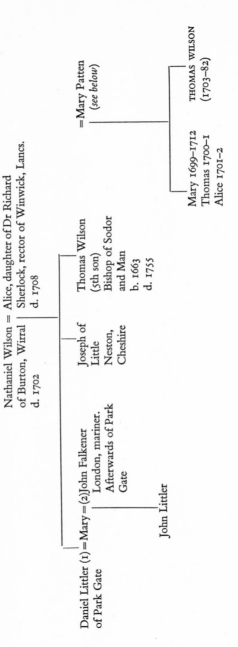

Nathaniel Wilson = Alice, daughter of Dr Richard
of Burton, Wirral | Sherlock, rector of Winwick, Lancs.
d. 1702 | d. 1708

Daniel Littler (1) = Mary = (2) John Falkener   Joseph of   Thomas Wilson
of Park Gate   London, mariner.   Little   (5th son)
    Afterwards of Park   Neston,   Bishop of Sodor
    Gate   Cheshire   and Man
           b. 1663
           d. 1755

John Littler

= Mary Patten
(see below)

Mary 1699–1712
Thomas 1700–1
Alice 1701–2

THOMAS WILSON
(1703–82)

[1] See John Keble, *Life and Works of Bishop Wilson* (Oxford, 1863), Vol. I, pp. 1–8.

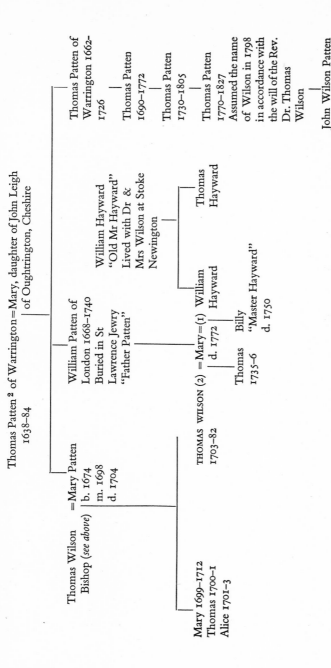

Thomas Patten [2] of Warrington=Mary, daughter of John Leigh
1638–84   of Oughtrington, Cheshire

Thomas Wilson   =Mary Patten   William Patten of   William Hayward   Thomas Patten of
Bishop *(see above)*   b. 1674   London 1668–1740   "Old Mr Hayward"   Warrington 1662–
                m. 1698   Buried in St   Lived with Dr &   1726
                d. 1704   Lawrence Jewry   Mrs Wilson at Stoke
                                         "Father Patten"   Newington   Thomas Patten
                                                                                         1690–1772

THOMAS WILSON (2) =Mary=(1) William   William   Thomas   Thomas Patten
1703–82   d. 1772 Hayward   Hayward   Hayward   1730–1805

                    Thomas   Billy   Thomas Patten
                    1735–6   "Master Hayward"   1770–1827
                             d. 1750   Assumed the name
                                                                                         of Wilson in 1798
Mary 1699–1712   in accordance with
Thomas 1700–1   the will of the Rev.
Alice 1701–3   Dr. Thomas
                                                                                         Wilson

                                                                                         John Wilson Patten

[2] For the descent of Thomas Patten from Richard Patten, brother of William—of Waynflete—Bishop of Winchester and founder
of Magdalen College, see Keble, op. cit., Vol. I, p. 224.

Introduction

Among the materials, preserved at Keble College, Oxford, which the Reverend John Keble assembled for his edition of the Life and Works of Thomas Wilson, Bishop of Sodor and Man, are two volumes of a Diary kept by the Bishop's son, Dr Thomas Wilson, Student of Christ Church, rector of St Stephen's, Walbrook, royal chaplain and prebendary of Westminster. The Diary, together with four volumes of Dr Wilson's correspondence, mainly between him and his friends John Leland and Philip Moore, had been supplied to John Keble by the Reverend H. Cruttwell of Bath, a son of the Reverend Clement Cruttwell who was the Bishop's first biographer, having produced an edition of his Life and Works, under the direction of Dr Wilson, in 1781. A new and enlarged edition, by the Reverend H. Stowell, the rector of Ballaugh, Isle of Man, had appeared in 1819.

For his book John Keble drew extensively on the four volumes of Dr Wilson's correspondence but made few references to the Diary as it was only indirectly concerned with the Bishop. Though only fragmentary, and covering barely a decade, it is concerned with what was the most interesting period of Dr Wilson's life and shows him to have been a shrewd observer of men and events.

Dr Wilson was a typical Whig clergyman of the period, but his father, though he passed the greater part of his life in the eighteenth century, is really a survival from an earlier age. Born in 1663, he is almost the contemporary of the Anglican Fathers of the seventeenth century and though consenting to the Revolution of 1688, there is much in him that was akin to the spirit of the Nonjurors. He "endured hardness" with unflinching courage which was the high quality of Laud. The standards he set in the spiritual life and in pastoral efficiency are reminiscent of Ken, and his devotional writings, especially his *Sacra Privata*, though now forgotten, long enjoyed a very wide circulation.

He was originally intended for the medical profession, and his son's shopping lists, which form interesting addenda to the last volume of the Diary, show that right up to the end of his life he was able to act as a physician of the body as well as of the soul to members of his flock, especially the poorest, among whom he was constantly resident. He was an early supporter of the S.P.C.K. and the S.P.G., was most active in the work for foreign missions, and drew up a scheme for the training of missionaries, and did much in his own diocese and elsewhere to promote the foundation of public libraries under the scheme established by Dr Bray.

Born at Burton in Wirral, a place which was afterwards visited by his son, Bishop Wilson was educated at Trinity College, Dublin. He was ordained deacon at Kildare Cathedral on St Peter's Day 1686, the same day the cathedral was consecrated, and priest three years later, on 20 October 1689 at Chester. After five years as assistant curate at Newchurch, near Winwick, Lancs., he was appointed chaplain to the ninth Earl of Derby at Knowsley, and in 1697 he was prevailed upon by the Earl to accept the remote and unrewarding see of Sodor and Man, which had been vacant ever since the death of Dr Baptiste Levinz in 1693.

"Forced to accept the Bishoprick of Man. Nov. 27. 1697. My Lord Derby even forced me to accept the Bishoprick" as he says repeatedly in his *Sacra Privata*. He was consecrated in the Chapel of the Savoy on 16 January 1697 by Archbishop Sharp of York, assisted by Bishop Stratford of Chester and Bishop Moore of Norwich. He was installed in St German's Cathedral on 16 April following, and as the see was a poor one Lord Derby offered him the living of Baddesworth, Yorks., *in commendam*; but he refused having set his face against pluralities and non-residence, a resolution which in after years he constantly urged his son to adopt. The year after his consecration he was married, on 27 October 1698, in the parish church of Winwick, Lancs., to Mary Patten of Warrington.

In its historical status and in its organization the see of Sodor and Man was in an exceptional position.[1] It was not until the Act of Revestment in 1765 that the Lordship of the Island was taken over by the Crown from the Duke of Atholl, the heir to the house of Stanley, Earls of Derby, who were Lords of Man. Before this the Church in the Isle was not bound by the English Acts of Parliament and the Bishop was free to rule it according to the ecclesiastical Law.

In 1704 at the annual synod of his clergy, Bishop Wilson promulgated Ten Constitutions which dealt with the duties of the clergy, church discipline, and education; and he set himself to enforce the discipline with a thoroughness which is reminiscent of Laud and of his most active coadjutor Bishop Wren, and with the result that the first twenty-five years in the see were turbulent ones.

Offenders were made to endure the full rigours of public penance. The Bishop proceeded against his own housekeeper, Catherine Crumbleholme, found guilty of the foul sin of fornication with a fellow servant, Zacharay Gaskill. She was sentenced to fourteen days imprisonment and made to stand at the crosses of the four market towns in the Island with a schedule of her crimes on her breast. Alice Cowley of Ballaugh and Isabel Gawne of Peel were imprisoned for thirty days and made to stand up in public in white sheets "for charming and sorcery". Slanderers were made to wear a bridle and prostitutes dragged through the sea after a boat. Some of those convicted, especially those sentenced to excommunication, which involved virtual outlawry, appealed to the Earl of Derby as Lord of the Isle—which brought the Bishop not infrequently into violent conflict with his patron.

But Bishop Wilson did not hesitate to attack the highest in the land. In 1721 Mrs Horne, the wife of the Governor of the island, was sentenced to do penance for slander, and in 1722 came the reverberating case of Archdeacon Horrobin who was suspended for heresy.

[1] For a short account of "The Church in the Isle of Man" see No. 13 in the *St Anthony's Hall Publications* by Anne Ashley for the Borthwick Institute of Historical Research.

3

The affair began three years before, in Advent 1719, when in a sermon preached in Castletown Chapel the archdeacon had declared himself a disciple of Bishop Hoadley in his opinion that the Gospels afforded no warrant for the existence of any visible Church authority. He followed this up with other sermons in which he impugned the doctrine of the Church as regards absolution and spoke of the Divinity of our Saviour as a point very much controverted in the Primitive Church, when, in the words of one witness, "it really appeared as if he would insinuate it to be a trivial controversy". The archdeacon was suspended, but his case became involved with that of Mrs Horne as he had admitted her to communion at the time she was under the Church's censure. Both cases were the subject of appeals to the Governor—which put the Governor in a rather peculiar position as judge, as his own wife was one of the appellants.

The result was that the Bishop and his two vicars-general were fined £90, and on their refusal to pay they were arrested and put in prison at Castle Rushen on St Peter's Day 1722. "St Peter's Day. See the Epistle," [2] wrote Bishop Wilson in his *Episcopalia*, and then adds, "I and my two Vicars-General were fined £90 and imprisoned in Castle Ryssin [*sic*] for censuring and refusing to take off the censures of certain offenders: which punishment and contempt I desire to receive from God as a means of humbling". The affair dragged on for another two years and ended with the submission of the archdeacon and the first half of Bishop Wilson's long episcopate came to an end with his refusal of the see of Exeter, which was offered him in compensation for all the trouble he had endured. The dampness of the prison had been particularly injurious to his health and so crippled his fingers that "he was constrained to write ever after with his whole hand grasping the pen".

From this time until his death in 1755 Bishop Wilson was constantly resident in the Isle of Man except for occasional visits to England which are recorded in his son's Diary; and during

[2] The account of St Peter's imprisonment, the Church praying for him, and his deliverance by the angel.

4

such visits he received the veneration of a large public, for his
reputation as a man of prayer and a devotional writer had
extended far beyond his own diocese. In the streets of London
crowds thronged him crying out "Bless me too, my Lord".
Queen Caroline, as we hear in the Diary, had a high opinion of
him as "an honest man" and said on his approach, "Here is a
Bishop who does not come for a translation", to which he replied,
"No, indeed, and please your Majesty, I will not leave my wife in
my old age because she is poor". In 1750 he was particularly
gratified to receive a message from Cardinal Fleury that "they
were the two oldest and the two poorest Bishops in Europe".

By then he was an almost incredible link with the past, and he
who was so much at one with the seventeenth-century piety of
Andrewes, Laud, and Ken lived long enough to see the revival of
personal religion in the early stages of the Evangelical and
Methodist Movement; and in 1749 he was made Honorary
President of the Reformed Section of the Moravian Church, a
dignity which he accepted gladly "because he was desirous of
doing everything for the brethren which lay in his power".

The last years of his episcopate were marked by the gradual
decay of the discipline he had done and endured so much to
enforce, but during this time he did what he could to eradicate the
evils of the contrabrand business—the running trade—the extent
of which is made abundantly clear in the Diary, and which he
denounced in a sermon at Kirk Michael on 1 July 1727 on the
perhaps not altogether inappropriate text, "At thy word I will
let down the net"; and in December 1733 he took advantage of a
sad occasion when six persons of Ramsey perished in the running
trade to instruct the rector of Kirk Bride, the vicar of Manghold,
the curate of Peel and the chaplain of Douglas "to lay before the
people out of the pulpit the great sin of the trade".

Bishop Wilson remained vigorous almost to the very last. He
died on 7 March 1755 in the ninety-third year of his age and in
the fifty-eighth of his consecration and not long after his son
had visited him. He was buried a few days later in the churchyard
at Kirk Michael in a coffin made from an elm which he himself

had planted, and his funeral sermon was preached by his son's lifelong friend Philip Moore from the text "The righteous shall be had in everlasting remembrance". It was "a hasty performance", as Moore afterwards told Dr Wilson, as he had only three days to write it in, "but it was neither preached nor heard without tears".

Dr Wilson had none of the heroism or the ruggedness of his father but the Diary reveals him as a generous and a kindly man. He was concerned to help people in trouble—an undergraduate who had got himself into difficulties, the necessitous widow of a dissenting minister—and the amount he expended in charity was very considerable. Though not qualified to give an intellectual lead in the burning theological issue of the day, the Deist controversy, he gave great help to those who were and did not hesitate to denounce, from the pulpit and in print, what he regarded as the worst evils of the age.

He was indefatigable in his work for the Church in the diocese of Sodor and Man during his father's lifetime and afterwards. Like his father he was greatly interested in the missionary cause at home and abroad and was a most active member of the S.P.C.K. and S.P.G. The real challenge of his life came when he was invited to join the Mission to Georgia, but one cannot really blame him for not taking it up as he was clearly not the man for the job.

"He was the heir of his father's virtues rather than his father's fortune," says his physician, and afterwards his protégé in the ministry, the Reverend Clement Cruttwell, piously; but what with his rich preferments, his private estate which accumulated over the years, and his wife's inheritance he was vastly more well to do than his father ever was and his numerous acts of charity, which are to his credit, did not make such heavy demands upon him.

He was the holder of more than one preferment in which he was non-resident for spacious periods, in spite of his father's disapproval and in spite of the strictures he himself makes in more than one place in the Diary on the evils of non-residence. He was careful to keep on the right side of "the great men", his devotion to good causes was not always disinterested, and his piety, scholarship, and ministry compare but poorly with his father in his devoted life of prayer and administrative energy.

It is true that he was often laid low by ill health, but he took good care of himself and, as is abundantly evident from the Diary, was inclined to be hypochondriacal and, as the years increased upon him, not a little cantankerous. He lived to be eighty-one but his life was one of cushioned ease—as he himself was prepared to admit—in comparison with that of his father. Perhaps a short account of his career will indicate more clearly the merits and the limitations of his life and work.

Born on 24 August 1703, he was the youngest of the Bishop's four children and the only one to survive infancy. His mother, Mary Patten, daughter of Thomas Patten of Warrington, was descended from Richard Patten, a younger brother of William Patten of Waynflete, the founder of Magdalen College. Towards the end of his life Dr Wilson undertook some researches into his Patten ancestry and wrote for assistance to his old friend Dr Wheeler, the Regius Professor of Divinity at Oxford, who replied that he had put such inquiries into the hands of a "young Master of Arts, Fellow of Magdalen College (whose name is Routh); one admirably skilled in English History, Biography and Anecdotes, and employed by the University in publishing some of Plato's *Dialogues*; if anything of recondite matter can be found he will search it out with eagerness". The result of these researches, though not included in the earlier editions of Bishop Wilson's Works, are given by John Keble.

Mrs Wilson died on 7 March 1704–5 when her son was barely two years old. The whole of his childhood and boyhood were spent at his father's house at Bishop's Court and the bishop seems to have made the Reverend Anthony Halsall, chaplain and schoolmaster at Douglas, tutor to his son. Another boy under Mr Halsall's tutelege, and who became his successor at Douglas, was Philip Moore who became Thomas Wilson's lifelong friend.

After a very short time at the Grammar School at Kirk Leatham in Yorkshire he was entered as a commoner at Christ Church where he matriculated on 20 April 1721. As an undergraduate he had to live under very straitened circumstances, for his father's resources were severely taxed at this time by the legal costs of the action he was taking against Archdeacon Horrobin. He seems to have run into debt, which gave rise to a number of stories which even as long as eighteen years later he found necessary to deny upon oath.

Several private letters of mine, wrote to my unkle and other of my friends about 18 years ago being industriously shewn and copies maliciously handed about, in order to blast my character (a Practice unheard of and as mean, as it is cruel and barbarous). And at present having no other way left to vindicate my Injured Character, do voluntarily make Oath before the Worshipful Thomas Pannwell Esq. one of his Majesty's Justices of the Peace for this County. Viz.

That the Crime which I ask pardon for, in these Letters, in terms I confess much too strong for the offence, was the exceeding by £30 a year or thereabouts, the small allowance given me by my father, which at that time I thought a Crime hardly to be forgiven. Tho' even that sum added to what my father allowed me was but barely sufficient to keep such company as became the son of a bishop.

I further declare that the illness of which I complain of in my letter aforesaid, was contracted by no Debaucheries (as this Person insinuates and gives out) but was occasioned by the fear of offending an Excellent Father who soon forgave me and with whom I have ever been on the best of terms.

And because the Person who shews these letters, takes upon himself the liberty of commenting upon and explaining the Meaning of the Expressions made use of in them and particularly of one—*of my returning or staying in Oxford with safety*—I do declare that *That* expression, as well as others of the same import, related to *The Small Pox* raging at that time in most of the colleges in Oxford and particularly at Christ Church, of which college I was then a member.

Kent. 11th. June 1740.   THO: WILSON.
Sworne before me
THO: PANNWELL.

On coming of age, however, he became possessed of the small estate left him by his mother, and a month before, on 8 July 1724, was elected a Student of Christ Church, in pursuance of the

Dean's recommendation in 1721, taking his B.A. on 17 December following. The Bishop visited his son once during the time he was an undergraduate, a visit also recorded by Thomas Hearne.

1723. Aug. 15. This morning the Right Reverend Dr. Thomas Wilson, Bishop of Man, called upon me. . . . He is a most excellent good natured pleasant man, and hath a son, a commoner of Christ Church, a pretty young gentleman.[3]

Shortly after taking his degree he visited his father in the Isle of Man and nearly lost his life by shipwreck, an adventure which was recorded by the Bishop in his *Sacra Privata*.

June 1st. 1725. My dear child coming to see me from Liverpool, was in tempest driven to the coast of Ireland, and there shipwrecked; but by the great mercy of God his life was saved, and this day (June 16) I have a letter under his own hand. The Lord make me truly thankful. The Master and he were left on board, the Master drowned and by the mercy of God *he* was saved. Blessed be God for this miraculous mercy.[4]

He was back again in Oxford the following year, took his M.A. on 16 December 1727 and two years later was made deacon by the Bishop of Oxford, Dr Potter, who seems to have held a high opinion of him and remained his very good friend and benefactor. Patronage which was of the greatest assistance to Wilson, especially after Dr Potter succeeded Dr Gibson of London as "the Whig Pope" and his unexpected elevation to the primacy on the death of Archbishop Wake in 1737.

Directly after his ordination Wilson returned to the Isle of Man, assisting his father at Ballough and acting as curate to his old tutor, Mr Halsall, at Douglas. This was evidently an experimental period and for the reasons he gave to Dr Stephen Hales of Teddington, an old friend of the family, and set out in the Diary for 4 October 1732, he soon decided that a ministry in his father's

---

[3] Hearne, *Collections* 1722–5 (Ox. Hist. Soc., 1907), pp. 127f.

[4] This incident is also recorded by Hearne, *Collections* 1725–8 (Ox. Hist. Soc., 1914), p. 282. "March 2. 1727. On Tuesday last called upon me Mr Wilson, Bach. of Arts of Ch. Ch. Son of Dr Wilson, Bishop of Man. He is lately come from that Island, where he has been detained a good while (about two years) which hindered him (he having been like to have been drowned) from coming to Oxford to determine last year, for which reason he determined this Lent."

diocese was not for him. He returned to England in September 1731 and was ordained priest by the Bishop of Oxford the following December. On the way he visited many of his mother's relations and was made particularly welcome by his uncle William Patten, whose daughter Mary had married William Hayward of Stoke Newington, whose death is recorded in the Diary and by whom she had one son, Billy, who died in 1750.

For just over two years he remained in Oxford, "living" as he said to Dr Hales "idly in a college". He pays visits to Stoke Newington, and in spite of the elaborate denial that there was anything between him and his widowed cousin their marriage seems to have been agreed upon by the time the Bishop visited England again in June 1733. They were married in the following February, his wife's father-in-law, old Mr Hayward, giving his consent "very freely", being "glad to live with us here" at Stoke Newington. This arrangement was convenient enough at first but did not prove successful in the end.

"God grant that I may be ever thankful and sensible of the blessing of so excellent a wife", he wrote on his wedding day. It seems to have been a very happy marriage, clouded only by the death of their son, and only child, when little more than a year old, and not long after he himself had recovered from an attack of smallpox which occasioned a break of three months in the Diary. "By a letter from my daughter in law", wrote Bishop Wilson on 28 April 1736, "I have an account of my son's recovery from the Small Pox, for which I cannot be sufficiently thankful." The little boy died on 7 May following. He never seems to have been a healthy child but the Diary gives touching evidence how precious he was to his parents, and the pathetic lines "On the Death of a Child" on the fly-leaf of the Diary, are the only example of Thomas Wilson's abilities as a poet.

Stoke Newington was a good place to be and on the spot "when anything dropps", as he put it in the Diary more than once. He decided to settle in London and embarked upon a pursuit of preferment which must appear to modern readers as quite shameless. He had only to hear that the holder of some rich

city living was ill, or even only indisposed, or likely to be preferred elsewhere and he was off doing the best he could to secure it
for himself; and taking into account that it was necessary for a
young man to keep himself in the public eye and that it was
impossible to get anywhere in any profession without the help
of a patron, Thomas Wilson really does seem to have overdone it
a little. Now and again some of the great men to whom he was
always applying were "coole". It is difficult not to believe that
Queen Caroline and the Bishop of London became a little weary
of his repeated demands and on one occasion he had to be told
that his interests would be better served if he did not go to Court
quite so often. It was a long and weary business, attended by many
disappointments, but in the end he did very well for himself, and
the first volume of the Diary ends with his institution to the
combined parishes of St Stephen's, Walbrook, and St Bennett's,
Sherehogg, a few months after he had been appointed a royal
chaplain.

He moved to his parsonage house in Walbrook. In 1739 he
proceeded doctor of divinity. He continued to act, as he had done
in former years, as his father's commissary in an unofficial
capacity and agent for receiving subscriptions for the clergy
widows in the diocese of Man; and in 1741 he was able to perform
a very great service at the time of famine and pestilence in the
Isle by obtaining a supply of corn, to be exported from Liverpool
and Whitehaven. For this he petitioned the King himself, and the
ships arrived at Douglas just in time to save many of the in-
habitants from starvation.

In April 1743 came his last and most notable preferment in his
appointment by the King to a prebendal stall at Westminster,[5]
and at the same time he was made Sub-Almoner to His Majesty
on the appointment of the Almoner, the Bishop of Salisbury.

On his first coming to London in 1731 Bishop Wilson had

[5] "1 Dec. 1743. This day the Reverend Dr Thomas Wilson was by virtue of his
Majesty's Grant and Mandamus installed one of the Prebendaries of this collegiate
Church, in the room of Dr Matthew Hutton promoted to the Bishopric of
Bangor" (Chapter Minutes).

commended his son to Auditor Harley and expressed the hope that his son would not be "tempted to hunt for preferment, to leave the flock he had taken charge of, nor without absolute necessity accept a plurality, which he knows I have ever been averse to". Dr Wilson did all these things and was to do them, but the Bishop expressed himself "both surprised and pleased with the unexpected favours conferred by the King and the Bishop of Salisbury". He wrote to the King in thanks for "so distinguishing a favour—may the King of Kings bless his Majesty with all the graces and virtues which are necessary for so high a station and for his eternal happiness". This letter was enclosed with one to Dr Wilson reminding him that such favours should be received with fear "lest you should be tempted to dishonour God by his own gifts. This was the case of the wisest and the greatest of men, whose history and fall was part of this day's service of the Church." (1 Kings 10—11.)

Later in the same year (1743) Dr Wilson visited his father, not having seen him since 1735. By the early autumn he was back in London. He moved from his house in Walbrook to Westminster and for the next few years he is heavily engaged in his duties at his parish church, where he was a frequent preacher, at Court and in Chapter business.

The year 1750 is especially clear, being covered by the second volume of the Diary. In the summer of that year, leaving his wife at Tunbridge Wells, he made another visit to his father which he believed would be the last time they would meet as the Bishop was beginning to fail. They were to meet again, however, when Dr Wilson paid another visit to the Isle of Man shortly before the Bishop's death.

From the Diary for 1750, and from the correspondence over the next few years with John Leland, it is apparent that Dr Wilson is ageing. Both he and his wife were often unwell and visits to Bath and to Tunbridge Wells became more and more necessary, and in 1755 when touring in Lancashire he suffered a bad fall from his horse which left him an invalid for months. It is also apparent that he was becoming somewhat eccentric, irritable and truculent.

Relations between him and his fellow prebendary, and Dr Johnson's friend and schoolfellow, Dr John Taylor, were anything but cordial.[6] His letters to Leland became more and more concerned with the evils of the times, this "gaudy, gaping, staring, thoughtless nation". But all these things were to be nothing in comparison with the tremendous and ringing row that blew up between him and the headmaster of Westminster School, Dr Markham, in 1758.

On his first becoming prebendary Dr Wilson lived in a house in the Little Cloisters, but in 1747 he "purchased Mrs French's house adjoining the Old Dormitory and also the Lord Bishop of Norwich's interest in the two houses in Dean's Yard fronting it".[7] with the idea of repairing the former and taking down the latter two houses to make a garden. But in 1756 Dr Markham came forward with a scheme for the demolition of this property for the purpose of enlarging Dean's Yard, making it a suitable playground for the boys and with the idea of building a new terrace which would serve as boarding-houses, thus bringing the school together in one place. The plan was presented to the Dean and Chapter on 28 May 1756 and received their approval with one dissentient, "I dissent to this. THO: WILSON" being scored heavily into the margin of the Chapter Book.[8]

Dr Wilson's fury knew no bounds and he gave vent to his feelings in *A Review of the Project of Building a New Square at Westminster. Said to be for the Use of Westminster School* printed in 1757. The pamphlet began by stating his case coherently but

[6] Dr Wilson and Dr Taylor collided over the matter of the Dean and Chapter's control of the Fish Market, the new Westminster Bridge, and over the perennial dispute concerning dilapidations. On 27 May 1749 Dr Taylor desired the Dean and Chapter's leave to apply in the name of the Court of Chancery concerning the dilapidations of the Chapel in the Broadway, Westminster, alleging that the Rev. Dr Wilson refused to pay anything for them—leave given to apply to the Chancery for Relief. (Chapter Minutes.)

In after years Dr Taylor was to succeed Dr Wilson in the curacy of St Margaret's, Westminster (1784-8). Dr Taylor was non-resident for even longer periods than Dr Wilson, spending most of his time at Ashbourne in Derbyshire, where he became a celebrated breeder of cattle. As Johnson said, "His talk is of bullocks".

[7] Chapter Minutes, 12 Dec. 1747.   [8] Chapter Minutes, 28 May 1756.

ends in a string of disjointed invective which suggests that he was almost apoplectic with rage.[9]

If we do our best to contrive *Immorality* and *Injustice* and, by the Dint of Practice *Inculcate Corruption* and a Love of DESPOTISM into our very boys at School—they will learn *there*, when they read the MAXIMS AND MANNERS of Antiquity, to despise HEROES and PHILOSOPHERS as so many MADMEN.

It was doubtless very annoying for him to be turned out of his house, on which he had spent a good deal of money, but one of the objections he made to the boarding-house scheme was a little curious. "That being thus collected they would find it easier to *combine*. And being once combined no *Porter* or *Gate Keeper* would dare to withstand them; and, when they sallied out they would bring *Terror* into the whole neighbourhood."

Dr Wilson went to law with Dr Markham over this affair [10] but he lost and the scheme went through [11] and the Terrace was built (on the site at present occupied by Church House) and Dr Wilson went to live at No. 6, Little Cloisters, the fine house built by Dr Busby which was destroyed by bombs in the late war. It had been let to the Moravian minister and evangelist, Nickolaus Ludwig Graf von Zinzendorf, who lived in England from 1749 until 1755, the Moravian Episcopal Church having been recognized by Act of Parliament in 1749.

In 1753 the Chapter appointed Dr Wilson curate of St Margaret's, Westminster,[12] where he was a fairly frequent preacher,

[9] A copy of Dr Wilson's *Review* in the possession of Mr L. E. Tanner has many, and even more furious, comments in the margin in the hand of the author himself. One of them is as follows: "Dr Wilson under Colour of Law has been robbed of his house in Dean's Yard and has lost by this Job near £2500. Such instance of Cruelty, Bribery, Lying and Corruption can be given before an Impartial Assembly in a country which boasts of its Liberty and Property."

[10] "17. April 1758. Ordered that the Registrar, Mr Gell, do attend the Trial in Ejectment between Dr Markham and Dr Thos. Wilson, with the Plan of Dean's Yard intended to be a Square" (Chapter Minutes.)

[11] "They have pulled down my house which cost me £2500 and have allowed me but £620 which was spent in the Law Suit I had with the Vile Projectors, who have sold the Jobb to Builders, who are to do nothing for the pretended good of Westminster School" (Dr Wilson to John Leland, 28 Nov. 1759).

[12] "26th. May 1763. Dr Wilson was made curate of St Margaret's, Westminster, in the room of Dr Kenrick, deceased" (Chapter Minutes).

and in 1764 he appears as the vigorous defender of his pulpit against the devotees of Enthusiasm, especially against the famous Evangelical divine, William Romaine,[13] lecturer at St George's, Hanover Square, and from 1768 incumbent of St Anne's, Blackfriars.

Dr Wilson's political views became more radical as the years advanced. He was the friend and correspondent of John Wilkes, whom he actually made his churchwarden at St Margaret's in 1759. Just before Mr Wilkes's churchwardenship extensive repairs and alterations took place in the church and just after it these became the subject of a reverberating lawsuit.

In 1757 a Parliamentary Committee was appointed for inspecting St Margaret's, Westminster, and £4000 was voted for its repairing and beautifying. The work commenced in the following year and included the reconstruction of the east end of the church in the form of a gothic apse to the designs of Kenton Couse who also designed the western gallery.[14] While these alterations were going on the parish had a stroke of luck. In 1758 the church-wardens were told of some magnificent early sixteenth-century Flemish glass which had been made by order of the Magistrates of Dort as a present to Henry VII for Henry VII's Chapel at Westminster. The King died before it was completed, but it came into the possession of the abbot of Waltham and in 1540 the last abbot, Robert Fuller, had it removed to a private chapel at New Hall in Wiltshire. New Hall eventually came into the possession of General Monck and John Olimus, who purchased the estate from him and pulled down the chapel and the glass was stored in boxes. The churchwardens were able to acquire

[13] "2. Feb. 1764. The Chapter Clerk ordered to write to Mr Romaine to acquaint him in the name of the Dean and Chapter that he is forbidden to preach or otherwise to officiate in the New Way Chappel in the parish of St Margaret's having no lycense from their commissary or consent of the Minister of the Parish" (Chapter Minutes).

[14] This arrangement lasted until 1799 when further alterations were carried out at St Margaret's by S. P. Cockerell (Colvin, *Biographical Dictionary of British Architects*, pp. 149, 155). St Margaret's was again extensively restored in 1876 during the incumbency of Dean Farrar (Charles Smyth. *Church and Parish* (1955), pp. 202ff.

it for £400. It was duly installed in the east window at St Margaret's and beneath it a bas relief, by Mr Alkin of St Ann's, Westminster, representing *Our Saviour at Emmaus* after the picture by Titian.[15]

In the window are figures of Henry VII and his queen, but the main subject is the Crucifixion and for this reason it became, in 1761, the matter of a lawsuit (Peirson *v.* Gell) on the grounds of idolatry. The case dragged on for the better part of a year but the defendants won and the window was retained. It was due in no small measure to the efforts of Dr Wilson that the defence was successful and the window remains to this day, perhaps the most satisfactory memorial of his incumbency at St Margaret's.

All these alterations and embellishments were described in *The Ornaments of Churches with a View to the late Decoration of St Margaret's, Westminster* by William Hole, with an introduction by Dr Wilson, published in 1761; and as regards idolatry Dr Wilson wrote:

I should prefer large historical paintings to single figures; and this the more willingly, because Adoration has at no time, nor in any place, been paid to them. Indeed it is scarcely possible to conceive, when a large number of objects are before the eye in one picture, that a particular one can be selected for this purpose. And yet it must be done, unless we can suppose men ridiculous enough to adore the Thieves that were crucified with our Saviour, or the Guards that attended.

In 1764 there was some talk of Dr Wilson's succeeding Dr Zacharay Pearce as Dean of Westminster, the Duke of Northumberland promising to further his interests as far as possible "as I know of no person so deserving of that dignity, or who would fill that situation with more credit to himself or advantage to his Majesty's service". But Dr Pearce did not retire until 1768—the first instance of the retirement of a dean in the long history of the abbey—and was succeeded by Dr John Thomas.

[15] Smyth, op. cit., pp. 197, 253. K. A. Esdaile, "Changes at St Margaret's, Westminster in 1761", in *Church Quarterly Review* (July–Sept. 1950), pp. 230–44.

Until 1760 Dr Wilson had been fairly frequent in keeping his periods of residence, but after that date his absences became more frequent and extensive and in 1766, even taking into account his prolonged ill health, this became a matter for comment. "I must desire you not to think of leaving to me the business of providing a Prebendary to attend the services in the Abbey during your absence," wrote Dr Pearce. "If you do not provide Dr Ballard, Dr Blair or Dr Fowler (if in town) to assist you, it will be a heavy disgrace to us if no Prebendary is to be seen for days together." [16]

Dr Wilson kept his house in the Little Cloisters, but after the death of Mrs Wilson in 1772 he found it very lonely and forlorn and he became continuously non-resident, making his permanent home at Alfred House, Bath.

During the last decade of his life he was more or less an invalid the whole of the time, but these last years were particularly enlivened by his friendship with the republican blue-stocking, Mrs Catherine Macaulay the historian, which lasted until Mrs Macaulay's second marriage to William Graham in 1778. Dr Wilson's resentment was reminiscent of Johnson's on Mrs Thrale's marriage to Gabriel Piozzi a few years later.

There was of course endless gossip about this love-affair of his dotage and he became a laughing-stock though it was hardly fair of Horace Walpole to describe him as "that dirty disappointed

---

[16] Prebendaries were fined 13s. 4d. for every day of absence during their period of residence except when "under the afflicting hand of God". In Sept. 1768 Dr Wilson was fined £19 6s. 8d. for 29 days absence. On 11 May he was fined £20 for the month of May.

The easy-going existence of such dignitaries as Dr Wilson and Dr Taylor remind one of the words of Crabbe in "The Church" in his description of *The Borough*:

> "What is a Church?"—"A flock," our vicar cries,
> "Whom bishops govern and whom priests advise:
> Wherein are various states and due degrees,
> The bench for honour, and the stall for ease;
> That ease be mine, which, after all his cares,
> The pious, peaceful prebendary shares."

17

hunter of a mitre".[17] It was at that time that Mrs Macaulay became renowned for her somewhat startling appearance. Wilkes describes her unkindly as "rotten as an old Catherine Pear" but Johnson said that it was better that "she should redden her own cheeks than blacken other people's characters". She had her own establishment in St James's Parade at Bath but Dr Wilson put Alfred House at her disposal—"Our little Tusculum", as he called it after the manner of Mrs Blimber, "which is honoured with the visits of all the Literary Persons who frequent this place; and forreigners particularly, for she is known and admired abroad

[17] To the Rev. Wm. Mason, Mar. 1778. (Toynbee, x, 207.)
There are a number of exceedingly ribald publications, as for instance a satire *The Female Patriot. An Epistle from C-t-e M-c-y to the Rev. Dr. W-l-n on her Marriage 1779*, and in *A Remarkable Moving Letter* (1779) are the lines:

> The Muse that shudders at that omened night
> When dreams and wild desires suggested flight:
> King *Alfred*'s head in frown the vision bore
> (Which I cast off, you stuck upon the door)
> A second spectre rose of skin and bones,
> Naked and Pale, and pois'd two dreadful stones.
> *St. Stephen Walbrook* was his ghastly name,
> Both grinned, both scor'd and shook my widow'd frame.
> When, from a Cloud prolific fancy drew
> Astride my *Quarto* Volumes Cupid flew:
> Gr-h-m was perch'd behind, and in his hand
> A Portly Syringe stood, or seem'd to stand:
> At sight of darts and squirts the ghastly pair
> Yell'd and dissolv'd into the Midnight air.
> Such were the portents of my love and fate
> And climateric widows cannot wait.
> I lose, forgetful of the storm that frown'd,
> Of *Alfred House*, of 17,000 £.
>
> .   .   .
>
> So shall no wily patriotic knave
> Bring thy white wig with sorrow to the grave,
> Gr-h-m and I shall watch our Patron still
> Soothe his departing hour and make his will,
> Then bear his sainted corse to *Walbrook*'s shrine
> And stick it in the nich that once was mine.

The case of Mrs Macaulay was also the subject of a successful farce first performed at the Haymarket on 17 July 1779 and called *A Widow or No Widow* by Richard Paul Jodrell, one of the Johnsonian circle and the last surviving member of the Essex Head Club.

more than at home". With increasing garrulity he writes to his old friend Philip Moore about "the *great* Mrs Macaulay—I talk of her to everybody in raptures. The brilliancy of her eyes is gone in a great measure, but her mind is as elevated as ever." "My *great* woman—the *first* woman in Europe for Virtues and Shining Literary Abilities." And so on until at last on 30 January 1799

To the great surprise of the world Mrs Macaulay without giving me the slightest notice at the age of 52 married a YOUNG SCOTCH LOON of 21 whom she had not seen for about a month before the fatal knot was tied. A mate to an East India Ship, without clothes to his back. She left this place the beginning of October on pretence of the health of her sister at Leicester whose Husband keeps a mad house, and there she is like to remain for I will never let her come to Alfred House. . . . It is a most beggarly Family in Edinburgh. How are the mighty fallen! The News Papers have been very free with my character. Those that know me, and the better part of mankind, and every person in this place are all of my side and if she had come here I could not have prevented her from being mobbed, for her ingratitude to me. I took her into my protection upon her Publick Character, and it could not be for any other motive. Whether she will exercise her Talents any more is impossible to tell. The world says I have spoilt her by Indulgence and so I have, but let that Pass. It gave me a shock at first, but I thank God it is over. . . . Sir Richard Brooke and his family are just returned to Neston and will I believe marry no more after the loss of his excellent lady and I am sure it will be the better for him, for the women are all gone stark staring MADD and when I see such a woman as Mrs Macaulay make one of the number, with the finest tongue and greatest mental faculties, what must we think? We must call it EPIDEMICAL.

Dr Wilson remained on good terms with his parishioners at St Stephen's, Walbrook, and St Bennett's, Sherehogg, in spite of the fact that for some years his appearances among them had been only occasional. In 1766 he presented to St Stephen's the large painting of the Burial of St Stephen by Benjamin West which was exhibited at the Royal Academy that year.[18]

[18] "1776. April 10th. Mr Lynn having reported to the Vestry that the painting given by Dr Wilson to the parish was ready and would be delivered in a few weeks it being necessary to brick up the large window at the east end of the chancel in order to fix the picture." It is curious that there is no note of thanks or recognition of this gift, which cost £700, in the Vestry Minutes.
On 2 March 1814 the thanks of the Vestry were conveyed to Benjamin West, R.A., for cleaning and varnishing the picture over the altar of St Stephen's, Walbrook.

In 1778, however, relations became a little strained after he erected in a recess in the chancel of St Stephen's, Walbrook, a white marble statue, by J. F. Moore, representing Mrs Macaulay in the character of *History*, pen in hand and leaning against a pedestal with her arm resting upon the four volumes of her *History of England*. On one side of the pedestal were engraved the words: "Government is a power delegated for the happiness of mankind when conducted by Wisdom, Justice and Mercy" and on the other the inscription: "Erected by Thomas Wilson D.D. Rector of this Parish as a testimony of the high esteem he bears to the Distinguished Merit of his friend Catherine Macaulay. A.D. MDCCLXXVII."

This was unveiled on 8 September 1778 but the Vestry took counsel's opinion and threatened their rector with legal action if he did not remove the statue forthwith. The affair dragged on for some months [19] but eventually when the statue was removed Dr Wilson did not mind as Mrs Macaulay had fallen from grace.

Dr Wilson was extremely generous to the parishes of which he was the incumbent. "The picture I made a present of to St Stephen's, Walbrook," he writes to Philip Moore, "is greatly admired, which draws Crowds of people of a Sunday and I take care of having an excellent preacher—I am going to erect a

[19] The entries in the vestry book are as follows:

"26 November 1777. Dr Wilson having erected a monument to the memory of Mrs Catherine Macaulay (now living) without a Licence or Faculty from the Ordinary. . . . The Churchwardens took the opinion of Dr Wynne of Doctors Commons to enquire whether the site occupied by the monument formed part of the Rector's freehold. Dr Wynne pronounced this not to be the case and Dr Wilson was ordered to remove the statue before December 19th next 'Mrs Macaulay never having been an inhabitant of the parish'."

"24 December 1777. Nothing having been done the Vestry informed Dr Wilson that unless the statue was removed within a month a suit would be commenced against him."

"17 July 1778 the Vestry Clerk was ordered to write to Mr Moore the statuary to know whether he had received orders from Dr Wilson or any person on his behalf to remove the statue of Mrs Macaulay from out of the Church."

"12 August 1778 it was ordered that freedom be given to Dr Wilson or to whom he may appoint to remove the statue of Mrs Macaulay from out of the Church."

handsome portico at my expense to the entrance of St Margaret's, Westminster,[20] which will cost more than I ever received from that Preferment, and I have laid out more upon the Rectory and Glebe Houses at Walbrook than would have purchased the perpetual Advowson of a much better living—And tho' I shall die rich, it is not accumulated from Church Livings." He also expended considerable amounts upon church buildings in the Isle of Man, and in 1776 entirely rebuilt the chancel at Kirk Michael, where his father was buried, the impropriate tithes of which parish he purchased from the Duke of Atholl for the benefit of the widows and orphans of the Manx clergy.

Philip Moore kept him in touch with events in his father's old diocese and he was on excellent terms with his father's successor in the see of Man, Bishop Hildersley. Bishop Hildersley, like his predecessor, was constantly resident in the Isle and continued Bishop Wilson's work with vigour. He completed the translations of the Bible and the Prayer Book into Manx. Though Dr Wilson gave great encouragement to this work, and persuaded the S.P.C.K. to take an interest in it, one cannot but agree with him when he wrote to Philip Moore on 26 January 1773, shortly after Bishop Hildersley's death, saying that he believed that the money left by his father for this project, and augmented by himself, would "have been better employed in the augmentation of poor Vicarages and the Schools. The Manks is a dead language and the books will hardly be wanted 20 or 30 years hence" and, by the time John Keble wrote, "the scanty prevalence and gradual extinction of the language have nearly reduced the book to a mere archaeological curiosity".

Bishop Hildersley was succeeded by Bishop Richmond, a very portly but grievously slack bishop whose negligence undid much of the devoted work of his predecessors. Dr Wilson's letters become increasingly full of denunciations of *The Fat Man*, "the great Pontiff", who was frequently in Bath but "to take care of his body only". It would appear that this was the reason why a good many people went to Bath, including Dr Wilson himself,

[20] The present portico was erected as a memorial to Dean Farrar.

but the Doctor was grievously offended when *The Fat Man* took no notice of him at all one day in the Pump Room "tho' I know he askt who I was". "I leave you to judge who behaved most like a gentleman." Such remarks were fully reciprocated by Moore, who gave his old friend a fearful account of Bishop Richmond's last illness and death in 1780. "Last winter he was tap'd in four different parts of the Abdomen—but not above a quart of any Liquid obtained—it was all converted into a thick Gelatinous Matter like Jelly. He had a miserable time of it for years with Gout, Asthma and Dropsy. When stripped for the operation no man on earth would take him for a human creature but for his face, he was such a monstrous figure of Fat and Blubber—like a Whale."

"I never heard where they *earthed* the Bishop," wrote Wilson in reply. "Not one word of him in the News, but that he died such a day. He lived here in a strange voluptuous manner caring for nothing but his Gutts."

Philip Moore's letters were even more garrulous than those of his old friend and they were always awaited with great eagerness at Alfred House. "*The Congé d'Elire* to a mitre in the Moon", he wrote after Wilson playfully suggested that he would be a suitable successor to Bishop Richmond, "is accepted with proper deference and respect to my generous Patron. Your choice could not have fallen on a better man, for age, incapacity and other imbecilityes of Mind and Body for the Dignity and Station. I have no objection, not the least *Nolo* etc. as I begin to find many symptoms of Lightness and Vacuity *in perecranio* that requires the Ballast of the *Pilei Bicipitis* to keep it steady. Which think ye is the greatest Monster? Pope Cerberus with three heads to one Body, or the Fool that wears these high crowned Grenadier's Caps on one Crazy Noddle?"

Bishop Richmond was succeeded by Bishop Mason. "I have heard a very good account of him", wrote Dr Wilson, "and the poor Church of Man never stood more in need of a Worthy Prelate. It was once, you know, made a sinecure of before my Father came to be Bishop there and so may be again for what I can tell." Dr Wilson's words were nearly prophetic and it was not until the active episcopate of William Ward, 1828–38, that the see was saved from extinction.

It is clear from his correspondence that Dr Wilson had long considered a biography of his father and a complete edition of his Works. It was not, however, until the last decade of his life that the idea began to take shape and by then he was too old and ill to undertake it unaided. He therefore put all his father's papers into the hands of his friend and physician, Clement Cruttwell, and so impressed was Mr Cruttwell at the Bishop's piety and example that his work was instrumental in making him decide to change his profession and become a clergyman. Dr Wilson wrote to several bishops commending his friend and protégé, with the result that Cruttwell was ordained by the Bishop of Bath and Wells.

The work proceeded apace. Dr Wilson lived long enough to see it complete and was much gratified to receive many appreciations of the book when it was published, especially one from the Convocation of the Church of Man. His old friend Philip Moore was particularly enthusiastic. "Hark ye friend Clement," he wrote to Mr Cruttwell, "It has just come into my mind that a very good parallel might be drawn between you and St Luke." Mr Cruttwell was indeed the beloved physician turned historian and biographer, but Dr Wilson would have been the first to admit that he would not be so happily cast in the role of St Paul.

During the last few months of his life Dr Wilson became very feeble and almost entirely bedridden. But he was still able to perform acts of charity, one of the last recorded of which is particularly happy. On hearing of a clergyman in Bath who was sick, very poor and with a large family, he gave £50 to Mr Cruttwell asking him "to give it to the sufferer in the most delicate way, as from an unknown person". Cruttwell said, "I will call upon him early in the morning". "You will oblige me, Sir," said Dr Wilson, "by calling directly. Think, Sir, of what importance one good night's rest may be to that poor man."

He died at Alfred House on 15 April 1784. His body was

brought to London with a procession of mourning coaches and 200 flambeaux and buried in great pomp in St Stephen's, Walbrook, on the 27 following amid a vast concourse of parishioners and friends.[21]

Concerning the Diary itself, the first volume covers the period September 1731 to December 1737, from the time of his coming into England at the close of his diaconate to his institution to the rectory of St Stephen's, Walbrook.

From the time of his arrival in England in the middle of

[21] *Gentleman's Magazine* for 27 April 1784, Vol. I, p. 379. His obituary notice was as follows (Vol. I, p. 317).

"His tenacity in the causes he espoused was no less conspicuous in his opposition to the building of the intended square at Westminster, than in his warm patronage of the celebrated female historian, to whom, while living, he erected a statue in his Church, which was boarded up until her death by authority of the Spiritual Court; and he continued his friendship and attachment to her 'till she forfeited it by entering into a matrimonial engagement against his consent. By deed of gift in his lifetime he made over to her his house at Bath, with furniture and library with £15,000. Also reported that he left £20,000 to John Wilkes and £500 to his Clerk, Mr Lind, at Walbrook. For these reports we do not vouch."

This account was later modified as follows (Vol. I, p. 395).

"Upon consulting the will of the late Dr Wilson we find that the legacy to Mr Wilkes was only £50 and a gold ring to Miss Wilkes £50. To his clerk, Lind, only directions to bury him, as Mrs Wilson was buried, in his Church at Walbrook, where he had in his lifetime put up a tablet undated and where he was buried April 27 1784 in great funeral pomp. The bulk of his fortune, and his estates in Cheshire, are left to his next of kin and executors Macklin and Patten, of which the latter, of the same family as Bishop Wainfleet, alias Patten, has in compliance with his will taken his name and arms."

Dr Wilson's memorial, also by J. F. Moore, still remains in St Stephen's, Walbrook, in the south aisle behind the pulpit. The inscriptions are as follows:

Sacred to the Memory of	To the Memory of
MRS MARY WILSON	THOMAS WILSON D.D.
The beloved and much	A Citizen of London
Lamented wife of	Rector of this Parish
THOMAS WILSON D.D.	Upwards of 46 years.
She died the 4th of	He died April 15 A.D. 1784
November 1772	Aged 80.
Aged 79	Only son of THO: WILSON
In the 40th year of	Late Lord Bishop of
Their Happy Marriage.	Sodor and Man.

September until the end of October he visits relations in Cheshire and Lancashire. By the beginning of November he is in London visiting his uncle William Patten and his cousins, the Haywards, at Stoke Newington. By the middle of December he has arrived in Oxford in time for the Bishop's Advent ordination on Sunday 19 December 1731.

From then until July 1733 he is in Oxford the whole of the time and we get another account of many of the same people and events, though from another point of view, recorded by Thomas Hearne in the last years of his life. During this time Thomas Wilson became friendly with the Wesleys and was evidently on the fringe of the Holy Club, though it becomes apparent that he was increasingly critical of Methodism, like Mr Wildair, the vicar of St Aldate's, for whom John Wesley and Thomas Wilson often officiated, who was at first attracted but eventually became a severe critic of the movement.

During the time he is in Oxford he makes several visits to Stoke Newington, which become more protracted as his affair with his cousin, "dear Molly", proceeds. Towards the end of July 1733 Molly and her brother visit him in Oxford and they go to Encaenia, hear a performance by Handel and an "excellent sermon" by the future Archbishop of Canterbury, Dr Secker. Unfortunately, though, there appears to have been a tiff between him and "dear Molly" at this time. His "vexation" made him "very ill" and occasioned a break in the Diary of nearly three months. By the middle of October, however, this had blown over and arrangements go forward for their marriage which took place on 4 February 1733–4. It will be noticed that the expenses for this were very considerable, including as much as £9 6s. for "a dinner for Molly's friends" and the services of "a poet" were required as well as those of the sexton, clerk, and ringers.

Up to this time Thomas Wilson enters his various expenses in the margin but from now on he discontinues this practice, except on occasions, and for the rest of the period covered by the book it is not so much a day-to-day diary as a journal written up subsequently and in which he records his impressions of the events of the day and of the people he meets. He is an excellent reporter, and in his company we can sit in on meetings of the S.P.C.K., attend the Court of George II and the levees of Sir Robert Walpole, listen to the conversation round the Master of the Rolls, Sir Joseph Jekyl's, table and in the summer of 1736 accompany Mr and Mrs Wilson to Tunbridge Wells for the season.

One is brought into contact with the great and famous men and women of the age—Queen Caroline of Anspach, Lady Walpole, who is seen to be not altogether eclipsed by Sir Robert's mistress, Maria Skerrett—and there are lively portraits of Miss Skerrett herself and of the Prime Minister.

The fear of Jacobitism is still very real and strong enough to disturb even the most secure and prosperous of Whigs, as for instance at the time of the Porteous Riots in Edinburgh in 1736.

We hear of some of the events which led up to the war with Spain which broke out in 1739, in particular the concern for the American colonies of Georgia and Carolina. Of General Ogle-thorpe and the S.P.C.K. Mission to Georgia we hear a very great deal, especially with regard to the settlement of the refugees from Saltzburg, and it is interesting to speculate what would have happened if Thomas Wilson had been appointed chaplain at Savannah—as he nearly was—instead of John Wesley after the Rev. Samuel Quincey had been dismissed for "very great impru-dences" in 1735. The time in America was not the most rewarding period of John Wesley's ministry but it is doubtful if Thomas Wilson would have been any more successful.

Thomas Wilson was also greatly interested in the work of the S.P.C.K. at home and also in the Society for the Reformation of Manners. The frequent references to "The Gin Affair" remind us that it is the London of James Hogarth, and Wilson goes on one occasion to see an exhibition of Hogarth's pictures. And we meet again and again that very great benefactor to the S.P.C.K., and the very good friend and patron of Thomas Wilson, Sir John Phillipps of Picton Castle, Pembroke, who at that time was nearing the end of his life and was almost totally blind but still continued with enthusiasm his active support for good causes, particularly the Charity Schools.

At Stoke Newington Isaac Watts was a near neighbour. Thomas Wilson appears as being of the greatest assistance to Watts in the publication of many of his books and he gave strong support to the side of orthodoxy in the Deist controversy, a topic which interested him all his life, and in after years John Leland's book *A View of the Principal Deistical Writers* was written in the form of letters to Thomas Wilson and published at his expense.[22]

The reader is also brought into contact with some of the burning events of the day—the popular clamour at the time of the Excise Bill in 1736, the quarrel between George II and the Prince of Wales, and the intrigue behind the Whig political machine, especially with regard to Church appointments. Thomas Wilson is deeply involved here, and throughout the whole of the period covered by the first volume of the Diary is his quest for preferment. This is not always edifying and it is startling to discover that the contest for the lecturership at St Sepulchre's, Holborn, almost led to fisticuffs among the clergymen themselves! But in the end the long delays and hopes deferred come to an end and he is rewarded with the rich and influential rectory of St Stephen's, Walbrook.

Throughout the period covered by the first volume Thomas Wilson is much concerned with his health. He evidently suffered from some kidney complaint from which it would seem he never really recovered, though he lived to a ripe old age. He took good care of himself; medicines—and especially "Rheubarb"—appear almost as frequently as in Parson Woodforde. Thomas Wilson shares with James Woodforde the ability to describe everyday things easily and naturally and here and there—as in Woodforde—there are some telling pen portraits.

[22] In the introduction Leland says: "The design was carried on in a series of letters written to my very worthy and excellent friend, the Reverend Dr Thomas Wilson, Rector of Walbrook and Prebendary of Westminster, and I choose to let them continue in this form, that the reader may have some resting places, which may be a relief to him as it was to the author."

Having been introduced to him we can no longer forget Woodforde's friend Mr Barnwell—"A gentleman of considerable property, much afflicted with the Gout, has travelled a good deal over England and well acquainted with Families"; and having met him in the company of Mr and Mrs Wilson during the season at Tunbridge Wells we cannot forget Mr Elton, the Minister of the Church of King Charles the Martyr—"of no great depth, reckoned an honest man because very blunt, when a little more civility might not be improper, tho' he knows, or his wife better, how to condescend and I think even to fawn upon those from whom they expect something".

The remaining portion of the Diary, which is entered in an interleaved copy of an Almanack, Rider's *British Merlin* for the year 1750, shows him well established in his rich preferments at Walbrook and at Westminster. It is again more of a day-to-day diary, but entered up on occasions and, as is the case with the first volume, some time after the events described had taken place. The volume, which is complete for the year 1750, is the record of a number of unfortunate quarrels and disputes, over the Dean and Chapter's control of the Fish Market at Westminster, over the building of Westminster Bridge, and there is a vivid account of the earthquakes in the February and March of that year in which Dr Wilson appears as one of those preachers ridiculed by Horace Walpole for making human shortcomings "a principal ingredient to the composition of earthquakes".

During the summer of 1750 the journey to the Isle of Man is given in some detail, in which we get an interesting account of the ways of smugglers—the running trade—and of the very considerable loss to the Inland Revenue occasioned by their activities. The expenses of this journey are interesting and are entered in detail in the fly-leaves of the Diary for 1750, together with a full account of his wife's housekeeping expenses at Tunbridge Wells during his absence, which I have set out in full, together with some of his shopping lists, which are also informative; especially those things which he obtained for his father. The diocese of Man was as remote then as one of the more distant missionary dioceses would be to-day, and many of the creature comforts and concomitants of the civilized life had to be obtained from England. One has, I think, a more intimate portrait of Bishop Wilson when one learns that in addition to some of the up-to-date theological works and books of devotion, spectacles and medicines worsted cambric for cassocks, bed linen and nightcaps, he was also in need of "2 yards and a half of Black Shagg".

In editing the Diary I have let Dr Wilson speak for himself, copying the MS. verbatim, only altering his spelling and extending his abbreviations here and there for the convenience of the reader. In the matter of footnotes I have been as sparing as possible, confining them in most instances to the identification of people mentioned in the Diary and the explanation of certain phrases and events which would otherwise remain somewhat obscure, and now and again I have put Thomas Wilson alongside other observers of society at the time.

I am most grateful to the Warden and Fellows of Keble College, Oxford, for giving me the opportunity of working on this interesting MS. and for their permission to publish it. My thanks are also due to the Reverend V. H. H. Green, D.D., of Lincoln College for reading the typescript and making many valuable suggestions; and to Canon Charles Smyth who has given me much help with the annotations and furnished much information with regard to Dr Wilson's incumbency at St Margaret's, Westminster.

I am also most grateful to the Dean and Chapter of Westminster for allowing me to consult the Chapter Books; to Mr L. E. Tanner for information concerning Westminster Abbey and Precincts in Dr Wilson's time; to the vicar of St Stephen's, Walbrook, the Reverend Chad Varah, and to the parish clerk, Mr Tom Matthews for putting the Vestry Books and other parochial records at my disposal.

Keble College, Oxford
November 1962

Thomas Wilson's Diary
1731–1737

SEPTEMBER 1731

Monday 13. Set out [1] from Douglass Bay at 3 a clock in the afternoon in a Wexford Sloop. Captain Scalian. Wind contrary in the night.

Tuesday 14. Tuesday at sea. Little or no wind bearing up to the Head.

Wednesday 15. At Ormestead. Lay at anchor. Stopt tides in the night.

Thursday 16. We gained close to the Welsh Shore and at the sunset turned the Rock and landed safe about 8 a clock. God be praised for all His Mercies. At the Talbot. Ill fategued.

Friday 17. Dined at Cousin Hugh Patten's. [2] Paid the Master of the vessel 10s. 6d. for my passage and 4s. to his men.

Saturday 18. Cousin Littler came to me from Park Gate and the two men that came with me returned with him at night. Dined with the Revd. Mr Stanley in the afternoon by ourselves. I gave him a full account of the Unhappy Differences in relation to the Church of Man, which he pittied us for, but would not meddle in them.

SUNDAY 19. Preached at the New Church [3] for Mr Stanley

[1] *Bishop Wilson's Journal*, 7 Sept. 1731. "I parted with my dear Child, he going for England. May our gracious God send us a happy meeting in this or a better world."

[2] Hugh Patten of Liverpool, died 1736: first cousin to the Diarist's mother (Keble, p. 902).

[3] St George's, Liverpool, built 1726–34 by the Liverpool engineer and architect Thomas Steers, whose docks were the beginning of the town's greatness as a port. The church was rebuilt by John Foster 1819–25 and demolished in 1897. Rev. John Stanley, son of John of Ponsonby, Cumberland, paup. Queens Oxon., rector of Liverpool 1726–50, of Workington 1726–53, and of Halsall, Lancs., 1750–7.

on Phil. IV.11. Dined with Mr Fryar the Mayor and very kindly entertained, his lady, 2 sons, daughter. Mr Halsal [4] in the evening at Cousin Verdon's. Cousin Hugh Patten. Cottam. Halsal. Pet. Peppard. Adderton.

Monday 20. Went with Halsal and Patten to Crosley. Saw the School House, an extraordinary stone building, but out of repair sadly in the inside. Dined at Harry Bridges.

Tuesday 21. Over the water to the Rock Boat. Cousin Gerard Macklin [5] met me with 2 horses. Dined at Stourton. T. Macklin's at night at Park Gate at Cousin Littler's. [6]

Wednesday 22. Went in Cousin Littler's Boat to Flint, a pretty little Town. One regular street, about the middle of it a ruined glass house built by Fotherby of Milk Street. A Town House on the other side, but they have removed the Sises [7] to Mould. At the further end of the street a handsome church, and a little further the Gaol. Just at the point of the Sea stands a ruined Castle, [8] the walls seem to have been designed only against arrows. Mr G. Mostyn, Sir Roger's son, Constable (with a sallary annexed to it) governs the town. Dined at the Flower de Luce (Jones). In the afternoon set out for Holywell, by the Shoar Side, about 100 Paces towards the sea stand Large Lead Work Houses, belonging to a Company in London, formerly in great business, but now pretty much at a stand. The road by the sea very pleasant, on the left hand about half a mile are Lead Furnaces, belonging to and managed by Mr Barker. A little further in this road is a fine Engine for removing water out of the Coal Pitts. On the left hand are the Furnaces for Lead belonging to Sir Richard Grosvenor and his steward. Then we come turning upon our left hand to the amazing brook of Holywell, where we come to 2 Wire Mills

[4] Rev. Anthony Halsall, his old tutor.

[5] Gerard and Thomas Macklin were the sons of Mr Garret Macklin who married the Bishop's elder sister Sarah (Keble, p. 494).

[6] John Littler of Park Gate was the son of Bishop Wilson's sister by her first marriage to Daniel Littler (Keble, pp. 261, 900). Her second husband, John Falkener, was also a mariner.

[7] I.e. Assizes.

[8] Richard II surrendered to Bolingbroke (Henry IV) at Flint Castle (Shakespeare, *Richard II*, Act III, Sc. iii).

and a Corn Mill. As you enter Holywell Town in the Bottom stand Lead Furnaces, belonging to Mr Fox, but upon some difference about the smoak spoiling the adjacent lands, are at a stand, after a Law-Suit cost 'em £2000 the matter is adjusted. You come to Holywell at the bottom of a steep hill, a wonderful spring, which turns a large Water Wheel ten yards from its rise, if it be not rather a stream under ground which breaks out there. The well is supported by a beautiful building but not so old as they pretend, it was a Popish Chappell, now a petty school! Brought Mrs Powell her letter from her daughter, waited upon Mr Fox, who entertained us with the utmost civility and respect. An old house but prettily furnished and delightful gardens. At the side pretty fields, with a gentle rising of some small hills with tufts of trees make a delightful prospect of this town and sea towards Hyle and the Bar of Chester and commands the ships that come up the Dee. Lay there all night. The Rev.d Mr Price,[9] Vicar of the place and a notable schoolmaster, very stiff and precise. Would willingly recommend himself to some Irish Bishoprick, lying in the way of the Lords Lieutenant whom he waits upon in their Journey. But after all in my opinion may end his days where he is and in a station suitable to his genius. Had a good deal of discourse about villainous pamphlets and vile clubbs set up in London of which I gave him a long account.

Thursday 23. In the morning visited Mr Price and staid with him 3 or 4 hours. Went to the well and bathed my foot, the water not so cold as I imagined. 2 Popish Conventicles and 3 Priests.[10] One of their Chappels at the Star Inn (the best in the town). They are very industrious in making converts. Pesterd at the well with 30 or 40 very troublesome beggars, who follow any stranger that goes down the hill and will have no denial. 1s. Mr Fox married

[9] Rev. Ellis Price, son of Andrew of Dublin, Pleb. Christ Church, vicar of Holywell 1700–63, rector and vicar of Ysceifiog, Flint, 1704.

[10] St Winifred's Well at Holywell remained a place of pilgrimage for long after the Reformation. James II visited it on 29 Aug. 1686. In 1805 Dr Milner, Vicar Apostolic of the Midland District, published *Authentic Documents Relative to the Miraculous Cure of Winifred White, of the Town of Wolverhampton, at Holywell, in Flintshire.*

first a rich widow, by whom he had this fine house, the lead works and a considerable estate and fine plate. To his second wife he married Sir T. Williams' sister, a pretty agreeable woman. Her brother died lately at Bath by which her sister is a fortune of £10,000. Lives at Chester.

Set out for Flint, Mr Fox along with us, and called at Mr Pennant's [11] of Bagg Hill, an ancient seat and fine estate. The old gentleman alive his eldest son married unfortunately, 3 sisters, one son sickly. The col. as they call him, a good humoured fellow, generous to the last degree, but drinks excessively hard and can't last long. He not at home. Came to Flint. Dined. Took leave of Mr Fox [Athanasius Fox Esq.], crossed the water and came to Park Gate at night. The Indentures in Mrs Littler's hands for Will. Quayle and J. Kegg finished and executed. 4 years 40s. per ann. Unkle Benjamin's daughter came to see me.

Friday 24. Went to Burton. The school [12] an excellent building but the additional work not finished, nor ceiled, no cellar. The garden not marled. Pickance and Cross not at home. The Church very pretty and nicely furnished. No Press for the Bookes.[13] Cousin Littler and I set forward to Squire Green's at Poulton. Dined genteely. His mother an extrordinary woman. 4 daughters, the eldest a pretty woman. The young gentleman very sober, governed by his unkle who lives with him and mightily respected in the country. An estate of £600 per ann. Went from there to Ridston, a village with excellent houses, the mansion a stately building upon a Rocky Hill, belonging to Mr Viner. Most of the families of the name of Wilson. Cousin Joseph [14] met us and went

[11] The same family as Thomas Pennant (1726–98), antiquary, topographer and writer of Tours.

[12] The school founded by Bishop Wilson at Burton in Wirral in 1724 and recorded in his *Sacra Privata*, A.D. 1724. "This year I built a school house at Burton in Wirral which cost me about £120. I have marled and am to marle twenty statute acres for a perpetual endowment, which when enclosed will make the school worth £20 a year. I have already laid out £138 upon marling."

[13] I.e. for a Dr Bray Library which Bishop Wilson had provided for the parish. Remains of it in 1849 (Keble).

[14] Joseph Wilson, the Bishop's nephew and one of the trustees of the school at Burton.

with us to Mr Bunbury at Poulton cum Secomb. Lay there all night. Poor man has lost the sight of one eye and in great pain though chearful.

Saturday 25. Went in the Wallisea Boat and came to Liverpool. At Cousin H's with Mr Halsal, Mrs Rowe etc.

SUNDAY 26. Was not asked to preach. The two Rectors out of town. At night at Cousin Cottams's. Mr Adderton and Mr Peppard. Sent unkle Will. Patten 2 Bills for £50 and another for £11. endorsed by H. Cottam.

Monday 27. At Cousin H's. Mrs Turton, Mr Bentley and his wife, Mrs Rowe etc.

Tuesday 28. Wrote to unckle Wm. Patten.[15] Sent him a promissory note in favour of Mr Austin Goldsborough by Jo. Williams in Monmouth Street for £30. endorsed H. Cottam. Dated 29 March 6 months after date. Dined at Cousin Cottam's. Mr Adderton. Mr Peppard.

Wednesday 29. At Mr Bentley's at night. Mr Halsal and Mrs Turton.

OCTOBER 1731

Friday 1. At Cousin Hugh's. Mr Cottam and lady. Mrs Hayes etc.

Saturday 2. Set out for Warrington with Cousin Hugh, daughter and Mr Halsal. Dined at the Three Leggs of Man at Prescot. Came to Cousin Patten's in the even [horse 2s. 6d.]

SUNDAY 3. Went to Winwick Church. Called at Sudworth. Hall. In the afternoon preached at Warrington for Mr Haddon. Prov. 13.4.

Monday 4. Went to Leigh with Cousin H. and Cousin Tho. Called upon Mr Ward (who never received my father's letter) and he went along with us to Grange. Looked at the barn. The back kitchen much out of repair and whole house out of order. To meet a Wednesday at Warrington to settle the accounts with Peter Morris. Supped at Sudworth.

[15] The Diarist's uncle William Patten, who became his father-in-law after the death of his daughter's first husband, William Hayward.

Tuesday 5. At Mr Worseley's at night. Mr Vaudrey, 2 sons and Cousin F. P. and son. Politicks.

Wednesday 6. Mr Ward came to town but Cousin F. P. could not find Morris' account. He paid me £10 for which I gave him a Receipt. This morning I received two letters from my father, 28th. Sept. and Ult. From my unkle Patten of London owning the receipt of the Bills I sent him 26 and 28 ult, and their acceptancies.

Thursday 7. Dined in the Lane. Cousin T. Murrey [16] supped and spent the evening with Tom and Ned Vaudrey, Dick Johnson, Ralph Wright, Fairclough, Taylor and T. Murrey. Navigation of the river Dee. Proposal to be in the Act that cannal shall go free of duty. No good understanding between Lord Warrington and his presumptive heir.

Friday 8. Went to Aston Parks to see Egerton Leigh, not at home. Dined with Hamlet Yates. George Leigh of Highleigh made but an indifferent bargain for himself at his marriage. Agreed to pay off debts and mortgages and sisters fortunes to the amount of £8000. Had only £6000 with his lady and is to pay £550 per ann. to his father, and the estates not worth above £1200 per ann. Came home at night and supped at Cousin Worseleys.

Saturday 9. Wrote to Mr. Hayward. John Lydyard came to town. A letter from Cousin Murray and Mr Woods. All friends well, God be praysed. In the afternoon at Mr Haddon's. Told me a story of Clayton,[17] Bishop of Killala, which he had from his own mouth. That Clayton lodging in St. James' parish gave five guineas to a Poor Man upon the recommendation of Dr. S.

[16] The Murrey family, merchants of Douglas, were relatives of the Pattens (Keble, p. 529).

[17] Robert Clayton (1695–1758), whose appointment to the see of Killala in 1729 was an example of Sir Robert Walpole's concern more for the genealogy than the orthodoxy of those whom he preferred (J. H. Plumb, *Sir Robert Walpole, The King's Minister*, p. 97). Bishop Clayton was the friend and disciple of Dr Samuel Clarke and in 1751 his *Essay on the Spirit with some Remarks on the Athanasian and Nicene Creeds*, presenting the Arian point of view, aroused a violent controversy; Waterland describing it as "the rubbish of old heresies".

Clark. The Dr. took it so kindly that he invited him to dine with him, asked him whether he was acquainted with Mrs Clayton at Court, which he denying the Dr. told him that the lady was to dine with him and accordingly introduced him in quality of a worthy namesake and relation probably. This acquaintance was his introduction to Court and by proper application was suddenly advanced to a Bishopreck.

SUNDAY 10. To Aston Parks. Preached at Budworth in the morning (Phil. IV. 11) in the afternoon (Prov. XIV. 17). Dined with Mr Yates. Came home at night ill fategued.

Monday 11. At night at Mr Vaudrey's. 2 sons, Mr Hawford. 3 Pattens. Mrs Wright. Mr Dennet. J. Murrey. Mr Worseley. About Mr Boolter's difference with Lord Derby—Liverpool Election—Col. Chartres Rape—Charitable Corporation—a great proprietor of it. Great Scandal.

Tuesday 12. Went to Oughtrington [18] with F. P. Corn Market. Dined with Cousin George and his wife and daughter in law. Civilly received and came home at night.

Wednesday 13. At Mr Worseley's at night. The Old Club. Mr William Murrey. Wrote to Mr Finch, Lady Hastings, Cousin Murrey, Phil. Moore, Mr Woods, Athanasius Fox Esq. at Holywell.

Thursday 14. Drunk tea with my aunt Patten. At night at Cousin Mollineux's. 2 F. P.'s, Mr Vaudrey. Cousin Goulbourn. T. Murrey. Mr Worseley. Mr Haddon told me an odd piece of Natural History. That in King Charles 2nd's time in the great frost there was heard out of Brereton Wood, Cheshire, the reports as of Minute Gunns, many 100 of them. The old man that constantly affirmed this thing is still alive and told his friends that he was sure most of the great trees were then shockt. Lately this famous wood was cut down and tho' it appeared sound, the bark firm etc., yet it proved most of it shattered in a wonderful manner and almost quite of no use. N.B. It is a swampy ground. The soil Marl.

[18] Mary, daughter of John Leigh of Oughtrington, Cheshire, married Thomas Patten of Warrington, who was the Bishop's father-in-law.

Friday 15.   Received the following Bills which I intend to send to unkle William Patten by the post tomorrow.

Halifax. Oct. 8th. 1731. £100.

One month after date pay to the order of Mr Giles Faircloth One Hundred Pounds Value received as advised by   E. Hoyle.

To Mr Nich. Skinner.
Mercht. London.

endorsed. Giles Faircloth
John Cheshire.

Sankey. Oct. 14. 1731.

[£100 received by my unkle Nov. 16.]

Twenty eight days after date hereof please to pay to Mr John Lyon or order the sum of One Hundred Pounds value received and place it to Accnt. and by advice from your humble servt. Thos. Blackburn.

To Mr George Suttere
Cheesemonger in
Thames Street, London.

endorsed. Lyon.

[£100 received by my unkle Nov. 16.,

For my own account.
S.N. 23.   £50.

Warrington. 10th Oct. 1731.

[£50 accepted.]

One month after date pay to the order of the Revd. Mr Thos. Wilson fifty pounds for value in Acct. and place to acct. by advice from

your humble servt.   Tho. Patten.

To Mr. Charles Pole. Mercht. in London.

Mr Fears Bill upon the Warden of the Worshipful company of Cloth Workers.

Saturday 16.   Went with Cousin F. P. and wife, Cousin Biddy and T. Murrey to Liverpool. Dined at 3 Legges of Man, Prescot, treated the company for their civilities to me. At night at H. P.'s Cousin Verdon and wife. Wrote to unkle Will. Patten. [Horse hire 3s.] Dined with Mr Brookes the Vicar. Came home in the evening with Mr Halsal.

SUNDAY 17.   Went to Walton and preached (Prov. XIV.17).

Monday 18.   Was entertained with the dirtiest Mob I ever saw which had been kept up 3 or 4 days at Bank Hall by Lord Derby, who came to town House about 12 to vote against Brereton. No friend to Brereton. At night at H. P.'s.

Tuesday 19. Drunk tea with cousin Clayton, Miss Leighs. Mr Hesket of Meath, a pretty gentleman.

Wednesday 20. At Mr Turton's. Mr H. H. P. and Mrs Rowe. Elegantly entertained at supper.

Thursday 21. Went over the water in the Kings Boat to the Rock, from thence to Cousin Macklin's of Stourton, sent his horses with me to Chester, lighted at the Golden Falcon (Mrs Kenness), sent for F. Aldersley. Told me an odd story of an amour he had with Dr. Greathead's Lady of Lincoln, which made that place too warm for him.

Friday 22. Dined with Mr Mapletoft.[19] At my own inn at night with F. Aldersley. They are repairing the Chapter House, long neglected. Mr Mapletoft Treasurer and intends to build a library. Bought Dr. Thomas' Bookes, value £100.

Saturday 23. Waited upon the Chancellor, Mr Gastrel.[20] Dined with Mr Mapletoft. Supped with Mr Hignet, 3 daughters, Aldersley in Fleshmonger Lane. Received the following Bills from Mr John Murrey of Chester.

Bolton 6th. Oct. 1731.

Sr. One month after date please to pay unto Mr T. Patten or order £200. Twenty Pounds for value received as by advice given and place the same to Acct. of yr. humble servant. Henry Layland.

[returned not accepted.]

Mr James Pickington at his Ware House near the Blossom's Inn, London.

endorsed F. P. Will. Murrey. John Murrey. Com. Chester. the 25. Oct. 1731.

Sr. at 10 days Date pay to the Rev. Mr Thomas Wilson or order Five Pounds for value and place to acct. by advice from John Murrey.

To James Creed Esq.
Merchant in London.

[19] *Rev. John Mapletoft*, vicar of Neston and treasurer of Chester Cathedral, who, together with the Diarist, was a trustee of Bishop Wilson's school at Burton.

[20] Peregrine Gastrel, LL.B., chancellor of Chester, d. 1748; buried in the Cathedral.

SUNDAY 24. Preached at St John's (Phil. IV.11). Dined at the Chancellor's. In the afternoon preached before the Mayor and Aldermen at St. Peter's for Mr Mapletoft who was to officiate for Dr. Fogg.[21] After prayers waited upon Sir Henry Bunbury, very civilly entertained. Came in Mr. Egerton of Oulton who had invited me to dine with him. Talked about Horse Races. Came in the Chancellor and Mr Mapletoft. Supped at an elegant entertainment. My Lady and 2 daughters (agreeable women) especially the eldest. Sir H. Bunbury a facetious gentleman very desirous to show his skill in Roman History etc. Too Pedantick for a fine gentleman, very censorious about other people's behaviour and faulty in that instance himself. The Chancellor entertained us with the Dispute he had with the Bishop about Rural Deans [22] etc. 'till near 12.

Monday 25. Set out in the Chester Stage Coach (2 Guineas and 6 shillings for baggage). Capt. Mayo, Lady Ungate, Miss Hargrave of Macclesfield Street. Dined at Burn Hill. Lay at Whitchurch, the George, an excellent inn (4s. 6d.).

Tuesday 26. Dined at the Red Lyon Newport. Lay at the 4 Crosses, a base extravagant inn. 5s. 2d.

Wednesday 27. Dined and lay at Coventry at the Bell. A Better Inn. 4s. 8d.

Thursday 28. Dined and lay at the Angel at Northampton. 5s. 6d.

Friday 29. Dined at the Swan at Newport Pagnell. Lay at the Bulls Head, Dunstable. 6s.

Saturday 30. Dined at the Green Man, Barnet. Came to Aldersgate Street at night. To my uncle Patten's. 3s. 4d.

SUNDAY 31. At. St. Laurence for letters. 2s. 6d.

[21] Arthur Fogg, D.D., vicar of St Oswald's, Chester, Dodleston, and prebendary of Chester Cathedral, d. 1738.

[22] The office of rural dean was in existence in Saxon times. Some bishops in the seventeenth and eighteenth centuries—Seth Ward of Salisbury and Martin Benson of Gloucester—sought to revive the office. Sodor and Man was the last diocese to receive rural deans, in 1880. See Hamilton Thompson, *The English Clergy,* pp. 63–70.

NOVEMBER 1731

Monday 1. My dear Cousin Hayward came to see me. Dined at unkle's (Dr. Best).[23] Went to Newington and exceedingly well entertained.

Tuesday 2. At Newington. Wrote to my Father.[24] Received a letter from Lady Eliz. Hastings [25] with a Bill for 25 Guineas on Mr Hoar for the clergymen's Widows and children which I paid in to my unkle Patten.

Thursday 4. Waited upon Sir John Philipps. Went to my Lord Ashburnham's, very civilly received, the young lady not well. My Lord mistakes in the successor imagining it to be Lord Dunmore. At night at the general Meeting for Promoting Christian Knowledge. Went to White Hall to the Bishop of London. Not at home.

Friday 5. Returned to Newington. Dined with Mr Rogers.

Saturday 6. The same place. Wrote to Lady Hastings. T. Patten of the Corn Market.

SUNDAY 7. Preached at Newington for Mr Thoresby. (Phil. IV.11).

Tuesday 9. Waited upon the Bishop of London.[26] Kindly

---

[23] Dr Wm Best, vicar of St Laurence, Jewry, and rector of St Mary Magdalen, Milk Street.

[24] *Bishop Wilson's Journal*, Nov. 1731. "Lady Betty Hastings has sent to my son twenty five guineas for the widows etc, Towards which good work I have given this year £100 which I pray God accept from his servant."

[25] Lady Elizabeth Hastings (1682–1759), daughter of Theophilus, 7th Earl of Huntingdon. The wife of her half-brother Theophilus was Selina, Countess of Huntingdon, the founder of "Lady Huntingdon's Connexion". Remaining unmarried, Lady Elizabeth Hastings devoted her life to acts of piety and charity, and besides Bishop Wilson her other directors were Archbishop Sharp, Robert Nelson, and William Law. She contributed very handsomely towards Bishop Wilson's expenses with regard to his lawsuit in the Isle of Man.

[26] Edmund Gibson (1669–1748), known as Dr Codex for his Digest of English Ecclesiastical Law—*Codex Juris Ecclesiastici Anglicani*. Bishop of Lincoln 1716 and translated to London 1720. He exercised a dominating influence on the Church of England during the last years of Archbishop Wake's life and Sir Robert Walpole was charged with treating him as "the Pope of the English Church" but he lost the minister's confidence—and the primacy—for his success-

received and ordered to attend any night at 6 a clock. Clear in the point of refusing resignations. Went to the Society. Dined with Sir John Philipps. Mr Arch.D. Deane, Mr Bundy. Mr Macbeth. Dr. Williams, 2 sons T. & H. [gloves 1s. 4d.]

Wednesday 10. Returned to Newington. Received a Bank Bill from Mr John Murrey and Co. Chester for £20 in lieu of that I returned to him viz. No. 215.

I promise to pay to Mr Jas. Parish or bearer on demand a sum of Twenty Pounds.
London the 4th. Day of May 1731.
For the Gov. and Company of the Bank of England. £20. Joshua Odams. [received bill at the bank Nov. 16.]

Received (Nov. 9th) of Mr Rogers £9. 2s. and £5. 4s. in all £14 7 as received by him for me from Starkey and Bound in full.

Thursday 11. At Newington.

Friday 12. At Newington. Wrote to Mr Bateman [27] about a Room and to Mr Moreton at Corpus Christi College.

Saturday 13. Went to London. at my unkle's. Mr Freke.

SUNDAY 14. Went to Wansted with Mr Waldo, lady and 2 daughters. Preached there (Phil. IV.11). Dined with Earl Tylney, very civilly received. With us my Lady, 2 daughters (Emma and Dorothy) and Mr Waldo. Came home at night.

Tuesday 16. Went to London. Waited upon Mrs Marshall etc. Went to the Society. Sir T. Gonson, Sir John Philipps and son, Mr Tylliam, Mr Sale, Mr Bundy, Mr Vernon, Mr Mead. Returned home at night. My Lord Tylney improving his gardens prodigiously but had not time to see 'em. Invited to come any time. Invited to my Lord Ashburnham's Gentleman to dine with his Lordship and Mr Anseley etc. on Thursday. [Tea Canisters for Molly Hayward £1 14s.]

ful opposition to the Quakers Relief Bill in 1736 designed to reform the method of recovering tithes and church rates. See *Edmund Gibson: A Study in Politics and Religion in the 18th Century*, by Norman Sykes (1926).

[27] Edmund Bateman, tutor at Ch. Ch. 1731. Close friend of John Wesley's, with whom he played cards in his unregenerate days. A member of the Holy Club and one of those Methodists who visited the prisoners in the Oxford gaol (V. H. H. Green, *Young Mr Wesley*, pp. 75, 160).

Wednesday 17. At Newington. At Mr Thoresby's.

Thursday 18. Dined with my Lord Ashburnham. Mr Anseley, Mr Hale etc. and talked about the succession of the Island in case of the demise of Lady Harriott. Marquess of Tullibarden,[28] elder brother to the Duke of Athol, attainted by Parliament, now in France. In the evening at the Bishop of London's, White Hall. Had a long discourse about the Island, much to the same purpose as he formerly wrote to my father. Very kindly received. Lay at my unkle's. [coach 1s. 6d.]

Friday 19. Returned to Newington.

SUNDAY 21. Preached at Newington in the morning (Prov. 18.14) for Mr Thoresby [29] and in the afternoon for the Lecturer, Mr Seers.

Tuesday 23. Went to town. Paid a visit to Mr Peters in Rolls Buildings, Fetter Lane and left a letter for Mr John Sharp in Southampton Buildings in relation to Mr Sedden. Went to the Society and dined with Sir John Philipps,[30] Sir John Gonson, Mr Mead, Mr Bundy,[31] Erasmus Philipps [32] and John and a Welch clergyman. Charitable Corporation affair will certainly my Lord

[28] William Murray, Marquis of Tullibardine. He joined James III in 1715 and after the defeat of the Rising he escaped abroad. He was attainted and his estates and titles were conferred on his younger brother Lord James Murray. He was one of the Seven Followers who embarked with Charles III at St Nazaire in June 1745 and was chosen to unfurl the standard at Glenfinnan. After the defeat at Culloden in 1746 he was captured and committed to the Tower, where he died in July 1746.

[29] Ralph Thoresby, Queens' Camb., son of Ralph Thoresby the antiquary, vicar of Rickmansworth 1723-8, rector of Stoke Newington 1728-63. Married Rhoda Stafford of London.

[30] Sir John Philipps, of Picton Castle, Pembroke, who appears frequently throughout the first volume of the Diary was a great benefactor to the S.P.C.K. and S.P.G. and the Society for the Reformation of Manners. He was instrumental in setting up over ninety free schools in Wales, most of them under the auspices of the S.P.C.K. For the last few years of his life he was totally blind but continued his interest in his many charities with unabated zeal. He was a great supporter of the charities organized by Wesley's Holy Club. Died 1737.

[31] Richard Bundy, D.D., royal chaplain, rector of Barnet and St Bride's, Fleet Street, preb. of Westminster, trustee of Georgia. In 1740 appeared his *Sermons on Several Occasions with a Course of Lectures on the Church Catechism.*

[32] Erasmus Philipps, son of Sir John. His cousin Catherine Shorter was the first wife of Sir Robert Walpole. Died 1743.

Chancellor says come before the House of Commons. Returned to Newington at night [coach. 1s.]. Billy's Birthday and Dear Molly's the 4th February.

Thursday 25. Wrote to my father dated 20th. Sent him Deeds of Trust for two original Bank Shares for the desolate widows and children of clergymen in the Isle of Man and 1 from my unkle for 1 Bank Share for himself. Went to the Tower and saw Mrs Tollet, Whitaker, deputy Master of the Assay Office. Called upon T. Parr and Mr Waterson. Dined with Mr Fox (a Broker in Johnson's Court, Fleet Street). Sir George Wynne. Mr Wright of Stretton. Mr Fox of Holywell and a younger brother at the Temple. [1 of the brothers dyed the other day of the bite of a Mad Dog.] Never to be led here again to drink above 2 or 3 glasses at a time. Lay at my unkle's.

Friday 26. Dined at Newington. A letter from H. Patten and T. Patten of the Corn Market.

SUNDAY 28. Preached at St. Mary Overs in Southwark in the afternoon (Phil. IV.11) at the request of Mr Kenwrick of Milk Street. Dined at my unkle's. Returned at night.

Tuesday 30. Went to the Tower to see the Duke of Lorrain. At Mr Whitaker's Deputy Assay Master. Dined at Pontaks. My unkle, Aunt and Cousins Hayward. [Treated them all 1. 11. 6.]

DECEMBER 1731

Wednesday 1. My cousin William Hayward taken ill. Returned to Newington. Poor Cousin Hayward much worse with cholicky pains.

Thursday 2. Dr. Monroe sent for. Thinks him in no danger.

Friday 3. Went to town in Dr. Monroe's chariot. Saw Bethlem Hospital where everything is kept with great exactness and Nos. of people sent out cured every quarter.

Saturday 4. Cousin a little better. Took leave of Sir John Philipps had a long discourse about Religious Meetings in the City of London. Had been with the Bishop of London to desire his patronage and protection. Liked the people but did not know what may be the consequence of taking such Publick Notice of them in a body. Bishop of Oxford much in the same way of thinking with the Bishop of London.

SUNDAY 5. Cousin worse and delirious. Stayed with him and prayed for his recovery if it should please His Almighty will.

Monday 6. Cousin a little better.

Tuesday 7. Much worse. Called in Dr. Leigh of Coleman Street whom I went for and he thought cousin rather better. I parted with him and my dear Friends with some pleasure [Servants there 12s. 6d.] and lay all night at my unkle's. [At my unkle's 7s. 6d.] With Mr Rogers. In the evening took a place in the Oxford coach, [Coach Hire In London 13s. 6d.] Received a letter from Mr. Hales advising me that he had a promise of £20 for our clergymen's widows and children.

Wednesday 8. Set out from the Black Swan in Holborn with one Martyn, Commoner of Merton. Took up Monsieur Fabre at Uxbridge. Lay at the Catherine Wheel at Wickham. [4s. 8d.]

Thursday 9. Dined at the White Swan at Tedsworth. Came at night to Oxford, to Mr Dewe's. [coach 10s.] A gentleman to whom my chamber was let gone out of town with my keys.

Friday 10. Had a letter from Mr Jos. Hayward acquainting him that his brother was much worse for which I am exceedingly concerned. God's will be done.

Saturday 11. Waited upon the Bishop of Oxford. Dined with him. Was mightily kindly received.

SUNDAY 12. Very ill of the Head Ache that I could not stir out of my room. Cupped 2s. 6d.

Monday 13. Wrote to Sir John Cheshire about our charity. Still ill of a violent cold. Answered 13th. Replied the next day.

Tuesday 14. A letter from F. Hayward telling me that his brother and my dearest Friend departed this life last saturday about 10 a clock at night without a sigh or a groan as if God would begin the happiness of the next life in an easy translation out of this. He was really a most excellent Christian, the best of friends and the kindest husband in the world. May my latter end be like his. Wrote to Mr. F. Hayward and Dear Molly upon this

Melancholly Occasion. Received a letter from my Father and one from Mr Hales advising me that the £20 would be ready to be paid the beginning of February.

Wednesday 15. Still ill of the Head Ache.

Thursday 16. At the 3 Tunns. Moreton. Walwin. Hayward and Parker.[33]

Saturday 18. I was examined by Dr. Rye [34] for Priests Orders and passed it to his satisfaction and in the afternoon subscribed to the 39 Articles before the Bishop.

SUNDAY 19. Was ordained Priest by the Bishop of Oxford in the Cathedral Church. God enable me to perform those solemn vows I then laid myself under. May his good spirit enable me to do my duty as a Minister of God to the Flock that may be committed to my charge, that none may perish for want of my care. That I may take no indirect methods to gain Preferment, and when I have any, constantly reside upon it. That I may rather study to be good than great, looking upon that state to be dread-fully dangerous, to be pitied rather than admired. That when it pleases God I am admitted to a cure of souls I study to lay out my whole time in saving my own soul and those committed to my charge. [To my Letters of Orders. 10s. Bishop's servant. 5s. Register 2s. 6d. Dinner 7s. 6d. Mourning Gloves 4s. Shoes 6s. Buckles 1s. (for W.H. 11s).

Monday 20. Confined to my chamber.

Tuesday 21. I this day with grateful acknowledgement re-member the Birthday of my ever dear Father [Aged 69 as I believe.] whom I pray God to preserve for the good of the Church, and as the best friend I can ever have under God, who has always treated me with the utmost Tenderness; Compassioned my Frailties and touched 'em gently with a Hand anointed with

[33] The Three Tuns was a noted inn in the High Street on the site of Staunton Hall between Catte Street and Queen's. Moreton (Corpus), Walwin (Univ.), Hayward (Pembroke), and Parker (Balliol) seem to have been the Diarist's especial friends.

[34] George Rye, D.D., rector of Islip 1717, archdeacon of Oxford 1724 and Regius Professor of Divinity 1737–41; also rector of Ickford, Bucks. 1729. His son William (Ch. Ch. 1739) became Doctor of Medicine in 1759.

Balm. May I coppy after so bright an Example and never do anything that shall grieve him, having afflictions enough, God knows, from other quarters, great enough to sink any other spirit but his, who is governed by such Principles as the world knows or at least practise very little of them. [3s. 8d. Dinners. Wine 4s.]

At the Common Room at the raising of the Censor Batteley.[35] All the M.A.'s of the college. [3s. 6d. as is customary.]

Thursday 23. Took Physick to carry off the remains of my cold.

Friday 24. Waited upon Dr. Cunnibear.[36]

XMAS DAY. Administered the Sacrament at St. Thomas for Mr Hayward who was ill of a cold in the head of which he died. Or rather died of a fall from the Terrass which broke some vessel in his Reins or hurt his kidneys. He was sober coming in the dark from the Common Room.[37]

SUNDAY 26. At St. Aldate's Church. Wrote to my father.

Monday 27–SUNDAY 2. Dr. Rye wrote to me word that he had had an ill fall from his horse which disabled him from performing his duty and sent his chariot for me and I went New Year's Day. Thanks to God for the greatest deliverance that ever man had, 6 years ago.[38]

JANUARY 1731-2

Monday 3. Returned from Islip. Servants 2s.

Tuesday 4–Friday 7. Much out of order with a pain in my back. Took some oyles and Syrups. Went off the 6th.

---

[35] Speeches were made annually at the "Burying" of the outgoing Censor and the "Raising" of his successor (J. Pointer, *Oxoniensis Academia*, 1749).

[36] Rector of Exeter College; soon to be Dean of Christ Church.

[37] Hearne, on the other hand, says: "A week or more before his death he came home much disordered with liquor and fell down from the terras in the great quadrangle at Xt. Ch. and broke two of his ribs which threw him into a raving condition." Rev. Samuel Hayward, d. 5 Jan. 1731/2. (Hearne *Collections*, Oxford Hist. Soc., xi, p. 14.)

[38] The shipwreck in 1725.

Saturday 8. Bought a chaldron of coales. Cost 1. 15. 6. and a quarter of one before cost 18s. 6d.

SUNDAY 9. Was sent for again by Dr. Rye. Buryed a Man in the night and got an ill cold. However performed duty on Sunday and came home Monday morning. Servants 3s.

Tuesday 11. Cought ill but I thank God much relieved next day.

Thursday 13. Wrote to Mr Hales [39] a letter to be laid before Corporation of the sons of the clergy, which God grant may succeed. [Paid Poland for letters 8s. 9d.] 3 Tunns. 2s.

Friday 14. Wrote to my unkle to pay £10 due to Cousin Will. Hayward.

Saturday 15. Much out of order with a pain in my back and voided red sand.

SUNDAY 16. Preached for Mr Lamprey [40] in the morning at Magdalen Parish and in the afternoon at Carrfax before the Mayor and Aldermen.

Monday 17. Dined with Mr Woods, schoolmaster of Abingdon. J. Dewe went with me. Returned at night. [servants 1s. horse 2s.]

Thursday 20. Received a most kind and affectionate letter from my Ever Honoured Father, dated on Xmas Day. At 3 Tunns 2s.

[39] Dr Stephen Hales (1677–1761), C.C.C. Camb. M.A. 1703, B.D. 1711, F.R.S. 1718, D.D. Oxon by diploma 1733. Physiologist and Botanist. Inventor of ventilators, about which he wrote to Dr Wilson in the 1750's with regard to their installation in hospitals. His medallion portrait in Wesminster Abbey by Joseph Wilton, R.A., was erected by Augusta, Princess of Wales and mother of George III, to whom he was appointed Clerk of the Closet in 1751. From 1708 he was perpetual curate of Teddington, where Peg Woffington was one of his parishioners. Pope was his near neighbour, who remarked: "I shall be very glad to see Dr Hales, and always love to see him; he is so worthy and so good a man." One of the Trustees for Georgia an ardent member of the S.P.C.K. Like Dr Wilson he took a prominent part in the "Gin Affair", publishing in 1736 *Distilled Spirituous Liquors the Bane of the Nation.* In 1734 he published *A Friendly Admonition to the Drinkers of Brandy,* which went into six editions. See Life by A. E. Clark-Kennedy (1929).

[40] Thomas Lamprey, vicar of St Mary Magd. Oxon. 1720–43, minor canon of Canterbury and rector of St Martin and St Paul, Canterbury, 1743–60.

SUNDAY 23. At home. Not well. Could not preach, nor stir out of my chamber without much pain.

Monday 24. Out of order.

Tuesday 25. Much pained in my kidneys. God's will be done. I deserve much greater punishments.

Thursday 27. At the 3 Tunns. 2s.

Friday 28. Wrote to Sir John Philipps and his son Erasmus.

Saturday 29. Sent for to Islip and came home a Monday after reading prayers. servants 2s.

Monday 31. Dr. Felton [41] preached before the University and rescued Lord Clarendon's Hist. from the Abusive Invectives raised against it by Oldmixon and others.

FEBRUARY 1731–2

Tuesday 1. Paid Poland for letters 9s. to this day.

Wednesday 2. At the Common Room. A great day for dancing and singing tho' I did neither. Cost us 7s. a piece to the Musick and Entertainment.

Thursday 3. The Dean [42] came to town from Bath. Looks very thin and declining. Waited upon him in a body this evening. At the 3 Tunns 1s. 8d.

SUNDAY 6. At Mr Tucker's Chambers.

Monday 7. Gave Councelor Brereton a Bank Note No. 181 signed by J. Collier for 20 Pounds Ten of which he paid me and is to bring a Banker's Note for the rest. *Feb. 27 Had not paid me.* Paid March 26 the remaining £10.

Tuesday 8. Set out to make Mr Wake a visit at Monks Risborough. Mr Brereton and Mr Dice. Wrote to Mr Jo. Hayward and Dear Molly.

Wednesday 9. At M.R. (a Dormitory formerly of the Monks

[41] "January 30 falling upon a Sunday this year the Commemoration of K. Charles' Martyrdom was kept Monday following when Dr Felton, Principal of Edm. Hall, preached before the University in St Marie's and I am told made such a sermon as many have said they will never go to hear him again" (Hearne, op. cit., p. 24; cf. John Oldmixon's *Critical History of England*, 1724–6).

[42] William Bradshaw, Bishop of Bristol and Dean of Christ Church (1724–32).

of Cant. a Peculiar of the Archbishop's). Set for £200 per ann. Firing found by the parish.

Thursday 10–Friday 11. Visited Mr Penn, Curate of P. Risborough. Spent the evening with him. An author against the Anabaptists.

Saturday 12. Went to see Hambden House, where the Rebellion against K. Charles I was concerted. The whole estate confiscated to the Government for a debt due from the late Mr Hambden. How soon does wickedness set like a Canker thro' the greatest fortune.

SUNDAY 13. Preached twice for Mr Wake at M.R.

Monday 14. Went to Missington 4 miles. The road between Ailsbury and London. Squire Fleetwood much in debt in spending money at elections. Lives in the town. Hambden's widow married Bradsbury the Presbyterian Parson.

Wednesday 16. Returned to Oxford. Dined with Mr Kiplin, Schoolmaster of Thame. In the Common Room at night. [servants 3s. 6d.]

Thursday 17. At the 3 Tunns. Moreton. Walwin. Wollin and Parker. [horse hire 10s.]

Friday 18. 2 Letters. 1 from H. Patten and another from Mr Halsal. Cousin Jonny Murrey gone to one Mr Davies an attorney (a Dissenter) in the Poultry.

SUNDAY 20. At home. Not well with my old pain in the back.

Monday 21. Took Physick. Much easier thank God.

Tuesday 22. At Mr Willis' Chamber. Demy of Magdalen. Mervin and Mr Tucker of Balliol and Mr Dewe.

Wednesday 23. Wrote to J. Hayward. At the 3 Tunns. Moreton. Walwin. Woolin. Parker and Mr Hayward.

Thursday 24. Wrote to My father. H. Patten.

SUNDAY 27. Went to Little Wittenham, Berkshire a mile from Dorchester, to preach. A sweet place, a good house, with £130 per ann. Huggins the Minister. Sir George Oxendon [43]

---

[43] Sir George Oxenden "married one of the Dunches. She is an extraordinarily pretty woman. But Sir George is not only a very ill natured man, but keeps other women company and lyes with them and will be out at his sports in Kent

married Dunchey's daughter and has a good house, a charming walk up a hill called Mrs Dunchey's Buttocks, and carried on thro' delightful woods. Returned at night. A letter from Mr S. Hales telling me that our widows and children may hope for a share of the money given to the Corporation.

Monday 28.   Answered the letter with thanks for the offer and wrote to my father to acquaint him with it.

MARCH 1731-2

2nd.   A letter from my father. Cousin J. Patten, Corn Market, died the 15th. last month. No letters yet gone for the Island.

4th.   I administered the Sacrament (by Mr Wildair's [44] leave) to old Mr Dewe who died the next night.

7th.   I buried Mr Dewe at St. Aldate's.

9th.   Wrote to my father by way of (Liverpool) Whitehaven.

25th.   A letter from my father dated the 13th. Wrote an answer the same day by way of Whitehaven he having received none of my former. The running trade goes on briskly. Especially tea from France in abundance.

APRIL 1732

Saturday 1.   Proctor Batteley spoke his speech. A dry one much hissed and clapt. Very unfit behaviour for a Theater of Scholars and Gentlemen.

SUNDAY 2.   Preached this morning (Palm Sunday) for Mr. Manaton.[45] at St. Thomas' parish Oxon. In the afternoon read

and other places and make his wife be sometimes six weeks or more together by herself at Little Witnam". (Hearne, op. cit. LXVII, p. 472). One of Sir George's more famous affairs was with the second Lady Walpole, and Horace Walpole wrote to Mann on 26 Feb. 1781 of his nephew's doubtful legitimacy.

[44] The Rev. John Wilder, Fellow of Pembroke 1703, vicar of St Aldate's 1724; d. 1742. John Wesley also officiated at St Aldate's for Mr Wilder, who afterwards became a severe critic of Methodism, publishing in 1739 *The Trial of the Saints or a Caution against Enthusiasm or Religious Delusions in opposition to the Methodists.* (V. H. H. Green, op. cit., pp. 113, 136.)

[45] Robert Manaton, Ch. Ch., Proctor 1728.

prayers for Mr Wildair at St. Aldate's. Wrote to Mr Joseph Hayward. In the evening at Mrs Hall's. 2 daughters and son.

Thursday 6. Not at the Tunns but at my own room.

Friday 7. A letter from Mr. J. Hayward in answer to mine of 2nd.

Saturday 8. Sent Erasmus Philipps Mr Wildair's sermons by Mr. Davis.

SUNDAY 9. *Easter Day.* Preached and administered the Sacrament at St. Aldate's for the rector Mr Wildair (Matt. 28.11, 12, 13).

Monday 10. Dr. Thomas preached a good sermon at St. Maryes in proof of identity of the same body.

Tuesday 11. Wrote to Erasmus Philipps esq. in answer to his of the 8th.

Thursday 13. At the Tunns.

Friday 14. A letter from my father.

SUNDAY 16. At St. Mary's.

Wednesday 19. A letter from Erasmus Philipps. Answered it next post.

Thursday 20. At the Tunns. 1s. 6d.

Saturday 22. Drew a Bill for £20 on my cousin Patten in favour of Daniel Whittaker.

SUNDAY 23. Mr. Ward preached an excellent sermon upon Lying. I preached in the afternoon at Binsey for Mr. Batteley.

Monday 24. Wrote to Mr. J. Hayward.

Tuesday 25. To my father in answer to his last.

Wednesday 26. A hard frost in the morning. Wind. NE. very cold.

Thursday 27. At the 3 Tunns. Moreton. Walwin. Woollin. 1s. 8d.

SUNDAY 30. Dr. Leigh, Master of Balliol, preached a good sermon against Tyndal [46] at St. Maryes.

[46] Matthew Tindal (1645–1733), Lincoln and Exeter Coll. Oxon., Fellow of All Souls 1678. For a short time a Roman Catholic under James II but returned to the Church of England at Easter 1688. He called himself a "Christian Deist" and in 1706 published *The Rights of the Christian Church asserted against the Romish and all other Priests who claim an Independent Power over it.* It maintained Erastian and

MAY 1732

Monday 1. Mr Jones, fellow of Jesus, told me that Mr Cockman was prevailed upon by the friends I wrote to in London to print his excellent sermon against *Christianity as old as the Creation*.[47] I am glad I was an instrument of doing so much good.

Wednesday 3. A letter from my unkle telling me that the half year's dividend for the clergymen's widows and children being 200 Stock in my name, was ready to be paid him. I answered it the same day and gave him the following order [ordered it to be credited to my father's acct.]

XT. Church. May 3. 1732
Pray pay to Mr Wm. Patten my Dividend due to Lady last on 200 Bank Stock and his receipt shall be your discharge
from your obedient servant Tho: Wilson.

My father received it for their use 6th.

Thursday 4. Sent away my letter to my father dated 27th. last month.

Saturday 6. Frost in the morning. Rainy winter weather these last 10 days. Snow in Scotland.

SUNDAY 7. Jones the Chaplain preached an indifferent sermon at St. Maryes. In the afternoon a gentleman . . . a worse.

Monday 8. A letter from Mr Bateman in which he owns himself debtor to me 19. 3. 0. for which sum I shall draw a Bill upon him in favour of my unkle. [received it by my unkle.]

Tuesday 9. A letter from Egerton Leigh about his bookes. Fanny Richmond going to be married to Mr Atherton.

rationalistic opinions. Four editions were printed but the author, publisher, and printer were prosecuted. Tindal answered in 1709 with *A Defence of the Rights of the Christian Church*, which was burned in 1710 by order of the House of Commons at the same time as Dr Henry Sacheverell's famous sermon on the wickedness of Whiggery and the duty of Passive Obedience to the Crown. In 1730 Tindal produced *Christianity as old as the Creation, or the Gospel a Republication of the Religion of Nature*, which became the "Bible" of the Deists. See p. 90, n. 125.

[47] "Dr. Conybeare, Rector of Exeter Coll. hath first published an 8vo. Bk. against Collins and Tyndal's *Christianity as Old as Creation* and dedicated it to Gibson, Bishop of London, who (he says) put him upon it" (Hearne, op. cit., p. 14).

Wednesday 10. Read Dr. De Lany's [48] *Revelation Examined with Candour.* An Excellent Dedication to the King and in the main a Curious Book. Dr. Middleton's [49] Letter to Dr. Waterland occasionally censured and confuted. My father approves much of it.

Thursday 11. Mr Cockman's [50] two sermons against Tyndal published this day and well approved by everybody at the 3 Tunns. Moreton. Walwin. Woollin. Parker and Hayward. I was the occasion of Dr. Cockman's printing his sermons. [candles 1s. 6d.]

Friday 12. Wrote to unkle Patten, the Bill enclosed for 19. 3. 0. upon Mr Bateman. He received it accordingly.

Saturday 13. At Mr Dawney's,[51] Gentleman Commoner of Hart Hall. Gave Mrs Hall a widow gentlewoman Half a Moidore 13s. 6d.

SUNDAY 14. Rawlins preached for Knipe [52] a Harangue about Searching the Scriptures at Christ Church in the afternoon. One Woodward of Brazennose preached the dullest sermon I ever heard at St. Maryes.

Monday 15. Wrote to Sir Jo. Phillipps for his opinion about Cockman's sermons that I recommended. Running of tea etc. brought from Dunkirk to the Isle of Man etc. Enclosed under cover of Erasmus Philipps Esq. To Mr Jos. Hayward about the receipt of Maderia Wine etc.

---

[48] Rev. Patrick Delaney (1685–1768), Dean of Down 1743. It was on his going to London to arrange for the publication of his *Revelation Examined with Candour* (1732; 2nd edn. 1734, 3rd edn. 1763) that he married a rich widow, Margaret Tenison, after whose death he married Mrs Pendaves, a close friend of John Wesley's who was George III's "dearest Mrs Delaney" often mentioned by Fanny Burney.

[49] Dr Conyers Middleton (1683–1750) published in 1731 *A Letter to Dr Waterland Concerning some Remarks on the Vindication of Scripture*, later in the same year *A Defence of his Letter to Dr Waterland*, and in 1732 *Some further Remarks on a Reply to the Defence of the Letter to Dr Waterland*.

[50] "Mr Cockman, Master of University Coll, hath just printed two sermons against Infidelity and Atheism, that he preached some time since at St Maries, Oxon." (Hearne, op. cit., p. 59.)

[51] See note for 28 Dec. following.   [52] Canon of Christ Church.

Wednesday 17. A letter from Erasmus Philipps. His father approves of the two sermons.

Thursday 18. Paid a Bill to the Common Room Man in full of all Accts. to this day. 1. 5. 3.

SUNDAY 21. Preached at St. Miles Church for Mr Vesey.[53] Dined at Mrs Halls. Sat at Brasennose Common Room with Mr Parker, Wilbraham,[54] Foxley,[55] Moreton

Monday 22. Wrote to my father.

Tuesday 23. Waited upon Dr. Rye at Islip with Moreton. Dined there. Dr. Cross (since dead) Archdeacon of Hereford, lives near Banbury, an only daughter, 16. Mr Pointer[56] of Merton returned with them. Found a letter from cousin Hugh Patten dated the 19th. with this Paragraph:

"We have a report in town (which I have heard several times) that you are on the point of marriage with Cousin Hayward. [Letter to my father.] That the Bishop is much displeased with it and is coming over very soon to prevent it if he can. I've contradicted this story in all Companies to be false and nothing of truth in it; for tho' you have a true Value for that deserving Lady, yet I think you have no intention to make her a wife. I have hunted the Crab (as we call it in the Country) and found the author to be Madam Clayton, but have said nothing to her of it. Miss, they tell me, but 19 next August. I wish she had no power to marry any other but him that I should name, and you should not want Preferment. But what could the old Lady mean by publishing this story? Pray consider of it."

To which I immediately returned him this answer:

"As to my marriage. Alas! They don't know me and you seem to be the only person of sense amongst them. They may make as free with me as they please. I have learnt to sit easy to the world, but they should not entertain such thoughts of a Lady under the deepest Affliction and whose Friends are all employed to support her spirits every day sinking. To deal freely with you—when I parted

[53] William Vesey, Fellow and Sub-Rector of Lincoln Coll. A friend of Thomas Hearne and one of John Wesley's closest friends during the time he was a Fellow of Lincoln (V. H. H. Green, op. cit., p. 88). St Miles', the City Church of St Michael and All Saints, in the patronage of Lincoln College.

[54] Henry Wilbraham, Fellow B.N.C. 1725. Afterwards rector of Shelford, Oxon.

[55] Thomas Foxley, Fellow B.N.C., Proctor 1731.

[56] See entry for 1 Dec. 1732.

from my father I solemnly assured him that I would never make any steps towards a married life without first acquainting him with it and this I have inviolably observed, and he will always be the first person that knows anything of it and I hope I have too much Religion ever to do anything of that kind without his free consent so that his friends may be easy. His Journey into England being purely to pay a visit to Lady Betty Hastings to anything relating to me, a line would be a determining on a 1000 Words from his mouth. I hope my friends will all have reason to approve of my choice. I am not very young. The warm blood is over and neither interest, love, nor money will singly ever determine me. I am obliged to you for contradicting a story for which there was no grounds, more for the sake of my dear cousin than myself. To her it would be a great grief to have the world imagine that she can forget the best of husbands or indeed so much as think of another. As for myself no Report of this kind can affect me. T.W."

Wednesday 25. At the 3 Tunns. Moreton. Walwin. Woollin. Hayward very silly.

Friday 26. Read the life of Dr. Barwick in which I find the great Dr. Wallis charged with decyphering King Charles I's Letters [57] taken at the Battle of Naseby for the Rebells and as a Monument of such Noble Performance deposited the original with the decyphering in the Publick Library at Oxford. Wood. Athen. Oxon. Vol. 2. Col. 415 and Mr Hearne says this very excellent book is or was lately in the library. See an acct. of our Bishop Barrow [Bp. Barrow of the Isle of Man.] and his character

[57] "Nov. 26, 1730. From another paper wrote by Mr Wood's own hand. March 1660. The latter end of this month Dr Wallis got by flatteries and good words etc., his book of decyphering the Kings Letters from the Publick Library from Dr Barlow which he altered where he pleased" (Hearne, LXVII, p. 358).

John Barwick (1612–64), Dean of Durham 1 Nov. 1660, but a year later transferred to the deanery of St Pauls. An ardent Royalist, he suffered imprisonment in the Tower in 1650 (Walker, *Sufferings of the Clergy*, ed. Matthews). In 1653 Dr John Wallis (1616–1703), the mathematician, deposited in the Bodleian a collection of letters deciphered by him. He was accused by Prynne and Anthony Wood of having interpreted the correspondence of Charles I at Naseby, but he "had this in him of a good subject, that at this time, in 1645, he discovered nothing to the rebels which much concerned the public safety, though he satisfied some of the King's friends that he could have discovered a great deal" (*Life of Dr John Barwick* by his brother Peter Barwick (1619–1705), Physician to Charles II, p. 251). After the Revolution in 1688 Dr Wallis was employed on behalf of William III by Daniel Finch, 2nd Earl of Nottingham. Some of the correspondence dealt with by him related to the alleged surreptitious birth of James III.

to our diocese. Wood. Athen. Oxon. Vol. 2. Col. 655, 670. Walker's Sufferings of the Clergy Pt. 2. p. 152.

WHITSUNDAY. Dr. Holdsworth of St. John's preached before the University.

Monday 29. Creed of Edmund Hall [58] before the University in the latter end desired them to stick to their old loyall Principles they were always famous for and reverence to the Princes of that Family to whom they had so many obligations. [Common Room 1s.]

N.B. Dr. Wallis vindicates himself fully from being guilty of this vile aspersion in a letter to Dr. Fell Dean of Christ Church, all I have seen at length in some of Mr Hearne's Collections. [59]

Tuesday 30. Spent the afternoon with Dr. Cunnibear at Exeter. Gave me an account of Lord Macclesfield's [60] [Ld. Macclesfield] behaviour just before his death, very surprising. After his physitians had declared that he could not have many hours he was not moved at all, but sent for his relations and friends, talked to them without any emotion, settled his affairs and said he was prepared and ready for another world. He was certainly loose in his Faith. He kept Mandevil [61] in his house and at table suffered him to abuse the whole Order of the clergy in

[58] "The Restoration of King Charles II. The sermon at St Marys was preached by Mr James Creed, Vice-Principal of Edm. Hall" (Hearne, op. cit., p. 64).

[59] Hearne, LXIII, p. 359.

[60] Thomas Parker, first Earl of Macclesfield, 2nd creation, Lord Chief Justice 1710, Lord Chancellor 1718. In 1725 he was impeached before the Lords for selling Masterships in Chancery and receiving bribes. Found guilty and fined £30,000 and committed to the Tower where he remained for six weeks while the money was raised to pay the fine. Retired to Shirburn Castle, Oxon. "He was a great villain and a great enemy to the Non-Jurors and 'twas he that was, among many others, who was so implacable to the late Bishop of Rochester, Dr. Atterbury" (Hearne, op. cit., p. 57).

[61] Bernard Mandeville (1670–1733), satirical writer especially famous for his *Fable of the Bees or Private Vices Publick Benefits* which went into three editions in his lifetime. He also had the reputation of being coarse and overbearing, but Benjamin Franklin spoke of him as "a most entertaining, facetious companion". Lord Macclesfield often entertained him for the sake of his conversation. He died 26 Jan. 1732/3 in the influenza epidemic. See p. 91, n. 126. See *Fable of the Bees*, 2 Vols., ed. F. B. Kaye (1924).

the grossest manner. He sold places when Lord Chancellor. Others did so what then? He suppressed and discouraged all the methods that were taking to find out and punish the vile management of the Masters in Chancery. Was not there a great many orphans and great losers by 'em? Was not Lord Macclesfield apprized of them? Is heaven so easily attained? The best men have their fears in the hour of death. The true reason say some why Mandevil had so many liberties given him, was his being an instrument in getting the Italian lady married to Lord Parker, to give up her pretensions and return to her Country—a dark piece of business.

Foulkes like to be Dean of Christ Church and Cross to succeed him whom they say is a clever man. They are going to print abundance of puerile things of Sir Isaac Newton's. The Dr. seems to slight Cockman's sermons. Professor Bradley [62] came in.

Wednesday 31. Mr Archdeacon Rye and Dr. Cunnibear Rector of Exeter and Mr Moreton, fellow of C.C.C. dined with me at my chambers in Christ Church. A vile book against the canonicalness of St. Matthew's Gospel. 3 Great men employed in answering it, himself I guess one. [Mr Briscow. Mr Leonard Twells].[63] This has hindered Waterland's going on with his 4th. Part of Scripture Vindicated. Talked about the Jews extirpating the Canonites etc. even supposing no Divine Command. [*see* Universal Hist.] They might lawfully be made slaves of and their hands tied up at least. 'Twas possible they might be guilty of many enormous crimes [Actually were so] such as would make them unfit for human society and the probability of it in part appeared in their barbarously sacrificing of their children etc. This is going to be treated of I find by a great man—2nd. Part of DeLanys book in the press indifferently talked of. In the afternoon Mr Thoresby and his brother in law Mr Jackson came to town. I shewed them the University. Supped at Dr. Manaton's.[64] Mr Manaton and

[62] Savilian Professor of Astronomy.

[63] Rev. Leonard Twells, Jesus Coll. Camb., Oxon. by diploma 1724, according to Hearne "by the interest of Dr. Conybear" (Hearne, op. cit., pp. 291, 335).

[64] Dr Pierce Manaton, Doctor of Medicine; died at Oxford 1743 and buried in the cathedral.

O. Batteley.[65] N.B. Mr Thoresby and his wife have been very rude to Cousin Haywards who always shewed them the utmost civility.

JUNE 1732

Thursday 1. Shewed the gentlemen the remaining curiosities of this place. Dined with them at the Angel.[66] Mr Jackson has been a very loose fellow. Spent £10,000. Member of the Temple and went at last into Orders. Married Thoresby's wife's sister. Formerly gentleman Commoner of Christ Church. They went out of town to Windsor. Sat at the Coffee House with one Mr Farewell and afterwards at Mrs Halls. A letter from Mr Baker of Plimouth about T. Moreton's affair. It was too late for him to go down.

Friday 2. Not very well. Tired with walking so much. Took Physick. An ugly pain in my kidneys. Sat at the Coffee House with Moreton, Smith and a Forreigner. [1. 7d.] Proposed to go to Cambridge all together this day fortnight.

Saturday 3. Breakfasted with Mr Brookes of Brazennose. Talked about Jones having Badesford and the injustice of it. Father Corear [67] intends the Bishop of Oxford a visit soon. Wrote to my aunt to bye me something for Summer Clothes. Paid Remmett the shoemaker £3.

TRINITY 4. Bishop of Oxford ordained a No. of Deacons and Priests. I assisted his Lordship in administering the Cup. Mr Douglas of Balliol preached the sermon. No very extraordinary one. Waited upon Miss A Maria Hall to be confirmed in the afternoon at St. Maryes. The Bishop confirmed young and old without any certificate of them. A great noise the whole time,

---

[65] Oliver Batteley, Ch. Ch., Proctor 1731.

[66] In the High Street between Queens Lane and the Eastgate.

[67] Presumably Pierre François Le Courayer (1681–1776), canon of St Geneviève at Paris and Professor of Theology in 1706. He corresponded with Archbishop Wake on the subject of episcopal succession in the English Church and upheld the validity of Anglican orders, for which he was excommunicated in 1728 and fled to England. He remained in England for the rest of his life but never joined the Anglican Church.

highly indecent. In the evening at John's with 2 Forreigners, Moreton, Gibson, Smith B.A. of Brasennose.

Monday 5. Terribly ill of the Toothe Ache, 4th. in left jaw tainted. Drunk tea with Mr Walwin of University a most conscientious tutor.

Tuesday 6. Spent the evening at Mrs Halls. Mr Mervin and Mr Willis Demy of Magdalen, who tells me that the Bishop of Winchester [68] threatens to come down and visit them in person. If he should do so he may expel a good many of them. 'Tis certainly in the interest of all colleges to ward off Visitations, most of the statutes having been broke one time or another. [Paid Moreton for Ridgwell £4. 16. 0. I have not paid it yet.]

Wednesday 7. I received a letter from my father dated Ascension Day which I shall answer next week and at the same time one from Mr Willis about his affair which I shall again recommend to T. Parr of Crutched Friars. These enclosed in one from H. Patten. Corn scarse in the Island. When they had Malt enough a year ago (if not basely consumed among themselves) to bye them Meal enough. The Governor has filled up the Body of the 24 Keys with 11 of his own men and gained his point. That seems a leading stroke to the further and entire loss of those poor people's liberties. Wickedness of all kinds encreases there since the Indignities offered to the Ecclesiastical Discipline. Cousin Murrey, son and daughter Sampson and Betty, gone to Dublin.

Thursday 8, Friday 9. Dined at Corpus Christi Gawdy. A very elegant entertainment. Cost at least £60. [servants 2s.] Went home exceedingly pained with the Toothe Ache and lay all night and next day tormented to the last degree. Tryed all kinds of medicines but found no relief. Such as Spirit of Turpentine, Sulphur, Harts Horn, Camphire, Laudanum etc. Resolved to send for the famous operator from Wickham.

Saturday 10. Dr. Perkins came and with a good deal of reluctance and he assuring me that it would spoil both the teeth it

[68] Richard Willis, Bishop of Gloucester 1714, Salisbury 1721, Winchester 1721 until his death in 1734. As Bishop of Winchester he was Visitor of Magdalen College.

touched upon, I suffered him to draw it out (an ugly kind of pain) being one of the worst kind and a part of the Jaw Bone forced away with it, tho' I thank God without much damage and the Toothe Ache quite gone for the present. [Paid him 10s. 6d.] Mem. To be very careful in keeping them clean washing behind the ears and combing the head to divert the Rheum that falls in great Quantities upon my Gumms. In the evening at the Common Room which was very wrong. Catched a bad cold in my mouth.

SUNDAY 11. *King's Accession to the Crown*. Dr. Cunnibear preached before the University.[69] I could not hear him being confined with a very sore mouth. A letter from Mr Woods of Castletown, begging something towards his house, but the person I was to speak to being dead (Madam Levinz [70]) I don't think I am obliged out of my own pocket to do anything for one who has formerly made but an ill use of charity from my unkle that he bought a Silk Coverlet. Cost 1. 6. 8. Stockings 4s. 3d. Lent Mr Godfrey Dawney of Hart Hall 2 Guineas which he promised to pay me in 10 or 12 days. Coffee House. Moreton. Gibson. A Forreigner.

Monday 12. Wrote to my father dated 15th. Cousin T. and Cousin H. Patten by cousin Tom. of Corpus Christi. In the evening at Mrs Halls.

Tuesday 13. Lent Cousin Tom. Patten [71] One Quinea to carry him into the country. Acquainted his father with it. [He has paid it me T.W.]

[69] "Yesterday being the Inauguration of George II the sermon at St. Maries this morning before the University was preached by Dr. Conybear, Rector of Exeter College, and I am told, 'twas a sad Puritanical Whiggish thing" (Hearne, op. cit., p. 69).

[70] Widow of Bishop Wilson's predecessor in the See of Sodor and Man. "30 Dec. 1730. Wed. Yesterday morning died in the Gravel Walk near Magd. College in Oxford Madam Levinz, commonly called Lady Levinz, the widow of Dr. Baptista Levinz, Bp. of Man.... This lady who was a Hyde and before she had the small pox a most beautiful woman, and continued very stately and she was very proud to the last" (Hearne, LXVII, p. 369).

[71] Tom Patten of Corpus was an early adherent of the Holy Club. Perhaps he was instrumental in introducing his cousin Thomas Wilson to the other members. He afterwards became rector of Childrey, Berks. (V. H. H. Green, op. cit., p. 176.)

Wednesday 14. Mr Phil. Moore, Dublin, of the Isle of Man made me a visit. From Bath and returned the same day.

Thursday 15. I set out towards Cambridge. Tom. Moreton, Mr Smith, Cousin Patten and Mons. Du Cange Hardin a Hugenot of Cambray. Called at Mervin's daughter at Bistow and went to the New Inn at Stowe that night. Very bad bedds and worse eating.

Friday 16. At 4 a clock in the morning went into my Lord Cobham's Gardens.

[Break in the Diary until 21 July.]

JULY 1732

Friday 21. Paid Poland for letters to this day 12s. Cleaning and mending clothes 13s. 8d.

Saturday 22. Wrote to my dear father by way of Whitehaven.

SUNDAY 23. This evening a woman poisoned her child with Liquid Laudanum. When examined they say owned she had murdered another formerly. Was put in the Bridewell and strangled herself with her garter. Begun with Adultery and ended in this tragical manner. They say a gownsman father of her child. I hope not.

Monday 24. The Jury brought her in contrary to all reason and sense Lunatick. Mr Anderson, mother and daughter and Mrs Blackwell supped with me.

Tuesday 25. Paid a visit to the Bishop of Oxford and dined with him at Cudsden. [Servants 2s. Horse 2s.] Mons. de Congee. Dr. Smith, Provost of Queens, and Dr. Mangey [72] who says that he had 2 MSS collated for him at the Vatican that had given him great light in his intended edition of *Philo Judaeus*. The discourse

---

[72] "Dr. Mangey who is about an edition of Philo Judaeus is an ingenious writer and a good preacher but his abilities for an editor of ancient authors I find much questioned" (Hearne, op. cit., p. 436). Dr Mangey was succeeded by Dr Thomas Sharp, younger son and biographer of Archbishop Sharp, in the office of official principal to the Dean and Chapter of Durham.

ran much against Talbot,[73] late Bishop of Durham, his putting a person into Orders and giving him the best living in his gift, who was highly immoral and grossly ignorant: his injuring his successors by letting leases to the great detriment of the Bishopreck in favour of his relations. Dr. M. told us that Dr. Bland, Dean of Durham, is likely to succeed Dr. Bentley if he is expelled by the Bishop of Ely.[74] Dr. M. told us that his brother Sharp [75] has a Diary of his father's ready for the press from 1679 to his death, contradicts Dr. Burnet in many instances.

Wednesday 26. Dined with Dr. Rye at his living of Ickford 7 miles off. A little village out of all roads and but an indifferent house. Woollin went with me. [Horse 2s. Servts. 2s.] The Judge came to town. Dr. Banner preaches the Assize Sermon tomorrow. My Lord Cornbury Pultney D. of Buckingham came to town. His Grace enters Queens, Brown his tutor. Magdalen College divided about election of fellows, almost equally between the Head's Friends and the Cabal. One man only may turn the scale, but 'tis thought Butler will carry it. Came home at night.

Thursday 27. I am told Dr. Banner preached against the Supremacy in Ecclesiasticks, talked of the Privileges of the University which were intended to be taken away etc.[76] Received a letter from T. Moreton [Moreton returns 19. Aug.] in which he tells me that he has heard something against me both at Warrington and at Liverpool. I wrote to him this day for particulars that I may be able better to ward against their Malice, not that it gives me much trouble since I know of no Provocation that I have given

[73] William Talbot, Bishop of Oxford 1699, Sarum 1715, Durham 1721; d. 1730.

[74] The famous dispute between Richard Bentley, Master of Trinity Coll. Camb., and the Fellows of the college lasted 38 years. He was brought to trial before the Visitor of the College, the Bishop of Ely, in 1714 and again in 1733 but remained in possession of his mastership until his death in 1742.

[75] See note 72.

[76] "This day preached the Assize Sermon at Oxford Dr Richard Banner of University College (who married a sister of the late Dr Henry Sacheverell and now lives with her at St Gyles, Oxford) and he made a very dull heavy sermon, little or nothing to do with the business of an Assize as I am told" (Hearne, op. cit., p. 88).

them. At the Three Tunns. Woollin. Walwin. Hayward and Parker. [2s. 6d.] Judge went out of town. Probyn supped with the Dean at Christ Church.

Friday 28. Sent my letter to my father and another to T. Moreton at Manchester.

Saturday 29. Paid washerwoman 10s. 6d.

SUNDAY 30. Preached for Mr. Wildair at St. Aldate's (Phil. IV.11). Dined with Mr Remmett and supped at Mrs Hall's.

Monday 31. Went to Eynsham. Saw Dr. Rogers' Monument.[77] Bought 40 Hundred Weight of Wood for 1. 16. 0.

AUGUST 1732

Wednesday 2. Wrote to Mr Joseph Hayward and Mr Hales of Teddington by Mr D. Hume

Friday 4. Wrote to Mr Finch, King Street near Bloomsbury Square and to Mr Erasmus Philipps about the Saltzburghers [78] and to the Bishop of Llandaff a compliment at White Hall.

[77] John Rogers (1679–1729), born at Eynsham. Corpus Oxon B.A. 1697, M.A. 1700. Vicar of Eynsham, also of Buckland, Berks., and lecturer at St Clement Danes and Christ Church, Newgate Street. Also for a short time vicar of St Giles, Cripplegate. He took a prominent part in the Bangorian Controversy and attacked Hoadly in *A Discourse of the Visible and Invisible Church of Christ* (1719). He was also a severe critic of the Deists, publishing in 1727 a volume of sermons entitled *The Necessity of Divine Revelation and the Truth of the Christian Religion.* For his work against Hoadly the degree of D.D. was conferred upon him by diploma at Oxford. In 1719 a canon and in 1726 sub-dean of Wells.

[78] *The Saltzbourg Emigration.* Prior to the Thirty Years War it was believed that Austria would be Protestant but afterwards proved not to be so and there was a vigorous persecution of protestantism, especially in the archdiocese of Saltzbourg from which there were 7000 refugees in 1731 and a further 10,000 in succeeding years. Over the years 1733, 34, 35 four Transports were sent to Georgia by the S.P.C.K. with more than 200 refugees. £47,000 was collected for this cause in England, the bulk of which was expended over the emigration. In June 1732 the S.P.C.K. published *An Account of the Sufferings of Persecuted Protestants in the Archbishopric of Saltzbourg From the Account with Extracts of the Journal of M. Von Reck.* (A nobleman from Hanover who was one of the commissioners who organized the emigration.) See also Carlyle's *Frederick the Great*, Bk. IX, Ch. iii. Also Allen and McClure, *History of the S.P.C.K.*, Lond. 1898, pp. 388ff. and Chapter 10 in *Henry Newman: An American in London 1708–1743*, by Leonard W. Cowie (1956).

SUNDAY 6. Preached at Binsea [79] for Mr Howes. Carried up and treated some friends there. [2s. 6d.]

Monday 7. Wrote to my father about Mrs Clayton's story of my marriage and another vile one told Tom. Moreton by Boardman at Warrington that I set my father against the Clergy of Man etc. Wrote and enclosed this under cover to H. P.

Tuesday 8. Rode out for the air. Mr Rogers of Milk Street came to town with his new wife, mother and sister in law and son. Shewed them the University. Spent the evening with me. Cost me in all expenses 1. 2. 0. I have been often obliged to them and could do no less.

Wednesday 9. They went to Worcester where his lady has an estate. Went part of the way with them. [2s.]

Thursday 10. Paid Mrs Stratford for the carriage of a Barrell of Ale to London and two Parcels for my friend Mr Hayward. A present. 15s. 6d. The Barrell of Ale cost 3. 4. 0. Barrell and all. [3. 19. 6.]

Friday 11. At Mrs Hall's. Gave her a Common Prayer Book.

Saturday 12. Gave an honest countryman that used to supply us with candles but now reduced. 10s. Read in the news this last Tuesday that my Lord Ashburnham's daughter died to our great seeming loss. [Lady Harriot Ashburnham dead. Died at Tunbridge.] The Island in all probability devolving after Lord D. to a Scotch Family who have generally a Notion of Vassalage and no very good friends to the Church. *But he who made the world best knows how to govern it and to him we must submit as to a wise Physitian, who knows and does what is best for us*

> We are all but actors on the world's great stage.
> Some play without, some with an Equipage.
> Death drops the curtain and the Farce is o'er.
> And all Distinctions cease 'twixt rich and poor.

SUNDAY 13. Wrote the following to my Lord Ashburnham on the Melancholly Occasion.

[79] I.e. Binsey.

My Lord,

Amongst the many that wait upon your Lordship with their Condolence at this season of Grief, none is more sensibly touched with the Loss than myself. As one of very many, whose Spirits were supported with the Hopes of being Happy under the Protection and Patronage of your Lordship's Family.

How great that Joy was of having a Lord to whom we could freely apply our selves upon all occasions can be truly felt, by none but those who have so long wanted that Happiness.

May this great Loss be in some Measure alleviated by a double share of Health and Prosperity to the rest of your family and that every happiness may attend your Lordship is and always will be the sincere prayer of your Lordship's most dutiful and obliged and humble servant. THO: WILSON.

To Earl Ashburnham.

Monday 14. At Mr Meadowcourt's [80] of Merton. Mr Fabre. Mr. Cowper,[81] Lord Cowper's brother. Talked of many things. Promised to supply for him at Holywell 2 Sundays in his absence. Received 3 books about the Saltsburghers and a letter from the Society to forward Charitable Subscriptions. [Mr Newman.] My father sent them £10. by Sir John Philipps.

Tuesday 15. Wrote to my father.

Wednesday 16. Waited upon Mr Cockman about the Saltsburghers who gave me great encouragement that a publick Collection should go forward in Michaelmas Term and that he would recommend it to his Society. But I am afraid it will come to nothing as I hear that Dr. Homes is not their friend.

Thursday 17. A letter from Mr Jos. Hayward telling me that his partner Mr Chambers and his lady designed me a visit.

[80] Richard Meadowcourt, Fellow of Merton, vicar of Oakley, Bucks. 1727. Canon of Worcester 1735, vicar of Quainton, Glos. 1738, rector of St Martin's, Worcester and vicar of Lindridge, Worcester 1751. d. 1766. An ardent Whig, he was Steward of the Constitution Club at which there was very nearly a riot when he proposed the royal toast at the time the Club was celebrating George I's birthday in 1716. On 29 May 1716 Meadowcourt presented the Professor of Poetry, Thomas Warton, to the Vice-Chancellor for his Restoration Sermon in which he stated that "Justice beareth all things, hopeth all things, and *restoreth* all things" (V. H. H. Green, op. cit., pp. 23, 25).

[81] Ashley Cowper, son of Lord Justice Spencer Cowper, uncle to the poet William Cowper and father of the poet's Theadora.

Friday 18. The Borlace Club [82] met at Oxford. One Mr Borlace of Magdalen left something yearly to be spent on this day. 'Tis a meeting of all the most considerable Gentlemen about Town in order as they say to keep up the Tory Interest and Secure elections for M. of Parliament. They have an elegant entertainment at the King's Head and choose a Lady Patroness. Miss Kitty Stonehouse. M.B. Last year the Marquess of Blandford drank so hard at the meeting that it was thought to have cost him his life, for he died of a Violent Fever a few days after.

SUNDAY 20. Mr Chambers and his lady (Mr Hayward's Partner at the Madeira) came to Oxford recommended to my friendship. Lodged at Barber's in St. Clements.

Monday 21. Shewed them the University. They dined with me and I exceeded in my civilityes to them, upon Mr Hayward's account in return for the many civilityes received from him. [£1. 6. 0.]

Tuesday 22. Went with them to Blenheim. Wrote to Mr Joseph H. Cousin Jonny Murrey and 7 or 8 of his companions & 3 more spent the evening with me. [Races began Wed. 23.] Cousin, I am afraid, by his company is in a very ill way, being a sett of very rakish young fellows. [13s. 8d.]

Thursday 24. I am 29 years old. I pray God grant I may make a better use of my time for the future and dedicate what remaineth of my life to His Honour and Glory. Alas! Quot Dies Perdidi—Almost the whole of it spent in doing very little good.

Friday 25. Cousin Jonny etc. went out of town but did not take leave of me. No matter.

SUNDAY 27. Preached for Mr Meadowcourt at Holywell and read prayers in the afternoon.

[82] "Aug. 20. Sun. On Friday last was the Borlace Club at the Kings Head Tavern in Oxford at which time as usual a fine Woman was pitched upon for the Toast next year. The youngest of Sir John Stonehouse's daughters, a most beautiful creature, was the Toast for the preceding year and now another of his daughters, also an Exquisite Beauty, was chosen for the following year. Mem. They will not allow it to be called a Club but only *The High Borlace*" (Hearne, op. cit., p. 99).

Monday 28. Received a letter from Mr Hales telling me that the £20 formerly mentioned would be paid in a month.

Tuesday 29. From Mr Chambers thanks for the favours I shewed him.

Thursday 31. At the 3 Tunns. Put up in a box for my father the following books. Puffendorf:[83] Law of Nat. and Nations. Cunnibear's Defence.[84] 5s. 6d. Minute Philosophers 2 Vols. 9s. Revelation Examined With Candour. 2 Vols. 8s. 6d. Waterland's 2 Charges 2s. [Candles 7d.]

SEPTEMBER 1732

Saturday 2. Mr Freke Mr Philipps and their ladies supped with me.

SUNDAY 3. Preached in the afternoon at St. Ebbes for Mr Warnford.

Monday 4. At Mr Fulford's chamber with a Limner. One Mr Billers.

Tuesday 5. At the Greyhound.[85] Moreton. Smith. Mons. Fabre and Segrave.

Wednesday 6. Dined with Woollin, Dr. Webster and Mr Hele. They spent the evening with me. [4s. 6.]

Thursday 7. Met with one Mr. Phipps Minister of Tilbury overagainst Gravesend. Shewed him the University. Brought him to our Meeting at the 3 Tunns. Woollin, Walwin and Mr. Hele Parson of North Stoke 3 mile beyond Benson.

Friday 8. At the Greyhound with Mr Phipps, Moreton, Woollin, Smith.

Saturday 9. Mr Phipps paid me a visit. Kind invitation from him to see him in Essex. To be heard of at Child's Coffee House, or by Mr Freke.

SUNDAY 10. Preached at Holywell for Mr Meadowcourt.

[83] *Samuel Pufendorf* (1632–94), Professor of National and International Law at Heidelberg (1661) and at Lund (1670). His most important work *De Jure Naturae et Gentium* (1672) of which an English Translation appeared in 1710.

[84] *Defence of Revealed Religion against the Exceptions of Tindal* (1732).

[85] At the corner of Longwall.

Dined with Fabre and Smith at the Red Lyon Inn. Spent the evening at More's Coffee House with Mr Phipps and Mr Holker, A.B.[86] Gentleman Commoner of Merton, a very good sensible young man, intends to travel.

Monday 11. A very high wind about 8 a clock this morning attended with a good deal of rain which was much wanted. At home in the evening by myself. The wind encreases and rains prodigiously. Wrote to Mrs Wake about her son's money that is due to me.

Tuesday 12. Wind continues high. I pray God have mercy upon those at sea and that I may never forget God's great goodness to me.

Thursday 14. At the 3 Tunns. Parker. Moreton. Wollin. 1s. 6d.

Friday 15. A letter from Mr Hales of Teddington to which I returned the following answer: Sun. 16.

Good Sir,

I received your kind favours of Aug. 21st and Sept. 14 and you have my sincere acknowledgements for both. I am very glad to find that your Colony in Georgia is likely to go on with the disinterested manner in which the worthy Trustees have undertaken the design, and will make every body the readier to promote it, since they are sure the Charity will not be misapplied. As to the Saltsburghers I have waited upon several of the Heads of Houses and they seem disposed to promote a general collection in their several colleges. Nothing of this can be done until next term, the University being almost empty. Before this time I should humbly think that a letter from the Society to each of the Heads of Houses, not much differing from the advertisement sent to their Members, would be very proper, and if that is approved of, if they are sent in a packet to me, I will take care to present them to each. Such a scheme as this might raise a handsome sum, without which I am afraid little will be done. If you will be so kind as to mention this to the Society, I shall receive the Directions with the utmost pleasure. We are exceedingly obliged to our Unknown friend for his most kind Benefaction to our Poor Clergymen's Widows and Children. [£20.] I can never enough acknowledge that Recommendation of our case. May God reward you and him with the Blessings of this world and the next. If it is convenient for our good friend to send me a Bank Bill or any

[86] *Gilbert Holker*, son of John of Billiter Square, London Gentleman, Merton m. 4 March 1726-7, aet. 17, B.A. 1730, B.C.L. 1733, M.A. 1734, B.MED. 1737, D.MED. 1741.

Bill of Exchange for the £20 it would be best, but otherwise in what manner you and he think fit.

The death of Lady Harriott Ashburnham has been a great shock to all true lovers of the Isle of Man, whose hearts were kept up with the thoughts of being some time happy under a good Nature of Government. I did myself the honour sometime ago to write to Lord Ashburnham upon the Melancholly Occasion and have since been mortified with the news of his Lordship's illness for which I hope he is now recovered. My most humble duty to his Lordship and none can truly sympathise with his Lordship in every Pleasure and Pain than myself, whose kind intentions to our poor Country and favours to myself, will always be gratefully acknowledged and continuance of your Correspondence and Friendship will be a very great favour to yours etc. T.W.

Wrote at the same time to Cousin Joseph Hayward and Mr Freke in Salisbury Court, Fleet Street, about my father's picture.

Preached for Dr. Cunnibear at St. Clement's (Prov. 14.18). Dined with Mr Dewe. At night at John's with Moreton, Patten, Du Cange, Smith.

Monday 18. Drew a Bill for £25 upon Cousin Patten in favour of Mr Whitaker to his daughter for kindness.

In great pain. Ridd out to see Mr Fox at Reading. 20 miles. About 15 mile off in the road Temple Stanyan Esq has a pretty house. Our college has a good curacy at Benson, a mighty pretty house and gardens. About £50 per. ann. At Caversham a little on this side of Reading we have another at 70. Mr Beaulew the present curate a sickly man. I should be glad of it. Came to Reading. Mr Fox not at home. Drunk tea with his lady and 2 daughters, pretty agreeable girls. Went to see Dr. Rye's boy [87] at Mr Hoyland's School. He has an excellent House and fine Outlet. 44 Boarders and a Cleaver Man. His Usher shewed me the Ruins of the Great Mitred Abbey which are very grand. Spent the evening with me at The Golden Bear. An excellent Neighbourhood of Persons of Quality about the town. Lord Cadogan. Lord Craven.—Caesar Esq etc.

Tuesday 19. In the morning saw the remains of a very fine chapel belonging to the Friary. 700 years old they say. It is covered and has 2 Rowes of Pillars of freestone. At present they make use

[87] See note 34.

of it as a Bridewell and the chancell of the great church belonging to the Abbey is now actually, I saw, a Hogg Stye. Set forwards towards Ipsden. A Living belonging to St. John's in Cambridge. Mr Heald the Rector. Kindly received by him. A fine sporting country. The Vicar of South Stoke (£60) per ann. belonging to our college. He supped with us. In the morning Mr Heald went with me to Wallingford. A little market town. Dined with Mr Aurgels the Mayor. An honest maltster. Very kindly entertained. Mr Hicks and Mr Lewin, Vintners of London Members of Parliament. Great buying and selling of Votes the last election. Came home much better for my ride. [Horse hire 6s.] Found a letter from my father dated 29. last month.

Wednesday 20. Gave Mr Wildair for Brookes (poor clergyman) £1. 1. 0.

Thursday 21. Dr. Rye told me that I had been very good in assisting him and that since I would not take any Recompense for it he desired me to accept £5 for the clergymen's Widows and children of the Isle of Man, but his name should be concealed; only that they were to thank me. I own therefore my Receipt of the said money and desire, if I should die, that it may be forthcoming to them or to the orders of the Trustees of that Charity. T. WILSON. Invited to dine at the High Table at C.C.C. by Mr Burton [88] who was just returned from Lord Palmiston.[89] He was hunting at Richmond last week with the Prince. Spoke kindly to him, expressed his Regard for our University and his desire of seeing it. Burton gave me the following paper: *E Registro Curiae Praerogat: Cant. Extra* (a copy of Lord Clarendon's Will 1675.

At the 3 Tunns. Moreton. Woollin and Parker.

Friday 22. Voted for Mr Creed [90] of St. Edmund Hall for

---

[88] John Burton, Fellow of C.C.C. and a Trustee for Georgia. In 1732 he published a sermon "occasioned by the Colony that in planting in Georgia". A friend and correspondent of John Wesley's and encouraged Wesley to accompany Oglethorpe to Georgia (V. H. H. Green, op. cit., p. 254).

[89] Henry Temple (1673–1757) created 12 March 1772/3 Baron Temple of Mount Temple Co. Sligo and Viscount Palmerston of Palmerston, Co. Dublin.

[90] According to Hearne (op. cit., p. 422) Mr Creed was again unsuccessful in an election to a University Living in Feb. 1734–5. This time 82 to 102.

a University Living but he lost it by 14. At Mores in the evening.

Saturday 23. Paid for mending chairs 5s. Waited upon Dr. Newton, Principal of Hart Hall, about Saltsburghers who seemed ready to promote a collection for them in his Society. Spoke to me about Mr Dawney [91] who has been exceeding irregular in every respect. He, Dr. Newton, has struck his name off the books this term so that I am like to be the loser by two Guineas. I deserve it, but really I did not know his character when I lent it him. [Mem. To write to Mr. Langford about it—his tutor.] Spent the evening at Mr Dewe's. Mr Fulford there.

SUNDAY 24. *Ordination Sunday.* About 27 Priests and Deacons at Xt. Church. I assisted the Bishop of Oxford in administering the sacrament. [Mr Airs of New Coll. preached the sermon.] Dined with the Bishop of St. Asaph at the Audit House where was Browne Willis Esq. [92] Asked me a No. of questions about the Isle of Man. Mem. I am to get the Bishop and he some of the silver Manks coins. Wrote to my father. Fleury's Hist. Tillemont's Universal Hist. etc. and to Cousin H. P. enclosed to Erasmus Philipps Esq to be franked downwards. At. John's. Moreton. Du Cange. Smith.

Monday 25. Begun the Universal Hist. which seemed to be very judicious and bears a good character in the learned world. Lord Derby, I hear, has given £50 a year for ever to the Trustees of the Colony of Georgia for the Incouragement of Botany. Spent the evening at home. Violent pain in my Left foot, like the cramp. The same kind in the right one. How it will end God knows. His will be done.

Tuesday 26. Continues very bad. Not able to go out. Paid my note of hand to Mr Jason, Cook, two pounds eight shillings for which I have his receipt in full of all demands. This was a debt contracted when I was ill of the Ague for 4 months for meat

[91] See note for 28 Dec. following.

[92] Browne Willis (1672–1760), the antiquary and friend of Gray, William Cole, and the historian of Ely, Dr Bentham. He lived at Whaddon Hall, Bletchley, was a notable eccentric, and eventually ruined himself on building Water Hall, Bletchley. He took an active part in reviving the Society of Antiquaries in 1717.

broths etc. and he never came for it until now. Spent the evening at Mores with Mr Heald and another Berkshire clergyman. Mr Heald [93] died suddenly in the pulpit.

Wednesday 27. Gave Tybald. viz. Mr Hall for releasing him. 2s. 6d. At Mrs Burrows'. Mrs Anderson and her daughter.

Thursday 28. At Mrs Hall's and at Mrs Dewe's who came this evening from London.

Friday 29. This morning I married Mr Rooke of Abingdon and Mrs Blackwall widow of this town (both Dissenters) at Wadham College Chapel by a Lycense from Dr. Brooke official to the Archdeacon. They thanked me for performing the office so well and their teacher was with them who said he never had so just a notion of the solemnity of the office before.

Dined with the new married folks at Mrs Burrows.

Saturday 30. Breakfasted with Mr Wesley [94] of our house. His brother of Lincoln there. Had some discourse about their Religious Society. A Particular piece of Providence in relation to the Jail.

OCTOBER 1732

SUNDAY 1. Letter from Mr T. Hayward inviting me to come to Newington.

Went to Sandforth. Administered sacrament and preached for Mr Moreton of Corpus Christi. Dined with Mrs Anderson, her son and Mrs Moreton. Called in on my return at Mr Tubbs of Iffley [95] and paid Mr Brookes a visit. He tells me that Dr. Cunnibear is like to be our Dean. I wish it may be so. Supped at Mrs Dewe's with Mr. Fulford.

Monday 2. Wrote to Mr Dawney to pay me 2 Guineas very pressingly and in answer tells me that I shall have them tomorrow

[93] See entry for 19 Sept. 1732. Rev. Whitley Heald, vicar of North Stoke and curate and lecturer at St George's Southwark. Died suddenly while preaching at at St Nicholas, Cole Abbey, Lond, 22 Feb. 1735-6.

[94] Charles Wesley and his brother John.

[95] Mr Tubb of Iffley "formerly lived near Carfax in Oxford and kept a milliner's shop, but leaving off trade he went and settled at his estate at Iffley and hath ever since followed Malting" (Hearne, LXV, p. 280).

morning which I much question and afraid he is so desparate, as to attempt either his own or some other bodyes life. He was one of the prettyest best behaved ladds when at Wakefield School that ever was, but he must go to Westminster from whence he came a finished rake.[96] Brought £100 with him. Had £100 per. ann. allowed him and in a year and a half's time spent all that and £150 in debt. I offered to do anything to recover him for his father and bretheren's sake but without the special Grace of God I am afraid he is ruined—for ever undone.[97]

Tuesday 3. Answered Mr Hayward's kind letter with hearty thanks for his kind invitation which I may probably accept of towards Christmas. No money from Dawney. I suspect he has gone upon another ramble. Spent the evening at Mrs Dewe's. Miss Hall. Mr Fulford. Gave a poor man in great distress 2s. 6d. For cleaning my cloth gown and cassock 5d. For 60 faggots 5d. 60 more 5d.

Wednesday 4. Just received a letter from Mr Stephen Hales with a Bank Bill for £20. No. 104 signed Joseph Collier for our Widows and clergymen's children. I answered the letter by the same post. P.S. I am answerable for this sum of money when called. THO. WILSON.

Dear Sir,

I had the favour of your kind letter etc. and Bank Bill for £20 and have just time by return of post to send you and our kind benefactor, my most humble thanks and assurances of laying it out to the best advantage for our widows and children. My father is of the opinion that our fund is sufficient for our present needs and exigencies and you have so many worthy designs that

[96] Cowper castigated the Westminster of the period in *Tirocinium, or a Review of Schools.*

> Would you your son should be a sot or dunce,
> Lascivious, headstrong, or all these at once;
> That in good time, the stripling's finished taste
> For loose expense and fashionable waste,
> Should prove your ruin, and his own at last,
> Train him in public with a mob of boys,
> Childish in mischief only and in noise,
> Else of a mannish growth, and five in ten
> In infidelity and lewdness, men.

[97] See note for 28 Dec. following.

will call for all your charity that we rest contented and thankful to Almighty God for raising up so many worthy friends. I am exceedingly thankful to you for the particular expressions of your kindness to myself, which will always be gratefully acknowledged. I presume my father's intentions are always grounded upon that he has always made resolutions with himself to lay out his whole revenues in charitable uses and to promote hospitality. Having no family estate all that is left for me is a small fortune of my mother's which he is appreciative would be a mean provision for me, and being advanced in years is under some concern for me, much more than I am myself, who have experienced the Divine Goodness in so many remarkable instances that I hope I shall never distrust the continuance of it and I am better pleased with the Blessing that will undoubtedly be left me by my father than £1000. I should indeed much rather be doing my duty than living idly in a college. As for any great Preferment I neither desire nor deserve it. As for the Isle of Man, I am not master enough of the language to perform my duty as I ought and my Lord Derby has too great an adversion to my father ever to prefer his son to any benefice there. You see I am very free with you, but I see so much Openness and Goodness in every thing that you do that I don't question the pardon and that you will continue the correspondence and friendship to, dear Sir, yours THO: WILSON.

I own the receipt of £20 for those of our clergymen's widows and children on the Isle of Man which I desire should be forthcoming if I should die. THO: WILSON.

N.B. The Bank Bill is in my large Pocket Book with the silver pencil.

At Mrs Dewe's in the evening.

Thursday 5. For painting my study and chimney piece. 9s. 6d. A pair of Knee Buckles. Silver. 8s.

Tongs, Fire Shovel. Poker. Snuffers and Bellows 12s. 6d.

Friday 6. This day the Vice Chancellor Dr. Butler having been so 4 years resigned his post and Dr. Homes, President of St. John's, was elected into his place. The late gentleman was very regular in performing the Publick Business but he was blamed for taking an exhorbitant fee of £500 from Mrs Bradgate [98] for a

[98] Mrs Bradgate was the landlady of the Three Tuns which has appeared so often already in the Diary. Mr Bradgate died 9 Jan. 1728/9. "She is a fine, stately beautiful young woman, but very proud and empty of sense, as her husband also was, and a great company keeper, particularly she is familiar with Mr Morley, M.A. a deformed rich gentleman, fellow of Merton College" (Hearne, LXVI, p. 85).

Lycense for a Tavern, which he had no right to demand. [He was roughly handled by Pardo just before he came into the Convoc. abt. giving his man the place of Keeper of the B.A. gallery at St. Marys.] In our present gentleman there are mighty expectations, being really very ingenious and declares his resolutions to restore the decayed Discipline of the University. I hope it may be in his power. It will never be thoroughly done until the Heads of the Houses are unanimous in promoting more worthy men to be Tutors and to see that they conscientiously perform their duty. As for the Publick Exercises, they are quite neglected. A Noble Design was formed some years ago by the Proctors to restore 'em, but they were succeeded by careless ones and so the matter has been dropt. What the V[ice-Chancellor] can do in this case I can't at present judge, but not much without the assistance of the Proctors. They both made very good speeches and the first spoke by heart and mighty well in the praise of Speaker Bromley. The latter was short but pretty excellent Latin. Rained all day. At Mrs Dewe's. Mrs Brookes. Mr Fulford.

Saturday 7. Great Rain. Wind SSW.

SUNDAY 8. Lame of both feet. Caused I suppose by the sudden alteration of the weather.

Monday 9. Still continues so. Wrote to unkle Patten and sent him an order upon the Bank for a Dividend due last Michaelmas last to the clergymans widows and children.

Tuesday 10. Took Physick which I hope will ease me being ill of my pain in the kidneys occasioned by having been confined at home so much in my chair.

Wednesday 11. Much better. Supped this evening at Mr Fulford's of Balliol. Mrs Dewe. Miss Slatford. Mr Upton,[99] Fellow of Exeter.

Thursday 12. Great Rain in the evening. Large thunder claps and lightning until 12 a clock. Sat at home all day.

Friday 13. Paid the Common Room Man his bill in full of all Accounts to this day. 1. 3. 2.

[99] John Upton, son of James of Ilminster, Somerset. Afterwards rector of Llandrillo, Denbigh and Great Rissington, Glos. Also prebendary of Rochester.

Supped at Mrs Katford's in New Inn Hall Lane. Miss Dorrell. Miss White. Mr Fulford. Mrs Dewe. Received a letter from Mr Hayward in which he seems to take it ill that I have not accepted his invitation. Wrote to my father dated 16th. by way of Whitehaven for leave to go to London. That he would write to my favour to Auditor Harley about the £20 Bank Bill.

Saturday 14. A proposal for buying a House for clergyman's widows and children in the Island. Wrote to Mrs Wake and desired her that she would pay the remaining sum due from her son being £11. 15s. to my unkle William Patten. This money I am to pay to Mr Dixon—as put against all Justice and Reason by the Dean a claim upon me in the year 1729 without my knowledge. Hard usage! Received a very kind letter from Mr Erasmus Philipps from Bath in which he tells me that he receives great benefits from the waters in his pain in the Breast.

Paid Poland for letters in full to this day 11s. 6d. Dr. Cunnibear returned from Exeter. Go to see him tomorrow.

SUNDAY 15. Mr Blakeway preached a very good sermon for Mr Burton at Christ Church. Sat in the evening at John's Coffee House [100] and took leave of my friend Mons. Du-Cange Hardin who sets out for France tomorrow morning. Mr Moreton with us whom I advised to apply to Lord Derby for Radsworth vacant by the death of Entwistle.

Monday 16. At Mrs Dewe's in the evening. Gave her maid, who was leaving her, for the trouble I gave her last winter when I was ill 5s. Found a letter signed W. Williams desiring I would call upon him at one Mrs Wooten's in St. Clements. Who he is I can't tell. Went to see the Rector of Exeter. Not at home. Mem. to breakfast with Mr Wesley of Lincoln on Thursday 9 a clock.

Tuesday 17. Spent the evening at Exeter with the Rector. Dr Waterland about a large Work. The Hist. of Moral and Positive Duties which Connibear thinks is built upon a Quibble. Told us he has misquoted Tyndal inadvertently in one point but

[100] In St Mary's opposite All Souls.

that it should be altered. Shewed us a pamphlet. Remarks upon the Minute Philosophers [101] in which he has been joked upon recently. Bishop of Norwich [102] a dying Tanner to succeed him. Methodists talked of. No friend to them. Saltsburghers. Objected that they had behaved in a civil capacity contrary to the Laws of the Country, appeared in arms etc. Endeavored to obviate and answer his objections but I am afraid little will be done for them in this place.

Wednesday 18. Drew a Bill upon my unkle for £5 in favour of Renton the taylor. Cunnibear told us that Dr. Bland [103] is one of the chearfullest companions in England. Dr. John Clark of Sarum another very agreeable man. Moreton at my room. Wrote him a letter which he transcribed and sent it to my Lord Derby to apply for the living of Badsworth in Yorkshire. I hope he will get it.

Thursday 19. No body met at the 3 Tunns. Went to Mrs Slatford's in the Lane. A gentleman of Corpus. This morning at Wesley's of Lincoln.

Friday 20. Young Wesley told me that he was informed I had married a couple without Lysence in Wadham College Chapel. Utterly false and convinced him of it.

Saturday 21. At home all day. Not well.

SUNDAY 22. Heard this afternoon a most excellent sermon at St. Giles of Dr. Holdsworth of St. John's Practical Considerations from the Omniscience and Omnipresence of God. Hour and a quarter long.

Monday 23. The heaviest shower of rain I ever heard at 6 a

[101] The reference is presumably the Bishop Berkeley's *Alciphron, or the Minute Philosophers*, two editions of which appeared in 1732 and a third in 1752.

[102] Dr Tanner had been chancellor of Norwich before his elevation to St Asaph but he never became Bishop of Norwich. Died at Christ Church 1735. A notable antiquary, his collections form the Tanner MSS. in the Bodleian, many of which were badly damaged in being brought from Norwich to Oxford in December 1731 by the sinking of a barge at Benson Lock near Wallingford (Hearne, op. cit., pp. 9, 16, 21).

[103] Henry Bland, Eton & King's Camb, Royal Chaplain from 1716 as also chaplain to the Chelsea Hospital, headmaster of Eton 1719, canon of Windsor 1723–33, Dean of Durham 1738, Provost of Eton 1733–46. d. 1746.

clock this morning. At Mrs Dewe's with Mr Fulford and Mr. Upton of Exeter in the afternoon.

Tuesday 24.   Staid at home all day. Spent the evening at Mrs Slatford's. Waited upon Dr. Brookes in relation to the marriage at Wadham College Chapel.

Wednesday 25.   For a Common Prater for my father 8s. Oxford Almanacks 5s. 6d. In the evening at Mr Fulford's chamber. Mr. Billers the Limner. Complin, Apothecary.

Thursday 26.   Went with Fulford and Mrs Dewe to pay Mr Brooks of Iffley a visit whose daughter married the Bishop of Lichfield. Was very kindly entertained. Came home pretty late in the evening. [Horses & Servants 4s.]

Saturday 28.   Mr Fulford's Birth Day. Supped with him at Balliol. Mrs Slatford, 2 nieces. Mrs Dewe.

SUNDAY 29.   Walked to Iffley. Preached there. Dined with Mr Brookes.

Monday 30.   Not well all day. In the evening at Mrs Dewe's. Mrs Clark. Mrs. Medcalf, doctor's lady.

NOVEMBER 1732

Wednesday 1.   Fell's Gawdy. Mr Batteley spoke the speech, a tolerable one. Moreton dined with me at the Hall. [5s. 6d.] Mark Mussendine [104] Law Beadle died this afternoon. I vote for Mr Beaver.

Thursday 2.   At the 3 Tunns. Walwin and Parker.

Friday 3.   Beaver for the Beadle's Place but not the Architypographus.[105]

---

[104] "A layman, excessive drinker, as well as a great glutton, and so bad a husband that some years ago was so much in debt that his creditors compounded with him for about half a crown in the pound, since when he ran into debt again very much, and so died leaving nothing to discharge his debts" (Hearne, op. cit., p. 124).

[105] "The beadleship of law be annexed to the Architypographus place, yet nowadays some Heads of Houses (such as the late Dr. Gardiner and Dr. Charlett) have so contrived the matter as to disjoyn them, and to let a mechanick enjoy the profits of the Architypographus place and indeed the office (tho' nothing of a scholar) too, . . . 'Tis true Mussendine was an ignorant man, but as he was chosen

Saturday 4. Paid my washerwoman in full 10s. 6d.

SUNDAY 5. Ratcliff[106] of Pembroke preached a very good sermon—"I came not to destry but to fulfil"—in the afternoon. Sylvester[107] preached upon Vows in opposition to Dr. Panten's[108] [A better sermon I think.] I heard Dr. Holdsworth of St. John's at St. Giles. Mem. He had 5 or 6 pages verbatim out of Barrow.

Monday 6. Gave Wesley of Lincoln leave to shew my father's letter about the Saltsburghers.

Tuesday 7. Wrote to Cousin H. Patten to enquire after my father's health having not heard from him of a long time. At Mrs Dewe's.

Wednesday 8. Paid Rushton at the Wheatsheaf in full of all accounts for horse hire, Barrel of Ale etc. and to have no further to do with him.

Thursday 9. At the 3 Tunns. Moreton. Walwin. Parker & Hayward. Vindicated myself in relation to the wedding at Wadham College Chapel.

Friday 10. At home. Gave a Poor Traveller 1s.

Saturday 11. 4 Oxford Almanacks 4s.

SUNDAY 12. Mr Burton preached twice before the University about Abraham's Religion, Circumcition etc. Historical, which they say he will print. I hope not. At St. Giles in the afternoon.

Monday 13. At the Common Room in the evening. Dr. Gregory. Allen. Burton etc.

Tuesday 14. Met Moreton at the Coffee House who tells me that the Bishop of Cork has wrote another book about Analogy in which he is severe upon the Minute Philosophers and remarks largely upon Dr. Cunnibear's sermon at St. Marys. In the evening at the Common Room. Methodists joked upon.

---

he ought to have enjoyed what he was chosen to, and so does Mr Beaver. . . . As to Beaver's election there were few that voted, there being no opposition" (Hearne, op. cit. pp. 124, 129).

[106] John Ratcliff, Master of Pembroke 1738–75.

[107] Edward Sylvester, New Coll.

[108] Thomas Panting, Master of Pembroke 1714–38, and vicar of St Ebbe's 1714–19.

Wednesday 15. At Mrs Dewe's. Mrs Clark. Horn. Mrs Woolton. Received a letter from Newman inviting me to go to Georgia. My answer in the latter end of this book.[109]

Thursday 16. Paid Mr Beaver for Brown's widow the cook and my bedmaker in full to Michaelmas last. [1. 10. 0.] In the evening at the 3 Tunns. Moreton and Smith of Brazennose. A letter from H. P. of Liverpool.

Friday 17. Wrote to unkle Patten about the Box of Bookes for my father etc. and to Mr Jos. Hayward.

Saturday 18. At Mrs Brookes, her daughter and Mr Horn.

SUNDAY 19. Preached at Carrfax in the afternoon (Eccles. 8.11). Dined with Applebee the Mayor.

Monday 20. Wrote to Mr Newman, my former having miscarried. St. John's Coffee House with Mr Horn. Total Eclipse of the Moon 9 a clock to 11.

Tuesday 21. At Mrs Brookes. The ladies.

---

[109] The letter is as follows:

To Mr Newman. 15. Nov. 1732.

Good Sir, I take the first opportunity of acknowledging your favour and kind letter and assuring you that none would more readily embrace every opportunity of promoting so good and charitable a design. Were I in my own Power my inclination would lead me where you mention, but having hinted it to my father, he seemed so uneasy that I would press it no further. His great age and the difficulties he meets with in his Diocese from the Enemies of Religion making it necessary for him to have one in England who he can trust, in order to aply for advise and protection for him, if they should proceed to extremities as they have often done. His great Tenderness for me, and the former hazards I have met with at sea weigh much with him and makes him tremble to think I would venture again. I speak to you with the utmost Freedom, and can assure you, that I am always ready to undertake anything for the service of religion, without regard to the difficulties that shall attend it; but you see how the case is, and will determine for me.

You will be so good as to let the Person only who gave you this trust see this letter. My Prayers and Wishes attend those Worthy Gentlemen who are embarking upon so noble a design. I have been so ill of late, that I am not able to pay my acknowledgements to good Sir John and his sons; pray make my humble service acceptable to them and believe me, dear Sir, Your very affec. and oblig'd servant.

THO: WILSON.

For Henry Newman, Secretary of the S.P.C.K. from 1708 until his death in 1743, see L. W. Cowie, *Henry Newman: An American in London, 1708–1743* (1956).

Wednesday 22. Mr Horn [110] and I had rather a warm dispute about the Methodists taking the part of Blair [111] who was found guilty of Sodomitical Practices and fined 20 marks by the Recorder. Whether the man is innocent or no they were not proper judges, it was better he should suffer than such a scandal given an countenacing a man whom the whole town think guilty of such an enormous crime. Whatever good design they pretend it was highly imprudent and has given the occasion of terrible reflections.

Thursday 23. At the 3 Tunns. Moreton. Walwin. Parker & Hayward. A poor traveller 1s.

Friday 24. At Mrs Brookes.

SUNDAY 26. Went with Horn to Iffley. He preached I read prayers.

Monday 27. Received a letter from my father dated 23 Oct. He has received the bookes safe that I sent him. Wrote to Mr. Dawney.[112] See in the end.

Tuesday 28. At Mr Horn's rooms in the evening. Mr Burton from Corpus and Mrs Brookes.

Wednesday 29. St. Andrew's Day. did not give the Bear Butler 2s. 6d. as formerly as it should not be pleaded as a custom which was only a meer favour.

Thursday 30. This evening I hear that Mr Pointer Chaplain of Merton 40 years standing was called before the Warden and Fellows upon a complaint made by one of the Commoners of the House whom he had got into his chamber, and after urging him to drink, would have offered some very indecent things to him. He has been long suspected of Sodomitical Practices, but could never be fairly convicted of them. They say he behaved

[110] Thomas Horn, Ch. Ch., a friend of the Wesleys, especially of Charles Wesley, and a keen member of the Holy Club (V. H. H. Green, op. cit., pp. 176, 191, 256, 257).

[111] John Wesley regarded Blair as suffering "unjust persecution" and this case took up a great deal of his time and attention as well as that of other members of the Holy Club. Blair was the subject of many entries in John Wesley's Diary but he never mentions what the accusation was (V. H. H. Green, op. cit., pp. 172, 184–5f.).

[112] See 28 Dec. following.

with the utmost boldness and confidence. At the 3 Tunns. Moreton. Walwin. Hayward.

DECEMBER 1732

Friday 1. This morning Pointer had the assurance to walk along under the wall when 40 people were there. They are certainly under the power of the devil, who has 'em at his will. They did I hear Wildair's Clerk brazen it out in the face of the Recorder, when the plainest proof in the world was given of him of sodomy. I am told the Warden and Fellows have ordered Pointer to leave the College.[113] But they should indite and bring him to condeign punishment, how shall we otherwise free ourselves from the guilt and Judgments that hang over us.

Saturday 2. At Mrs Dewe's. Mrs Clark and Miss White.

SUNDAY 3. Went to hear Dr. Holdsworth. In the evening at the Coffee House. Moreton and Smith. I hear they have only rusticated Pointer for 4 months until the talk is over and then he is to return again. [He has resigned they tell me.] Shameful if it be true.

MONDAY 4. At Iffley. Mrs Brookes. Dined and supped there. Horse hire and servants 3s. 6d. Returned with Horn to college in the evening.

Tuesday 5. Sat in the Common Room in the evening. Brush Wood 3s.

Wednesday 6. Rode out to bury a corpse at Cowley. This morning came on the election of a 13 in the room of Mr Bacon deceased. Lord Abingdon set up Lawrence and Mr Rowney Knib the Upholsterer. The latter was chosen by a vast majority and my Lord was hissed and shamefully treated by the Mob. He has lost their interest by removing the Bucks and Does from Oxford to

---

[113] This affair is referred to at length by Hearne who says that Pointer "went into Nottinghamshire where he had a vicarage. He staid out a little while, returning to Oxford . . . taking a house in St Giles where he now lives." 8 June 1733.

An even more startling case of this nature which involved the Warden of Wadham, Robert Thistlethwaite, took place in 1739 (V. H. H. Green, op. cit., p. 31–3).

Cumnay and by his disregard of the populace by this means 'tis imagined Sergeant Skinner will lose his election for Member of Parliament. Horn's Birth Day. Aged 25. He treated us at Mrs Dewe's.

Thursday 7. Went with Moreton to see Dr. Rye at Islip. Dined with him and came home in the evening. At the 3 Tunns. Walwin. Parker and Hayward. The Bishop of Norwich died a Tuesday at Bath. Tanner they say to succeed him. Dr. Baker [114] lived freely in his youth and spoilt a good natural constitution. St. Giles in London now vacant. Given to Dr. Gully, Chaplain to the Lord Chancellor.

Friday 8. This day began a very hard frost which country people say is like to continue a long time. At Mrs Slatford's in the evening. To her niece 5s. for to give to two very poor families. God be thanked that I am able to relieve others.

Saturday 9. Very cold with great spews of snow. This day was put up in our Dormitory a fine bust engraven by Cheere [115] of Dean Aldrich and a black marble stone upon his grave. Both given by Dr. Clarke our member of Parliament.

SUNDAY 10. Mr Stone of Wadham preached a good ingenious sermon before the University rescuing the command of God to Abraham to sacrifice his son from the objections made against it. At John's with Moreton and Smith.

Monday 11. Frost continues hard. In the afternoon at Dr. Medcalf's who is much out of order with Pheumatick Pains, lives

---

[114] William Baker, Warden of Wadham, Bishop of Bangor 1713, Norwich 1717. "He was a very personable man and had been a good tutor . . . but a man of little learning. And as to his being universally respected it seems to be a sneer. He was a great drinker of the true Whiggish stamp" (Hearne, op. cit., p. 137).

[115] Sir Henry Cheere (1703–81) was doing much work in Oxford about this time and was responsible for the statues of Law, Physic and Poetry and of Queen Caroline at Queens in 1733, that of Christopher Codrington at All Souls in 1734, the busts of 24 fellows of All Souls being made by him in 1756. In 1738 he made the busts of Lord Clarendon and Archbishop Sheldon for the Sheldonian Theatre and in 1739 supplied many chimney pieces at Ditchley, Oxon. for the second Earl of Lichfield. Sir Henry Cheere became very friendly with Dr and Mrs Wilson and became the tenant of Dr Wilson's prebendal house at St Margaret's, Westminster.

very low, bleeds much and takes Rhubarb and Manna Purges.

Tuesday 12. A letter from Mr Fulford.

Wednesday 13. Walked with Horn to Iffley. Paid Mrs Brookes a visit. Archdeacon Brookes at home. Came back in the evening to our Common Room. At the burying of the Censor (Battelley) which cost us 3d. a piece. A letter from Mr Gibson from London.

Thursday 14. At the 3 Tunns. Moreton. Walwin. Parker. Alma Mater a Satyr against the University published.

Friday 15. At home all day. Wrote to Gibson and Fulford in answer to their last.

Saturday 16. Letter to my father. Paid a visit to the Principal of Jesus. Mr. Ascue advises me to put off our collection for the Saltsburghers till Lent. He told me that Lord Hunt. told him it was in his interest to get the Dean's friendship. That he should still retain his old Principles.

SUNDAY 17. A letter from Bath that our Dean [116] dyed there yesterday morning about 3 a clock. He had the unhappiness to be so much disliked being very hasty and yet easily bullied. Gave too much ear to little stories but what confirmed the students in their disregard for him was his putting by Blakeway in a living and giving it Jones his junior. Aged 60. They say either Fawkes or Cunnibear to have the Deanery. I hope the latter. In the Common Room.

Monday 18. Windy rainy weather.

Tuesday 19. Erasmus Phillips came to town from Bath. Not well recovered yet and is advised to go to a more favourable climate. At Dr. Medcalf's.

Wednesday 20. Dined with Moreton at Corpus and Dr. Rye who is of the opinion that the Isle of Man reverts to the Crown as a forfeiture upon the death of the present Earl.[117]

Thursday 21. Waited upon Mr Philipps to the Principal of

[116] William Bradshaw, Bishop of Bristol and Dean of Christ Church. Hearne says he was "great under the Dutchess of Marlborough and other noted Whiggs and yet several Whiggs did not much care for him" (Hearne, op. cit., p. 138).

[117] After the Act of Revestment in 1765 (V Geo. III, Cap. 26) the Lordship of the Isle of Man was taken over by the Crown from the Duke of Atholl, heir to the house of Stanley, Earls of Derby, Lords of Man.

Jesus. Dr. Thistlethwaite. Mr Wright etc. Spent the evening with Dr. Cunnibear. Vindicated the Saltsburghers upon the footing of Riot and Resistance. Talked about the late Dean's behaviour and wished he might succeed him. Promised him my best services tho' I am aware what treatment the late Dean's friends met with. Candles 16s. 6d.

Friday 22. At the Common Room. Wrote to Mr. Jos. Hayward.

Saturday 23. At home. In the afternoon at Walwin's read Alma Mater—a silly thing.

SUNDAY 24. *Ordination Sunday.* Assisted the Bishop of Oxford in administering the Sacrament. 13 Deacons and 8 Priests. Langford[118] preached the sermon.

Monday 25. Dr. Terry preached before the University[119] some Oratoricall Stokes out of Barrow upon the same text almost verbatim. In the Common Room.

Tuesday 26. Waited upon Dr. Cunnibear. He has no account as yet of being appointed Dean but I believe he expects it. I gave him some account of our exercises which he liked well and is resolved to see them performed. Will be pretty strict in knowing whether the tutors do their duty. Is resolved to put Ladds of merit into his turns as Students and not before they are a year of the House at least. I hope he will make an excellent Dean tho' the Westminsters object that he is no friend to Verses and indeed I think a more substantial kind of study might be carryed on. Aiscough[120] preached a sermon about his own case before the University in which he charged Lactantius for a Position which the criticks say is not his works. Some very loose expressions about thinking and following a mode of worship equally edifying. Have considered the Saltsburghers.

[118] Emmanuel Langford, Ch. Ch. A friend of John Wesley's and a member of the Holy Club (V. H. H. Green, op. cit., pp. 73, 176).
[119] Dr Thomas Terry, canon of Christ Church and Regius Professor of Greek. Hearne says that the service was at 11 a clock "the first instance of the sermon at that hour on Christmas Day . . . that people might lye in bed the longer" (Hearne, op. cit., p. 140).
[120] Francis Ayscough, Fellow of Corpus.

Wednesday 27. Rainy weather. Very much out of order with pains in my back and left Testicle. I am afraid the stone is in my kidney.

Thursday 28. Dawney admitted upon his humble submission into Hart Hall.[121] I hope he will behave well here again.

[121] Wilson wrote to Dawney at Sarum on 27 Nov. 1732 as follows:

Sir. If you had let me see you when you were last here I might have said something which might have proved to your advantage. And since you did not think fit to do so I can't excuse myself from writing to you and assuring you that none can be more sincerely your friend than myself. If it were not so I could easily excuse myself and you from this trouble. I know very well that your circumstances have made you uneasy, and well they might, but the way you are in will every day encrease the trouble and every day make your friends less able to serve you. You know better than I can tell you what temper your father is of and you have already tryed it very far. It is time to soften it by your dutyful and becoming carriage. Both the Laws of God and Common Prudence direct you to this, as he is your parent, whom you must obey, and as one upon whom you entirely depend for subsistance. It will not be in your brothers' power (tho' they have the tenderest regard for you) if you go on to slight their advise and his command. They all know the debts you have contracted here and if you were sensible of the amount of them I believe it would startle you. Can you possibly be easy to be daily at the mercy of your creditors who can arrest you and throw you into prison; and if you think your father, out of regard to his family, would not let you lie long in prison, you may be mistaken in this, for perhaps he may think that such a heavy chastisement is the only thing to bring you to a serious way of thinking. Promises of amendment will little avail at present. You must all at once throw off the habit of idleness you have got into. You must throw yourself at your brothers' feet and entreat them to intercede for you to your father and in the meantime get into some retirement, where you may be concealed, till matters here can be somehow or other adjusted. How far this scheme may prevail I am not able to promise, having no authority to propose any method, only 'tis the liklyest way to appease an angry father and regain the esteem of the world, and if you will come heartily into it I assure you that I will take pains to reconcile your friends to you, but then you must be in earnest. A miscarriage after such resolutions will be fatal. Your father's character and your brothers' excellent behaviour in the university, justly entitle them to the respect of every good man. One of that family was sure of meeting regard. Every body must expect great things from such an example, such an education. If you have in some measure forfeited the esteem of your friends, consider what aggravation such bad behaviour is attended with; but at the same time I would not have you despair; upon your return to your duty and Amendment of Life every body will readily forgive and forget and esteem you upon your own as well as your family's account. I have a great deal more in my mind, but my intention is not to trouble you, but waken you to a lively sense of your duty and wretchedness of your condition, for no other reason but that you may the better amend it. Your manner of life at the moment must be very extravagant

Xmas Boxes to College Servants, Tradesmen, Prentices as usual. 12s. 6d. I hear the Bishop of Winchester is dangerously ill at Chelsea. This wet weather has been fatal to abundance of old decayed constitutions. At the 3 Tunns. Moreton. Woollin. Duffield. Marshal of Univ. Page and Hayward of Magd.

Friday 29.   At home. In the evening at Mrs Slatford's.

Saturday 30.   *This Day* I am more particularly bound to commemorate with the most profound thanks to Almighty God for the greatest preservation that ever man had, from Ship-Wreck. His Holy Name be praised. May I be more careful of my wayes, more sollicitous to please him who has done such wonderful things for the unworthyest of his servants. This day we had the confirmation of Dr. Cunnibear being our Dean.

SUNDAY 31.   Paid Dr. Medcalf a visit. He is much better tho' still very weak. In the Common Room.

JANUARY 1732-3

Monday 1.   I waited upon Dr. Cunnibear at Exeter who took a coach for London this morning to kiss the King's hand. Wrote to the Bishop of London. Wesley of Lincoln preached at St. Mary's about Circumsition of the Heart etc. Enthusiastick. Dined with Moreton at Corpus. In the Common Room.

and far from becoming a young person in your circumstances. If you have any true friends where you are they must tell you so, but there are few that care for the ungrately task of reproving, even where it is their duty. Far be it from me to add weight to your concern. I would lessen it if I could, but that can never be done unless you let us know your design, which I can't guess at at present. When your creditors in Oxford find out that your father will not pay your debts they will grow very uneasy and it will be no difficult matter to find you out. You will excuse the haste I write in, being engaged in a great deal of business, which I should chearfully lay aside to serve you if you would let me. I desire an answer to this letter and let it be a sincere one. I am your sincere well wisher.   T. W.

N.B. I shewed this to Dr Newton the Principal of Hart Hall and he very much approved of it.

N.B. The effect of this letter was the bringing him to town and upon his humble submission was admitted again to Hart Hall, where I hope his behaviour will be more answerable to that resolution he has made. I pray God it may and then I shall be sufficiently pleased.

N.B. I am afraid he has since returned to his old courses.

Tuesday 2.   At home all day. A letter from my father dated 29th.

Wednesday 3.   At Mrs Dewe's. His sister very ill. Wrote to him to come up.

Thursday 4.   She made her will. At Dr. Medcalf's. Supped there. His sister and wife.

Friday 5.   Gave Mrs Dewe the sacrament by leave of Mr. Wildair. Woollin, Moreton, Duffield at my chamber. A letter from the Bishop of London,

Saturday 6.   12 Day. In the Common Room. Did not play at cards. The Recorder there. He intends to stand as Member of Parliament.

SUNDAY 7.   Preached at St. Ebbes for Jones in the afternoon. Wrote to my father in answer to his of Nov. 29th.

Monday 8.   Mrs Dewe's will lodged in my hands by her sister Wotton. Back into Mrs Dewe's hands.

Tuesday 9.   At Duffield's chamber. Parker. Woollin. Moreton.

Wednesday 10.   Lent my bedmaker 5d. more. Jan. 16. 5s. in full to Xmas 1732.

A Pair of Breeches. Knit. 17s.

A Silk Sash from London 17s.

A Pair of Stockings 5s. 6d.

Night Capps. 6s. 6d.

A letter to my unkle.

Two persons tryed for writing a sham letter to Mr. Griffiths of Magdalen to get money out of him upon a pretence of his having a girl with child. Found guilty and to be pilloried a Saturday.[122]

Thursday 11.   At the 3 Tunns. Mr Goole [123] and all our

[122] "13. Jan. Sat. One Bubb and one Moll Wells ... they were pelted with dirt but pretty favourably" (Hearne, op. cit., 147).

[123] This case was heard at Doctors Commons before Dr Bettesworth, Dean of the Arches, on 9 June 1733. Margaret, daughter of Dr John Hudson, was married to John Boyce, son of Sir John Boyce of Oxford, Kt. The Rev. Mr Goole, Vicar of Eynsham and schoolmaster of Witney, claimed that there was a marriage contract between him and Margaret prior to her marriage with Boyce. The judge pronounced in favour of her marriage with Boyce. Hearne (op. cit., pp. 220, 351-2) says "it appears that there was a most solemn contract between them and that Mr Goole acted very honourably with respect to that contract". Goole stated his case in a book entitled *The Hasty Marriage or the Contract Violated.*

own company. He gave us a long account of his contract with Mrs Boyce by which I am apt to think she will be separated from her husband. Mr Goole was easy, tho' as a clergyman he acted very unworthily. Drunk tea at Woollin's. Moreton and Parker.

Friday 12. At Woollin's. Moreton. Parker and Walwin.

Saturday 13. At Mrs Dewe's. His sister worse. A letter from my father dated 9. Dec.

SUNDAY 14. At John's. Moreton. Smith.

Monday 15. A letter from my dear father. 2 Enclosures. 1 for my Lord Chancellor and the other for Auditor Harley recommending me to their favour.

Tuesday 16. A kind letter from Mr Hales telling me that Sir John Philipps will readily wait upon my Lord Chancellor upon my account. Returned my thanks. At the Common Room.

Wednesday 17. At Duffield's. Woollin. Parker and Langford.

Thursday 18. At the 3 Tunns. The usual company.

Friday 19. At Moretons

Saturday 20. Wrote to my father in answer to his last kind letter. Enclosed with frank to Cousin Hugh Patten. At Parker's room. All our own company.

SUNDAY 21. At the Common Room at University. Entertained by Walwin.

Monday 22. A strange infection in the air [124] by which Nos. in London and in the country are violently seized with pains in their head and coughing. It has last proved universal here. I find myself very much out of order. The doctors bleed immediately, give sweating draughts and as soon as the body is cool give physick and they have hitherto had good success.

Tuesday 23. Wrote to Mr Jos. Hayward.

Wednesday 24. Am much better. Live low and drink warm water with my wine.

Thursday 25. At the 3 Tunns. Ward with us,

Friday 26. Dr. Conybear came to town with Mr Cowper. Paid my compliments to him at Exeter. Gave him a full account of the exercises, discipline etc. of Christ Church. Long neglected.

[124] Influenza epidemic. See note for 3 Feb. following.

Was very thankful and promises all acts of friendship to me.

Saturday 27. This morning Dr. C. was installed Dean of Christ Church [125] by the SubDean. I gave an entertainment in the evening to a few of his and my friends at my chamber. [8s. 9d.] Find myself much out of order with a sore throat.

SUNDAY 28. Continue ill. Keep my chamber. Drink water gruel with Honey in it, broth etc. Wrote to unkle Patten to pay Ridgwell what Moreton owes him. A letter from Jos. Hayward.

Monday 29. Paid for binding my father's Common Prayer Book 8s. Much worse with my throat. Eat no meat but live entirely upon water gruel. Fluxt my throat with burnt allum to prevent a Quinsey.

Tuesday 30. Much worse and fever attending it. Drank sack whea and spirit of Hartshorn, warm water and orange and sweetened with Honey. Could not sweat. The Master of University preached a plain sermon as they tell me at St. Mary's. Horn and Dewe sat with me in the evening.

Wednesday 31. Dr. Medcalf came to visit me. Told me my pulse was wavering and tending to be worse. Water very foul. Ordered a cooling purge to be taken in the morning. Eat nothing but water gruel.

FEBRUARY 1732-3

Thursday 1. Wrote to Mr Hayward the reason for my not coming up to London. Took physick. Agreed with me well. Drank Bath water and took Spermacetea Bolusses. Beginning to cough and run at the nose much.

Friday 2. A thin Gawdy. The Canons all out of order with this

[125] "Jan. 28. Sun. On friday last about noon came very privately to Oxford in a coach and four Dr. Conybear, Rector of Exeter College, being met by not so much as one soul and yesterday at ten o clock in the morning he was installed as Dean of Christ Church, but very little, or no rejoicing on the occasion. He owes this piece of preferment to Mr (he is not a university Dr.) Edmund Gibson, Bishop of London, who hath some private by-ends in view, to whom he dedicated his reply to *Christianity as Old as Creation*, which book (I am told but I have not read it) is spun out at great length, wherein all that is material might have been contracted as brought into almost a sheet of paper" (Hearne, op. cit., p. 152).

cold and most of the Masters of Art. I am, I thank God, much better tho' advised to take more physick. Manna and Glauber Salts.

Saturday 3. Took another dose of physick a little stronger than the last. Agreed well with me and am much easier in my stomack. I find that the Bills of Mortality in London are higher this last week than they have been since the Plague, above 1586.[126] Very stormy weather yesterday and today. Mr Harrison sent me a 2nd. Hand Gold Watch at 12 Guineas, made by Burckham London as good as new, the size perfecly fashionable. I wrote to him that I desired to try it for 8 or 10 days. (Returned it being very slight.)

SUNDAY 4. Very windy and in the afternoon rained hard. I am afraid the weather will make these colds more general and fatal. The Doctor bids me keep up close in my chamber and take physick often while my water is so foul. I am to drink nothing but Bath water and a little sack in it.

Monday 5. Drew a Bill in favour of Daniel Whitaker on Cousin T. Patten of Warrington for £10 10s. of which I gave him advise by the same post.

Tuesday 6. I ventured out. Visited the Dean. Abundance of people ill. Sent 9s. to 3 poor families by the hands of Mrs Slatford. Dr. Ailmer [127] taken ill this afternoon of an Apoplexy and 'tis feared will go off. Dr. Ailmer died this afternoon at 7 a clock, very much regretted by all that knew him.

Wednesday 7. Ash Wednesday. Pretty much out of order it being very cold. This day I received a Bill from Mr Richardson our University Treasurer for £25 drawn at sight upon Sir Robt. Furnesse, Dover Street, Pickadilly by his son Henry in favour of William Ives endorsed by him and Richardson. [A Bill of £25 in my pocket Book with the Silver Pencil.] Wrote to Mr Harris on the case of the Gold Watch, much too slight and that I should

---

[126] The winter of 1732-3 was exceptionally mild and damp and there was a bad epidemic of influenza, especially in London (Plumb, *Sir Robert Walpole, the King's Minister*, p. 253).

[127] Dr George Aylmer, M.D., Fellow of C.C.C.

return it by Mrs Slatford's wagon on friday—sent it. Woolston,[128] author of the Discourses against the Miracles of our Saviour died last week and said he resigned with great chearfulness. Terrwit [129] is to be Canon Residentary of St. Paul's and Dr. Secker [130] made Rector of St. James. Dr. Godolphin,[131] an excellent man, died last week. [60 years.] Bland to be Provost of Eton.

[128] Thomas Woolston (1670–1733) was chiefly concerned to discredit the miracles of Christ, speaking of the Gospels as "an emblematical representation of the spiritual life in the soul of man" and the miracles as "figures of His mysterious operations". He was especially bitter against the clergy as "the physicians under whose care the woman with the issue grew worse". The most popular of the Deist writers, Swift refers to him as follows:

> Here's Woolstan's Tracts, the twelfth edition
> 'Tis read by every politician.
> The country members when in town,
> To all their boroughs send them down;
> You never met a thing so smart,
> The courtiers learn them all by heart.
> The maids of honour who can read
> Are taught to use them as a creed.

Hearne says "about four or five minutes before he died he uttered these words 'This is a struggle, which all men go through, and which I bear not only with patience but willingness.' After which he closed his eyes and shut his lips with a seeming design to compose his face with decency, without the help of a friends hand, and then he expired. But whether he shewed in the time of his illness any sense of conscience or any signs of repentance for his having invalidated in his Discourses the Miracles of our Saviour we don't hear."

[129] Dr Tyrwhit, son-in-law of Bishop Gibson of London.

[130] Thomas Secker (1693–1768), who often appears in the Diary, was appointed rector of St James's, Piccadilly, on the recommendation of Bishop Gibson of London. Bishop of Bristol 1734, Oxford, in succession to Dr Potter, in 1737, Archbishop of Canterbury 1758. Educated at the Nonconformist academy at Tewkesbury with Joseph Butler, Bishop of Durham, and Isaac Maddox, Bishop of Worcester, he remained in constant friendship with such leading dissenters as Isaac Watts and Philip Doddridge. Like Bishop Sherlock of London he tried unsuccessfully to get bishops consecrated for the American colonies. As Bishop of Oxford and afterwards as Archbishop of Canterbury he was outstanding among the bishops of the time in attempting to make the organization of the Church more efficient and insisting upon a higher sense of pastoral responsibility among the clergy.

[131] Dr Godolphin, "commonly called Mother Louse, because his nose reached near to his chin" (Hearne, op. cit., p. 157), presumably because of his resemblance in this respect to Mother Louse, the latest woman in England to wear a ruff and who was the subject of a rare print by Loggan (illus. in Tuckwell's Reminiscences of Oxford (1907), p. 290).

Thursday 8. At the 3 Tunns. Moreton. Woollin. Parker. This night the Dean ordered the gates to be locked up a quarter after 9.[132] I hope he intends to revise the ancient discipline of this House long neglected.

Friday 9. Mr Wade, Prebend of Windsor died, my Lord James Beauclerk to succeed him and Lewis of Kew to succeed Bland in his Canonry of Windsor. My Lady Countess of Buckenborough used to say that he used to hear her speak to the Queen about preferment. This day I wrote to my father by way of Liverpool an account of my illness, Some of our House angry that Dr Medcalf visited me. This grounded upon a false presumption of my sending for him when he only came to see me as an acquaintance in return for the visits I made him in his late illness. At Mrs. Slatford's in the evening.

N.B. This short illness, Physick, Attendance etc. stood me in £2. 15. 6d. An extravagant place to be ill in as any in the world.

Saturday 10. Paid the Candle Man £1. 1. 0. N.B. I owe him 9s. A letter from Billy Hayward that all our friends at Newington are well. At the Common Room. Decreased in the Bills of Mortality at London this week 422. The greatest part that have died by this late disorder have been children between 2 and 3 and old people. Those that have had bad lungs have gone off very suddenly.

SUNDAY 11. At home.

Monday 12. At the Dean's with F. Moreton. Supped and spent the evening with him. Very kindly entertained. Tells me that the Students have no right by seniority to Livings and that we M.A. are as much obliged as the undergraduates to early prayers.

Tuesday 13. The Dean gave me a letter to Counselar Carter (Treasurer of the Temple) to let me have a turn to preach there, which he did.

Wednesday 14. Set out for London in Smith's coach with Hall

---

[132] Dr Conybeare makes a great stir in the college at first pretending to great matters, such a locking up the gates at nine o clock at night, having the keys brought to him, turning out young women from being bedmakers, having the kitchen (which he visits) cleansed, and I know not what, aiming at a wonderful character" (Hearne, op. cit., p. 169).

of Brasennose Cheney the Taylor. Dined at Tedsworth. Supped and lay at the Catherine Wheel at Wickham. [2s. 8d., 3s. 9d.]

Thursday 15. Dined at Uxbridge. Lay at the White Swan, Holborn Bridge. [3s. 4d., 2s. 6d. Coach 10s.] Waited this evening on Mr Carter who set me down to preach the 15 April at the Temple. At the Devil Tavern with Mr Freke. 1s. 10d.

Friday 16. Waited upon Mr Newman. Went with him to the sermon before the Society for Propagating the Gospel in Forreign Parts. Bishop of Lichfield and Cov.—Smalbroke.[133] Went to the Society. Dined with Sir John Phillips. Received most kindly. A letter from my father the 2nd. inst.

Saturday 17. At a Committee for the Saltsburghers affairs with Sir John. Desired that I would draw up a Sketch of a Preface for a further narrative of their sufferings. Dined with Sir John. Went to Newington and received with great affection.

Tuesday 20. At the Society. I read the Preface I had drawn up. Put into Mr Vernon's hands to peruse and alter. Dined with Sir John. Coach hire 1s. 1d.

Wednesday 21. At Newington.

Thursday 22. At the Saltsburghers Committee. Read over and sent part of the narrative to the press.

Friday 23. Wrote to my father.

Saturday 24. At Newington. Ridd out with M. to Endfield. 4s. 6d.

SUNDAY 25. At Newington.

Monday 26. At the Saltsburghers Committee. Went through more of the narrative. Dined with Sir John, Erasmus and Buckley. Mr Fox. Mr. Macbeth. Gave him in private an Account of the Methodists, how ill they had disposed of his charity in relieving a Sodomite.[134]

Tuesday 27. At the Society. Waited upon Auditor Harley. Well received.

---

[133] Richard Smalbroke, Bishop of Lichfield and Coventry 1731–49. In 1746 he published a charge to his clergy on "Methodism akin to Romanism".

[134] See note 95, Sir John Philipps was a great supporter of the Holy Club's charities.

MARCH 1732-3

Thursday 1. *The Queen's Birth Day.* Went to Court with Mr Rogers. A numerous assembly of ladies to compliment her Majesty. Dined with Mr Rogers.

Saturday 3. At the Society. Proposed Dr. Conybeare as a member.

SUNDAY 4. Cousin Jonny Murrey dined with us. Pretty much of a Fopp. I preached this afternoon for Mr Seers.

Monday 5. Waited upon Lord Ashburnham (in Bullingdon Street, Pickadilly). Found him in bed. Very kindly received. Promised to serve me with great chearfulness. Desired me to get a letter from Dr. Conybear in my favour and that he would present it to the Bishop of London.

Tuesday 6. At the Society. Brought my abstract of the Sufferings of the Exiles. Approved of. Dined with Sir John. [Coach 1s.]

Thursday 8. Mr Hayward and I went to dinner with our society at the Rose Tavern, Cursitors Alley. Mr Earl inveighed against the Charity Schools in the House of Commons as the cause of Street Robberies. Sir J. Bernard and Mr Harley defied him to produce any that were hanged educated at those places. My Lord Duke of Argyle abused the clergy in the other House as the curses of education in all ages.

Saturday 10. At the Saltsburghers Committee. Dined with Sir John.

SUNDAY 11. At Newington. Wrote to Dr. Conybeare for a character. To Moreton.

Tuesday 13. At the Society. Paid a visit to Mrs Marshall. Dined with Sir John Phillips. Mr Tylliard. Mr Sale. Dr. Humphreys talked of the citizens going down in a Mobbing Way to Westminster tomorrow to shew themselves averse to the Excise Bill. Wrote to my father.

Thursday 15. At Bow Church. The Anniversary sermon for the Trustees of Georgia. Preached by Burton of C.C.C. Very long and dry. Dined with Moreton and Horn at Truby's, St. Paul's Church Yard. In the morning I visited the Bishop of Oxford

(Palace Yard). Shewed him the Dean's letter and told him my design of getting some preferment which he wished me all success in. Went to see Bishop Tanner (Union Street) in the afternoon. Saw Hogarth's paintings (Piatazza's Covent Garden). Was at the Saltsburghers Committee.

Friday 16. Went through the narrative. Spent the evening with Mr Gibson. Breakfasted with Sir John Phillips. He desired the Dean's letter to shew the Lord Chancellor. Very heartily in my favour. Returned to dine at Newington.

SUNDAY 18. At Newington. Wrote to Tom. Moreton.

Tuesday 20. Took an airing with Cousin Hayward to Hyde Park. Came round by Westminster and went to the Society. Appointed by them to draw up a Preamble to an Account to be published at the latter end of the Anniversary Sermon before the Charity Children. Undertook to get it finished by that time tho' a laborious task for I shall be forced to look over all the Minutes of the Society from 1698. Dined with Sir John Philipps. Dr. Colbatch. Dr. Bundy and talked about the Excise Bill and the heat the whole country seemed to be in about it. Returned in the evening.

Thursday 22. Waited upon Lord Ashburnham. Civilly received. He told me he had not yet an opportunity of seeing the Bishop of London about my affair, but certainly would not forget it. Returned in the evening.

Saturday 24. Proceeded in the Account and made great Progress in it.

SUNDAY 25. *Easter Day.*

Monday 26. Finished the Preamble.

Tuesday 27. At the Society. Read over. Approved of and a Committee was ordered to meet a friday evening to consider of what the Appendix should consist. Dined with Sir John. Mr Sale. Mr Bedford.

Wednesday 28. At Newington and looked over the matter of the Appendix.

Thursday 29. At Ditto. Looked over and corrected a sermon which I am to preach at the Temple next Sunday.

Friday 30. At the Society. Went thro' the affair and ordered it to be printed and brought to me to be corrected. Dined with my unkle. Cousin Hayward.

Saturday 31. At Newington. About my sermon. Told Dear Molly of my great Inclination to have her and I have reason to believe she will consent when I have preferment.

APRIL 1733

SUNDAY 1. Went to town. At St. Sepulchre's received the Sacrament from Dr. Knight. Dined with Mr Freke and preached at the Temple to a large congregation. Appointed by the Treasurer Richard Carter Esq, Treasurer of the Inner Temple. A Welch Judge. [Coach Hire 6s.]

Monday 2. Went with Mr Hayward and Dear Molly to Rossy Green 9 miles off. Treated them there with a coach and dinner. [1. 4. 6.] Returned home in the evening.

Tuesday 3. At the Society. A Proof Sheet [135] brought of the Account but not yet correct.

Wednesday 4. Dined with Sir John.

Thursday 5. At Anniversary Sermon at St. Sepulchre's for the Charity Children.[136] The finest sight my eyes beheld and the

[135] "The Committee went through the Preamble to the Account of the Society's Proceedings to which several amendments were made and Mr Copping and Mr Wilson were ordered to wait here by 8 next Tuesday morning to give directions for preparing a draught of what is now doing" (S.P.C.K. Minutes, 7 April 1733).

[136] The anniversary services for the Charity Schools of London and Westminster, which were established in 1704, drew vast congregations which increased over the years, and after 1782 they were always held at St Paul's. The procession of Charity Children with their masters and mistresses and their parish clergy going before them was, as Strype says, "a wondrous surprising as well as pleasing sight" and was described by William Blake in his poem *Holy Thursday.*

> 'Twas on a Holy Thursday, their innocent faces clean,
> The children walking two and two, in red and blue and green,
> Grey-headed beadles walk'd before, with wands as white as snow,
> Till into the high dome of Paul's they like Thames waters flow.

Bishop Wilson was a great supporter of the Charity Schools movement and with the assistance of Lady Elizabeth Hastings opened thirteen schools in the Isle of Man, imposing a fine of one shilling on parents who neglected to send their children. See *The Charity School Movement*, by M. G. Jones (1938).

best Musick in the world. The Bishop of Peterborough [137] preached an indifferent sermon. I dined with the Trustees of the Charity Schools at Auditor Harley's. A fine entertainment. Very severe on the Prime Minister and large Encomiums upon the minority in the House of Commons. Returned home in the evening. A letter from my father dated 19 March. He has not received my 3 last.

Saturday 7. Looked over and corrected a sermon I am to preach the 15 of this month at the Temple.

Tuesday 10. At the Society. Dined with Sir John Phillips. Dr. Colbatch. Mr Bedford. Mr Copping. Returned to Newington.

Wednesday 11. This morning the Sheriffs attended with 130 Coaches full of merchants. Went solemnly from the Guildhall with the Petition against the Excise Bill which after a smart debate was admitted to be read, they having an undoubted right to be heard against any Bill depending. Sir Robert finding the Tide ran so high against him proposed to put it off and so it was unanimously to the 12 June, that is dropt for good and all. The news was received in the City with the utmost joy and thanksgiving and the night concluded with Bonfires, ringing of Bells etc. The Mob broke all windows that were not illuminated at the Post Office. An Effigie representing Sir Robt. was drawn from New Prison and burnt at Temple Bar and other places. *This is I am afraid but the beginning of troubles* the whole Nation being disposed to follow the same riotous doings.[138]

Thursday 12. Went to town. Paid the Bishop of London a visit. Very well received. Told the Bishops were resolved not to give up their rights, their temporal ones I presume he means. Dined with Mr Harrison at Charing Cross. Returned in the evening.

Friday 13. Wrote to my father in answer to his of March 19.

Saturday 14. At Newington. Finished my sermon for tomorrow.

SUNDAY 15. Went to London. Preached in the morning for Dr. Best at St. Laurence. Dined with my unkle. Preached in the

---

[137] Robert Clavering, Bishop of Llandaff 1725, Peterborough 1729–49.

[138] See note for 19 April following. Also J. H. Plumb, *Sir Robert Walpole, the King's Minister*, pp. 254ff.

afternoon at the Temple. Bishop Sherlock [139] and 2 other Bishops being by. Returned in the evening. [Coach Hire 6s.]

Monday 16. At Newington. Not very well. Took Physick. Am better. Dear Molly shows how dear a wife she would make.

Tuesday 17. At the Society. Carried my Aunt and Dear Molly to the Park. Very pleasant. Mr Hayward gave us a handsome entertainment at Truby's. Returned to Newington in the evening.

Thursday 19. At the Society. Dined with Sir John. Dr. Brydges. Mr. Copping, who told me that there had lately been great Riots in Oxford,[140] even to proclaiming the Pretender. I hope 'tis not true. In the evening Sir John carried me to the Lord Chancellor who hoped it would be in his power to serve me which he should be glad of. Supped with Sir John. Lay at Mr Newman's our Secretary's.

Friday 20. I walked across the fields by Islington to Newington which fateguee me much.

Saturday 21. Mr Dewe, Mr Fulford and Mr Maitland came to pay me a visit. Were most kindly received by Mr Hayward

[139] Thomas Sherlock (1678–1761), Bishop of Bangor 1728, Salisbury 1734, London 1748, who often appears in the Diary, is like Bishop Wilson in that he displayed many of the characteristics of an earlier age. The eldest son of William Sherlock (1641–1707), Dean of St Paul's, he succeeded his father in the Mastership of the Temple, an office which he held from 1704 until 1753 and where he established a reputation as a preacher. He was a voluminous writer, the most celebrated of his works being *The Trial of the Witnesses of the Resurrection of Jesus Christ* (1729). In 1716 he preached a sermon in favour of the Non-jurors and in 1718 was deprived of his position as Royal Chaplain for writing against Hoadly. A great supporter of the S.P.C.K. and S.P.G., he tried unsuccessfully to get bishops consecrated for the American colonies, and in 1746 pleaded for the Scottish Episcopal clergy in the House of Lords. He is said to have refused both archbishoprics, York in 1743 and Canterbury in 1747.

[140] "April 15. Sun. Sir Robert Walpole, King George's Statesman, having received a very great disappointment last Wednesday in the Parliament House with regard to an unheard of Tax he had projected upon Tobacco & Wine etc. there was such rejoicings in London at it, that the like thereof hath not been heard, and the news thereof being brought to Oxford late at night on Thursday following Apl. 12 the bells rung between ten and eleven a clock at night till two or three in the morning at most of the Parish Churches etc. and there were Bonfires also. Likewise the next night were Bonfires, throwing of serpents and other rejoycings at Oxford upon the occasion. But the Vice Chancellor and Mayor last night prohibited the proceedings" (Hearne, op. cit., p. 185).

and they invited us to dine with them at Pontacks next Tuesday.

Tuesday 24. At the Society. Dined at Pontacks. Treated very handsomely by Mr Maitland.

Thursday 26. In town with the Society. Dined with Sir John.

Friday 27. Wrote to my father.

Saturday 28. A letter from my father.

SUNDAY 29. At Newington. Preached in the afternoon for Mr Copping at Hackney. A very large congregation.

MAY 1733

Tuesday 1. The Society desired I would join Dr. Bundy. Mr Copping in drawing up a short account of the Rise and Progress of the Society to be annexed to the sermon preached at St. Sepulchre's, which I undertook and we are to meet a friday.

Friday 4. Met with Dr. Bundy and he left the business.

Saturday 5. In Town. Bought a set of Tea Spoones cost 2. 0. 6. 2 Table Cloths 12s. 6d. Gloves, 6 pair 7s. 8d. A Portmantua 1. 1. 0. 4 Handkershiefs, Cambrick. 1. 0. 0. A Pair of Shoos 5. 6d. Coach Hire 1s.

SUNDAY 6. Preached in the afternoon for Mr Seers.

Tuesday 8. At the Society. Read part of the Account of our Society which was approved of. Dined with Sir John.

Wednesday 9. Waited upon the Duke of Athol who is Presumptive Heir to the Isle of Man. Gave him a short account of that place. Paid my father's and the clergy's compliments to him. Was mightily kindly received and promised us his Favour and Continuance of it when he becomes our Lord. That he would himself come over and settle all our differences. Wrote to my father word of this. Returned in the evening. [Coach Hire 2s. Horse 1s.]

Friday 11. In town about the Account corrected for the Press and am to have a proof sheet tomorrow.

SUNDAY 13. At Newington.

Tuesday 15. At the Society. Was directed to proceed in the Account according to the Method proposed by myself. Dined with Sir John.

Wednesday 16. Rode out with Mr Hayward and his sister to Endfield and dined abroad. [8s. 6d.]

Thursday 17. At Newington.

Friday 18. Very sore eyes.

Saturday 19. Worse. Took Physick.

SUNDAY 20. At Newington. Preached for Mr Seers, his son being lately dead and he under great affliction.

Tuesday 22. At the Society. Dined with Sir John.

Wednesday 23. Received my father's book concerning the Sacrament and design to shew it on Friday to Sir John Phillips.

Friday 25. Read over my father's little Book to Sir John and he altered a few words. He desires it may be printed soon.

Saturday 26. At Mr Downing's. Gave him the copy and he promises me a Proof Sheet next week and I am to correct the Press. Dined with Mr Rogers and his lady.

SUNDAY 27. At Newington.

Tuesday 29. At London. It was moved in the House of Commons for a sermon but if it had come to a devision Mr Phillips tells me that he believes it would have been carried against by a great Majority.[141] The Lords had none and did no business this day. Dined with Sir John.

Thursday 31. At Newington. Went to Fulham. Dined with Mrs Gibson and her 3 daughters and 2 sons. Kindly received. Sat afterwards with Mr Carthwright the Chaplain. Returned in Dr. Watson's coach with Dr. Crowe.[142] Went home in the evening.

[141] After the Restoration it was the custom for the House of Commons to attend St Margaret's, Westminster, for the State Services on 5 November, 30 January, and 29 May. The House of Commons appointed the preacher and his sermon was afterwards printed. By the middle of the eighteenth century, however, this observance had become largely a formality (Charles Smyth, *Church and Parish: Studies in Church Problems, illustrated from the Parochial History of St Margaret's, Westminster* (1955), p. 26).

[142] William Crowe, D.D., Fellow of Trinity Hall, Cambridge, chaplain to George II. vicar of St Mary Magdalen, Fish Street 1722, prebendary of St Paul's 1726, rector of St Botolph's, Bishopsgate, 1730 and of Finchley 1731. d. 1743. A popular preacher and published many sermons during his life and a collected edition—*Dr Crowe's Favourite and Most Excellent Sermons*—appeared after his death in 1759.

JUNE 1733

Monday 4. Dined with the ArchBp. of Canterbury. His grace not at dinner. 2 sons in law. Col. Broadrop and sat with the Chaplain and Mr Bateman.

Tuesday 5. At the Society. Dined with Sir John. Dr. Colbatch. Dr. Denne. Mr Tylliard and Mr Vernon. They lamented the great increase of Popery and proposed that in all the counties our correspondents should be desired to give accounts of the stepps taken by these people.

Wednesday 6. At Newington.

Thursday 7. Mr Downing brought me the proof sheet. Looked it over and corrected it.

Friday 8. Ridd out with Dear Molly to see her mother at Edmington and afterwards to Mr Downing's Lodgings at Southgate. [Coach hire 6s.]

SUNDAY 10. At Newington.

Tuesday 12. At the Society. Dined with my unkle.

Tuesday 19. Took leave of the Society and they desired me to undertake the collection for the Poor Sufferers at Saltsburgh.[143]

Wednesday 20. At Newington. Spent the evening in town with Mr Fulford and Mr Harrison at Bentley's Charing Cross.

Thursday 21. Set out in Dewes coach for Oxford. Dined at Wickham. Called at Tedsworth. The coachman had the impudence to leave Sir William Osbalson and I there, we rode to town and complained to the Vice Chancellor who promises to make the fellow repent of his insolence. [dinner 2s. coach man 1s. carriage hire 5s. 6d.] Spent the evening with Sr. Wm. at the Cross Inn. Lay at Mr Dewe's.

Friday 22. Wrote to Mr Hayward and to my father who is just arrived in England.

Saturday 23. Dined with Horn at the Coffee House. A differ-

---

[143] "Agreed that the Rev. Dr Conybeare, Dean of Christ Church, Dr Pardo, Principal of Jesus Coll., Dr. Smith, Provost of Queens and Dr. Cockman, Master of University Coll. in Oxford be desired to further Mr Wilson's endeavours for promoting a collection in Oxford in favour of the Saltsburg Exiles" (S.P.C.K. Minutes, 19 June 1733).

ence between the Vice Chancellor and our Dean. The latter would have Verses spoke in Honour of the Royal Family. The former against it. I hope it will be accomodated.

SUNDAY 24. Preached and read prayers for Mr Lamprey at Magdalen Church. Dined with Mr Dewe. Wrote to Dear Molly.

Monday 25. Waited upon the Dean the 2nd. time.

Tuesday 26. A letter from my father at Liverpool.

Wednesday 27. A Dear Letter from My Charming Molly which I answered the same post.

Thursday 28. Dined with Mr Fulford at Balliol.

Friday 29. Wrote to my father. Mr Newman. Mr Downing.

Saturday 30. Went to Wickham and met Molly and her brother. Dined with them. [5s. 6d.] Brought them to Oxford. They lay at Mr Dewe's.

JULY 1733

SUNDAY 1. They dined with me.

Monday 2. Molly not well.

Tuesday 3. I hope a little better. Mr Patten and Mr Shipley dined with me.

Wednesday 4. Dined at Mr Fulford's. At the Oratorio.

Thursday 5. At my room. Cousin Jonny Murrey came to town. This day Molly promised to have me supposing I had no preferment at Xmas. I resolved never to play any more at cards.

Friday 6. The Act [144] began. We were in the Theator from 11 to past 6

Saturday 7. A letter from my father.

SUNDAY 8. Act Sunday.[145] Dr. Cockman in the morning and Dr. Secker an excellent sermon in the afternoon.

[144] At this Act (Encaenia) there was a performance by Handel and, according to Hearne, "his lousy crew, a great number of forreign fiddlers" on the invitation of the Vice-Chancellor, Dr Holmes (Hearne, op cit., pp. 224–5).

[145] "This being Act Sunday the sermon was preached at St. Maries in the morning by Dr. Cockman, Master of University Coll. and in the afternoon by Dr. Secker of Exeter Coll, both inceptors, the ladies both morning and afternoon sitting as usual in Act time in the Gentlemen's Galleries" (Hearne, op. cit., p. 227).

Monday 9. At an Oratorio. 10s.

Tuesday 10. At Kat Mundey's.

Wednesday 11. Upon the water.

Saturday 14. Dined with me.

SUNDAY 15. I preached at St. Aldate's in the morning.

Monday 16. They were with me.

Wednesday 18. My dear friends parted with me this morning for London.

Thursday 19. Paid my Bills.

To the Cook.	6.	19.	6.
For Wine.	4.	15.	8.
Attendance.		10.	0.
Pocket Expenses.	2.	2.	6.
	14.	7.	8.

Friday 20. A kind letter from Molly which I answered.

Saturday 21. A letter from Mr Hayward.

SUNDAY 22. Wrote to Molly. Preached for Dr. Rye at Islip. There was there Dr. Evans.

Monday 23. Wrote to my father.

Tuesday 24. Wrote to Molly. No letter from her which I am surprised at.

Wednesday 25. Wrote to Molly to know what was the matter.

Thursday 26. A very severe letter from Molly charging me with Galantries and not being true to her, everything very false. Answered the same day.

Friday 27. Very ill occasioned by vexation etc. Vomited blood. Much worse in the evening.

Saturday 28. Very much out of order. God grant I may bear this stroke with tolerable Resignation.

[Break in the Diary until 10 October.[146]

[146] During this time the Diarist went down to Lancashire and bade farewell to his father at Liverpool on his return to the Isle of Man.

Bishop Wilson's Journal Sept. 14. 1733: "Having the day before parted with my son and dear friends at Liverpool I landed this day after twenty two hours, with Captain Richmond, at Douglas. Deo. Gr."

OCTOBER 1733

Wednesday 10. Went to pay Dr. Hales a visit at Teddington. Found him at home and very civil.

Thursday 11. Went to Court. *Coronation Day.* A Grand Appearance. Dined with Mr Eccleshall, a Lancashire Gentleman (Clerk of the Kitchen), Mrs Kane, the Col's Lady, Mrs Marriott, Housekeeper at Windsor, Dr. Charleton, Sub-Dean, Dr. Tessier.

Friday 12. Paid Sir John Cheshire a visit at Thistleworth. Recommended our charity for clergymen's widows and children in the Isle of Man. Promised me £25.

Saturday 13. Hunted the Hind with the King. All the Royal Family there.

SUNDAY 14. Preached for Dr. Hales. Dined with Mr Mather who formerly kept a toyshop between the Temple Gates. Drank tea with Mr Edwards, Capt. Nicholson, Mr Hammond of Queens and 2 sisters.

Monday 15. Went to Court. Introduced to the Queen by Lord Grantham. Said she would be glad to see my father in London. Kist her hand. Dined with Dr. Regis [147] and Dr. Briggs,[148] Chaplains, Dr. Naylor, Dean of Winchester, Dr. Maddox told me that the Duke of Atholl had promised to see the Reversion of the Isle of Man to the Crown.

Tuesday 16. Returned to Newington. Saw the Duke of Devonshire's house afire. At the Society.

Wednesday 17. Dined with Sir John Cheshire in Essex Street. Went to see Lord Ashburnham in Charles Street near St. James' Square. Not at home. Drunk tea with Mr Harrison. Supped with Sir John Phillips. Talked of the Rise and Progress of Popery and how to put a stop to it. Lay at Newman's.

---

[147] Balthazar Regis, D.D. Trin. Coll. Dublin, Incorp. at Trin. Coll. Camb, Royal Chaplain 1727–57 and canon of Windsor 1751–7.

[148] Henry Briggs, D.D., son of William Briggs, M.D., Physician to William III and author of *A Theorie of Vision.* Rector of Holt (1721–48) and of Letheringsett (1742–8), Norfolk.

Thursday 18. At the Society. Made a Motion [149] to petition Lady Harold Penyston Lamb Esq etc. for a Legacy to Charitable Uses of £40,000 left by the late Lord Thanet. Not well. Returned to Newington. Wrote to my father setting forth in the fullest manner the reasons of my request to him etc.

Things bought:

Linnen.	14.	6.	8.
A Night Gown	3.	15.	0.
Shoos. 3 Pair.	8.	18.	0.
Pocket Expenses since			
I came to London.	5.	6.	0.
Expenses on the			
Road.	4.	18.	6.
	37.	4.	2.

Wednesday 24. At Newington. Mem. for tomorrow. To see Lord Ashburnham to put him in mind of his promise to see Auditor Harley to get a Chaplain's Place in the army.

[Break in the Diary until 15 November.]

[149] "The draught of such a memorial was laid before the Committee and read and with some amendments approved in the following words. viz. To the Rt. Hon. the Countess of Harold, John Coke and Peniston Lamb Esquiers, Surviving Trustees of the late Earl of Thanet's Charitable Bequests. The Memorial of the S.P.C.K. Sheweth:

"That for many years past the said Society has been engaged in promoting the several Religious and Charitable Designs mentioned in a little Tract entitled An Account of their Origins and Designs lately printed and herewith presented. That the Society is informed that the late Earl of Thanet hath left a considerable sum to Charitable Uses to be distributed at the discretion of the Trustees mentioned in his Lordship's Will with particular regard to such good designs and works as he had in his lifetime encouraged. The Society therefore begs leave to represent to the said Trustees that the Earl was in his lifetime a very great benefactor at different times to their designs and so now make it their request that the said Trustees would be pleased to favour them with their assistance in such manner as they shall think proper. Agreed that the Rev. Mr Wilson be desired to go with the Secretary to wait upon the Rt. Hon. the Countess of Harold and the other Trustees with the said Memorial in the name of the Society" (S.P.C.K. Minutes).

NOVEMBER 1733

Thursday 15. At Newington.

Friday 16. Waited upon Lord Ashburnham. Kindly received. He spoke in my favour to the Bishop of London who assured him that none stood fairer in his opinion than myself.

Saturday 17. At Newington.

SUNDAY 18. Preached for Dr. Baker at St. Michael's Cornhill. Dined with him in Basinghall Street. He promises Mr Hayward to use his interest for me to the Dean of St. Paul's and to introduce me to him.

Monday 19. At Newington.

Tuesday 20. At the Society. Sir John tells me he proposed me as a member of the Society for Propagating the Gospel abroad.

Wednesday 21. At Newington.

Thursday 22. Dr. Littleton, fellow of Eton, dead. Only 2 strangers to be elected, except from King's.

Friday 23. Wrote to Sir John about the vacant fellowship at Eton Coll. He applied for me to the Bishop of London who said it was promised to one Burcket his son's tutor.

Saturday 24. At the Society for the Saltsburghers Affairs.[150] Mr. Butjenter and Capt. Coram sent to Dover to meet the Emigrants from Rotterdam going to Georgia. Dined with Sir John.

SUNDAY 25. Went with Mr Waldo to Wansted. Preached

---

[150] "Agreed that Mr Butjenter be desired to go down to Dover on Monday morning next to visit and encourage the Emigrants going to Georgia and that Mr Vernon be desired to defray the expenses of his Journey thither and back again out of the same collection" (S.P.C.K. Minutes).

The same meeting also arranged for the salaries of the two Ministers, the Lutherans John Martin Bolzius and Israel Christian Gronau with Christopher Ortmann the schoolmaster. Their salaries "to commence from the time of their embarkation from hence, the salaries to continue until such time as they can be provided from Georgia". At the same meeting it was also agreed "that Mr Ziegenhargen be desired to provide a proper Chalice and Paten in plate to be sent with the Ministers of the Saltsburghers for the Communion Service, and that the Society provide for the same service a Flagon in Pewter according to instructions now given" (S.P.C.K. Minutes, 24 Nov. 1733).

there. Dined with Earl Tylney, Lord Castlemain, Mr Child.[151]
I hope to make interest with him for one of his Livings. Wansted,
Woodford, Ickford.

Monday 26. At Newington.

Tuesday 27. At the Society. Letters from Professors Catenburg
and Franks.[152]

Wednesday 28. At Newington. Wrote to my father enclosed
to H. Patten.

Thursday 29. Waited upon the Lady Harold in Burlington
Gardens with the Memorial from our Society. Not at home.
Upon Peneston Lamb [153] No. 7 Lincolns Inn. In good hopes that
we shall succeed. Dined with Sir John Philipps. Wrote to Lord
Tylney.

DECEMBER 1733

Saturday 1. Went to Court with Cousin Billy. At the King's
Levee. General Wade [154] told his Majesty that Mantua was
scituated like Mexico and could not be taken by starving. The
King asked what way the Emperor could march his Troopes into
Italy and he says no way but thro' the Venetian Territories. Dined

[151] Sir Josiah Child, the banker.

[152] "Professor Franks at Hall in Saxony 19. Nov. that Mr Ulsperger having
desired time to help him to two gentlemen qualified to attend the Georgian
Colonists into America, he has procured two viz. Messrs John Martin Bolzius
and Israel Christian Gronavius." (S.P.C.K. Minutes).

[153] Peniston Lamb, d. 1734, left the considerable fortune he acquired as a
barrister to his nephew Matthew Lamb who died in 1768 leaving £1½ million.
His son Peniston was created First Viscount Melbourne in 1781 and was father of
William Lamb, 2nd Viscount Melbourne, the instructor of Queen Victoria.

[154] General, and after 1743, Field-Marshal George Wade. Chiefly memorable
for his construction of roads in the Highlands of Scotland where he had been
Commander in Chief.

> Had you seen these roads before they were made
> You would lift up your hands and bless General Wade

were the words inscribed on an obelisk on the road between Inverness and
Inverary. He was in Scotland at the time of the Porteous Riots and Porteous was
reprieved on Wade's application to Queen Caroline. His monument in Westminster Abbey by J. F. Roubiliac was regarded by the sculptor as his best work.
See entry for 14 Sept. 1736.

at the Chaplains Table. Dr. Pearce [155] and Dr. Cobden. The first spoke on the Ecclesiastical Courts which be again struck at by the Parliament and perhaps entirely taken away. That what had led to this was the different opinions among the Bishops about the Regulations, the abuses in them. That there were certainly very great abuses, but yet that the whole should not be abolished. Dr. Tanner, Dr. Cobden says, very ill at Oxford occasioned by the drying up of his Legg. It is said out of Complaisance to his lady. Mem. to endeavour at a Canonry of Christ Church, a Promise of his Place—by Sir John, Lord Ashburnham, the Bishop of London.

SUNDAY 2. At Newington. Sacrament. Assisted Mr Thoresby.

Tuesday 4. At the Society. Waited upon Dr. Pearce at Court with a letter from Mr Ulsperger about the Persecution of the Protestants in the Emperor's Hereditary Dominions. He told me that he believed nothing would be done this next Sessions. That he believed both sides would be glad to make an advantage about the growth of Popery. That he preached against it last Sunday at Court and that the Queen thanked him for telling them the truth. That the Investiture of Bremen and Verden [156] would be the first thing insisted upon by the King of the Emperor before he would assist him from thence. Lay at Mr Newman's. Spent the evening with Sir John who promised to to speak to Lady Walpole about the Canonry of Christ Church.

Wednesday 5. At Newington.

Thursday 6. Went to town. Sir John went to my Lady. Left a paper with her setting forth the promise made to my father. That he desired nothing but to see me preferred in the world. That I was

[155] Zacharay Pearce (1690–1774), who appears time and again in the Diary as vicar of St Martin-in-the-Fields, found, in after years as Dean of Westminster, that Dr Wilson was one of the most difficult members of his Chapter. In 1739 he became Dean of Winchester, and Bishop of Bangor, on Matthew Hutton's translation to York, in 1748. In 1756 Bishop of Rochester with the deanery of Westminster *in commendam*. In 1768 increasing infirmity made him resign the deanery—which was regarded by many of his contemporaries as an extraordinary proceeding—but he retained the bishopric until his death.

[156] The threat to Bremen and Verden by Prussia had been one of the causes for the formation of the Alliance of Hanover by Great Britain, France, and Prussia in 1725 (J. H. Plumb, *Sir Robert Walpole, the King's Minister*, pp. 120–1).

the best friend to the present King and Administration in England etc. Her Ladyship promised to interest herself strongly with Sir Robert in my favour who is to return a Sunday from Norfolk. Dined with Sir John. Capt. Hudson. Mr Curtiss, 2 sons. Spent the evening with Mr Rivington at the Church Coffee House. Lay at Newman's.

Friday 7. Dined with my unkle. Wrote to Lord Ashburnham in Sussex desiring him to write to Sir Robt. about my affair. With the Bishop of London. Received civilly. He directed me to preach at St. Paul's a Sunday morning. Returned to Newington in the evening.

Saturday 8. Wrote to Dr. Hales that he would write to Lord Ashburnham and press him as above.

SUNDAY 9. Preached at St. Paul's in the morning. Dined with Dr. Terwit, Residentary Canon. Talked about the Great Growth of Popery and the Great Animosity of the Dissenters against the Bishop of London. Returned home in the evening.

Monday 10. Went with Sir John to the Bishop of London. He told us that Sir Robert was surrounded with Lords and Commons and had a number of engagements for preferment but he had and would speak to Sir Robt. in my favour as well satisfied in every respect of my character. From there to Horace Walpole [157] next door to the Treasury, Whitehall. Not at home. From thence to Sir Robt's where I was introduced to Lady Walpole and sat with her a hour and a half. Talked about the riot at Yarmouth and her son Ned's [158] having dirt thrown in his face by the Mob. The Parliament not to be dissolved. The Growth of Popery upon which I delivered the following paper:

"There is a design carrying on, of having a Petition signed by a No. of Clergy and laid before the House of Commons the next Sessions by a Certain Party complaining of the Growth of Popery, and the Lenity of the Present Administration towards the Papists in order to cast a Reproach upon the King and His Ministry. This information is humbly submitted to Sir R. W. that he may be on his guard against the secret attemps of his enemies.

N.B. The reason of this step is because they suppose the Court will make use of the Papists in the next Election."

[157] Horatio Walpole, 1st Baron Walpole of Wolterton, the Prime Minister's brother.
[158] Sir Edward Walpole, K.G., second son of the Prime Minister.

Her Ladyship was mightily pleased at this Information, ordered me to wait upon her often and correspond with her and that she would never be denied to me. A sensible shrewd woman. She has promised to speak in my favour strongly to Sir Robt. for the next Canonry etc. The last Craftsman [159] the greatest abuse upon the King and Queen of any that has been writ. Dined with Sir John. Returned in the evening.

Tuesday 11. Went to town. At the Society. Spoke to my unkle and aunt upon my marriage with Molly. They made the same objections as formerly. Preferment. Differences of Ages etc. I endeavoured to answer them as well as I could. In pretty good humour. Returned in the evening. Wrote to my father. Mrs Tollet. T. Moreton. Mr Duffield. Mr Goss about the rent of my chambers. Received a letter from Dr. Hales that he had wrote to Lord Ashburnham as above. I intend to go to Oxford tomorrow. At the Feathers Tavern in the Strand.

Wednesday 12. Went towards Oxford. A very rainy day. At Beaconsfield King's Head sat with Mr. Smith the Dissenting Minister. [3s. 6d.] The Post Master there an enemy to the Government. Waller—an Anti Courtier. Wrote to Molly.

Thursday 13. Dined at Stoken Church. At night at Oxford. At Mr. Dewe's. Wrote to Molly.

Friday 14. Waited upon the Dean. Dined with him. Told him of my design for applying for a Canonry. Told me that Gregory [160] had applied by the Duke of Newcastle, that he would fain keep him out. That Atwell would give the Bishop of London but a very indifferent character of him. He has entirely neglected his Duty as Professor of Modern History. Spoke 2 speeches. False Latin and False Quantities in the

[159] This organ of the Tory party which first appeared in December 1726 and for ten years continued to vilify the government, and Sir Robert Walpole in particular. After 1736 its popularity began to wane and in 1748 it ceased to be an opposition newspaper. It continued publication until 1750 (see p. 156, n. 213).

[160] Daniel Gregory, D.D., son of Daniel Gregory the Savilian Professor of Astronomy at Oxford. Canon of Ch. Ch. 1736, Dean 1756–7. The First Regius Professor of Modern History and Languages.

speaking. Gilbert [161] expects preferment that will make him quit his canonry. The Bishop of Oxford if removed Cockman to be Professor. To represent Knipe's character one if an exchange might not be made for a Prebend of Westminster and force him to go down to College. Spent the evening with Moreton at Corpus.

Saturday 15. Visited Dr. Smith and Dr. Cockman. Put him upon petitioning the King with the Expensive Fees in passing them were statutes consequent upon the King's Visitatorial Power being secured. At Mrs Slatford's.

SUNDAY 16. Not well. Dined at Mr Dewe's. Mr Moreton and Mr Upton.

Monday 17. Dined with Dr. Smith, Provost of Queen's. Spent the evening at Jesus with the Principal Dr. Pardo. Talked about the late riot when the Pretender's Health was drunk and Sir R. W. burnt in effigie. That the Vice-Chancellor neglected to look into and punish these offences. April 11. 1733.

Tuesday 18. Finished and settled all my affairs and paid my debts in Oxford. Spent the evening with Moreton at Corpus. Dr. Pardo and Dr. Conybear. Promised to nominate Moreton a member of our Society.

Wednesday 19. Set out for London. Lay at Beaconsfield. With Mr Smith again.

Thursday 20. Came to Newington. I thank God safe and sound. Dear Molly very well. My dear father born.

Friday 21. Went to town. Found Sir John at Archbishop Tenison's Library. Said my Lady Walpole enquired twice after me. To wait upon her tomorrow with the Memorial about the Vice Chancellor. Dined with Sir John. Mr. Thorold.[162] Mr Westley,

[161] John Gilbert, Dean of Exeter 1726. Canon of Ch. Ch. same year which he held *in commendam* after being made Bishop of Llandaff in 1740. Bishop of Salisbury 1746, Archbishop of York 1757 until his death in 1761. Horace Walpole describes him as "a mixture of ignorance, meanness and arrogance".

[162] John Thorold was John Wesley's immediate predecessor as Fellow of Lincoln. He succeeded to a baronetcy in 1748, was a noted Evangelical, and died in 1775. Mr Westley was a well-known City merchant and his two sons had been undergraduates at Lincoln College (V. H. H. Green, op. cit., pp. 76, 94, 134n, 135).

his two sons. He has lately lost his grandson. Came to Newington in the evening.

Saturday 22.   In town. Waited upon Lady Walpole. Not at home. Called at Sir John Cheshire's. Returned to Newington.

SUNDAY 23.   Preached Charity Sermon at St. George's Bloomsbury. Collected £23. 14. 6. Dined with Mr Vernon. Mr Green. Returned to Newington.

Monday 24.   In town. Dined with Sir John, his two sons. He promised to speak again to Lady Walpole. Sir Robt. is hardly pressed by Dr. Bland to prefer his relations, Dr. George, Mr Neal etc. but that she would use her interest. This evening I opened my mind freely to Mr Hayward about marrying Molly and he gave his consent very freely and will be glad, he says, to live with us here. I laid before him the state of my affairs and shewed him that I could have £200 this next year and my father has promised us £50 p. ann. for 2 or 3 years if I have not preferment in that time. I think the matter will at last be settled, tho' my unkle and aunt talk so various that there is no contending with them.

Tuesday 25.   At Newington. Assisted at the Sacrament.

Wednesday 26.   Went to Town.

Thursday 27.   At Newington.

Friday 28.   At the Society. Sir John Phillips.

Saturday 29.   At Newington.

SUNDAY 30.   Preached for Dr. Baker at St. Michael's Cornhill.

Monday 31.   At the Society. Undertook a further Account of the Sufferings of the Saltsburghers.[163]

JANUARY 1733-4

Tuesday 1.   At Court. Dined with Mr Harrison at Charing Cross.

---

[163] In the report made to Mr Vernon at the meeting "The Trustees for establishing the Colony of Georgia in America have made no distinction between the Saltsburghers and those of the English who went in the last embarkation and have never granted them better terms than the English in the late Embarkations" (S.P.C.K. Minutes, 31 Dec. 1733).

Wednesday 2. At Lady Walpole's. Left a Memorial to beg Sir Robt. to speak to the Dean of St. Paul's for Foster Lane if Dr. Maddox should resign it. She promised to do it and that Sir Robt. would be my friend when anything dropps.

Thursday 3. At Newington. Wrote to my father and I accepted his offer with thanks and that I believed the Match would now go forwards.

Tuesday 8. At the Society. Waited upon my aunt who at last gave me their consent that I should marry Molly.

[Break in the Diary until June 1734.]¹⁶⁴

¹⁶⁴ During this time the Diarist was married. On 4 Feb. 1733/4. He gives the following account at the end of his Diary:

This day I was married by the Bishop of London at White Hall Chappel to dear Molly, which, by the Blessing of God, will be the happiest day I ever saw. God grant that I may be ever thankful and sensible for the blessings of so excellent a wife. There were by Father Patten, Mrs Jackson, Mr Hayward and Billy."

Presents to my wife
Expenses just before my Marriage

A Diamond Ring *of my Mother's*			
A Pair of Diamond Earrings. Cost.	115.	0.	0.
A Cornelian set in gold.	5.	5.	0.
A Snuff Box.			
Altering of some jewels.	2.	15.	0.
A Piece of Gold.	4.	18.	0.
Gave my wife to the value of	150.	0.	0.
Linen.	17.	3.	6.
A Gown and Cassock Waistcoat and Breeches.	14.	6.	4.
A Scarfe.	1.	10.	0.
A Beaver Hatt.	2.	5.	0.
A Lycense Fee at the Chappell etc.	4.	15.	6.
Bishop's Servants.		10.	0.
Our own servants.		16.	6.
The Musick	1.	16.	6.
A Pair of Gold and Purple Fringed Gloves for the Bishop. A Pair of gold ones for Mr. Haward and a Pair of Silver for Billy.	6.	9.	6.
Coach Hire at different times.	3.	6.	0.
Expenses when we read and sealed the Articles.	2.	2.	6.
A Dinner for Molly's Friends. At Timbrey's	9.	6.	0.
Stockings and Bands and Gloves for myself	2.	10.	0.

JUNE 1734

SUNDAY 16. Preached a Charity Sermon at Lambeth. Dined with Arch Deacon Denne.[165] Collected £7. 6. 0.

Monday 17. Dined with Mr Rogers. Waited upon the Salters Company and put in for their lecture.

[SUNDAY] 23. Preached for Mr Trebeck [166] at St. George's Hanover Square.

[*Thursday*] 27. Went to Hampton. Dined at Kingston with Dr. Hales at the Castle. He paid me as a gift from an Unknown Benefactress £25 for the buying of New Testaments for the Converts to Christianity at Fort St. George and Madras as a benefaction to our Mission there. And I accordingly paid it to Mr. Benjamin Hoare Treasurer for the East India Mission and have his receipt for it.

[Break in the Diary until 9 July.]

JULY 1734

[*Wednesday*] 9. Stood for the Lectureship of St. Dunstan's in the East in the gift of the Salters's Company. Mr Watkinson threw up his interest to Berryman for which reason I lost it 126 to 108.

[*Tuesday*] 15. Went to see Lord Tylney with my wife. Well received.

[*Wednesday*] 16. At the Society.

[*Friday*] 18. Waited upon Col. King over against Charles Street, Soho Square. Received of him as a benefaction for our Poor Clergy Widows and Children five Guineas as left in his

---

[165] John Denne, D.D. (1693–1767), Corpus Christi Camb., Archdeacon and prebendary of Rochester, rector of St Leonard's, Shoreditch, and St Mary, Lambeth, and many other preferments. Prolocutor of the Lower House of the Convocation, historian and antiquary; arranged the archives at Rochester.

[166] Andrew Trebeck, D.D. (1681–1759), Ch. Ch., vicar of Croydon, royal chaplain and rector of St George's, Hanover Square, 1725–59.

hands for this use by Mrs Tollet. I own the recipt of so much money and am accountable for it to them. THO: WILSON.

[*Monday*] *21.* Preached for Mr Smith at Old Gate. Dined with Mr Boswell, a Butcher. Common Council Man.

Tuesday 22. At the Society. Received and gave Mr Williams who lives at a Butcher's in Abingdon Buildings near Old Palace Yard the following receipt.

"Mem. Received by the hands of Mr Williams the sum of Sixteen Pounds Sixteen Shillings from an Unknown Benefactor towards furnishing a No. of the Bishop of Man's last Treatise upon the Sacrament and also dispensing them in the Isle of Man amongst the Poor. Which sum I promise faithfully to lay out upon this Design and beg the favour of Mr Williams to return my father's and my thanks to the Unknown Benefactor." [Paid it into my father's Bookes.]

Mr Williams has promised me a Silver Salver for the New Church at Kirk Onchan in the Isle of Man and gave it me the 30th. inst. With an Inscription—*Deo Sacrum.*

Wednesday 24. I received a Commission dated the 23 from The Trustees of Georgia empowering us to collect and receive any charitable benefactions that shall be paid to me and remit it for their use. Given under their Common Seal.

SUNDAY 28. I went with Dr. Crowe to Westham near Stratford (Mr Wyat Minister). Waited upon Mrs Tollet in the morning, who lives at Mrs Comperes at Stratford. Dr. Crowe collected for the Charity Schools in the morning £40. I preached in the afternoon. Dined with Mr Curtise a Grocer at Stratford, Treasurer of the School.

Tuesday 30. Received a letter from Cousin H. Patten that my Aunt Patten died the 16 and was buried the 18. Wrote Biddy upon the occasion. At the Society. Dined with Sir John Phillips. Mr Vernon. Mr Thorold. Mr Tylliard. Mr Erasmus Philipps. Spoke to the Bishop of London about giving me St. Christopher's but he said he had Chaplains to provide for. Nothing ever to be expected from that quarter. A.D. 1737. So I have found in experience.

AUGUST 1734

Thursday 1. I went with some of the Trustees to Kensington to see the Indian Chiefs [167] from Georgia presented to the Royal Family. They behaved with a becoming Gravity not much admiring the furniture or the Dress of the Court tho' very splendid —being introduced by the Duke of Grafton and Sir Clement Cottrell to his Majesty. *Tomo Chichi* spoke to some such purpose.

"This Day I have seen your Majesty to your Face. The Greatness of your House. The number of your People. Tho' I am old myself and can't be supposed to see the Advantage of it myself, yet I am come for the good of the whole Nation called the *Creeks*, to renew the Peace which long ago they had with the English. I am sure for the good of the children of our Nation that they may be instructed in the knowledge of the English."

Then two of his Captains spreading a Deer's Skin before the feet of the King *Tomo Chichi* laid upon it Eagles Feathers fixed to two pointed sticks fann wayes and said:

"These are the Feathers of the Eagle, which is the noblest of birds, and which flock all round our Nation. These Feathers are a sign of Peace in our Land and have been carried from town to town there and we have brought them over to leave with you, O Great King, as a sign of Everlasting Peace."

They were afterwards introduced to the Queen, the Princess, Prince and Duke.

Saturday 3. I waited upon the Archbishop of York [168] at Edmunton. Found him in very good health. Was received with the utmost civility. Dined with him, Mr ArchDeacon Hayter, his Chaplain Mr Crewe. Talked about the Indian Chiefs. Ward's Pill—laughed at it. Chiselden an impertinent fellow. Would have

[167] Tomo Chichi, Chief of the Lower Creeks, his wife Sarauki and his nephew Tooanaliomo, were brought by General Oglethorpe on his return to England in 1734. Besides this interview with the King and Queen they were received by the Trustees of Georgia and Archbishop Wake, of whom "they had an apprehension that he was a conjurer, but the kind reception he gave them altered that imagination" (Lord Egmont's Diary, II, 121f.).

[168] Lancelot Blackburn, Dean of Exeter, and Bishop 1717–24. Archbishop of York 1724–43. Mr Archdeacon Hayter, chaplain to George II and tutor to George III, became Bishop of Norwich in 1749, translated to London in 1761.

have the Archbishop subscribed for Chubb's Works, called Polly Peacham a Heroine in virtue.[169] He has a great opinion of Westbrook the surgeon. Foulkes made Canon of Christ Church. His ingratitude both to the Court and him, pride etc. Not liked as a preacher at Court. Of the Dean Conybear, that is like to do no great good to the Wesleys in the college. By his choice of a favourite Gregory, a mean wretch, by being opposed by a set of Jacobites amongst the Students and Dr. Foulkes underhand. Miss Gastrell married to Speaker Bromley's [170] younger son the clergyman late Student of Christ Church. At my return received a letter from Dr. Hales telling me that Lady Harold would be very favourable to another petition from our Society which must be presented some time before Christmas. Mr Lamb and Mr Cook to be particularly applied to. He has this Paragraft in his letter— "I am told by one that converses much in the world that there are many servants in town turned *Muggletonians* [171] and that the infection spreads amongst them." That they believe God to be a Material Being. This 'tis to be feared arises from too many of their unhappy masters who have no belief at all of Him. Qu: Is not this worthy the Enquiry of the Society for Promoting Christian Knowledge. There is a Tract advertised at the end of Tillotson's sermons called The Pernicious Practices of the Muggletonians. Printed for Chiswell.

[*Thursday*] 15. Wrote to my father.

SEPTEMBER 1734

[*Wednesday*] 4. Waited upon the new Bishop of Winchester. Grosvenor House (Dr. Hoadley) with my compliments upon his

[169] Many political lampoons appeared at this time in the style of the *Beggar's Opera*, the *Craftsman* in particular making use of Gay's Polly Peachum in its vilification of the government.

[170] William Bromley (1664–1732), Speaker of the House of Commons 1710 and Secretary of State 1713. Never held office again after the death of Queen Anne and the fall of the Tory Government.

[171] Sect founded *c.* 1651 by Ludowicke Muggleton and his cousin John Reeve, who claimed to be the two witnesses of Rev. 11. 3–6.

MRS MACAULAY

From the statue by J. F. Moore erected in St Stephen's, Walbrook. Print by
J. Caldnall as frontispiece to Vol. 4 of her *History of England*

THOMAS SHERLOCK

Bishop of London, 1748-1761

translation. Told him of the charity collecting for our poor widows and children. Said he would be a benefactor to that design.

[*Friday*] 6. *Downing* our printer being dead Mr Rivington desired my interest and I have used it accordingly. There is like to be very great struggles. Sir Jo. Gonson would have one Ackers have the Printer's Place and the Bishop of London's Clerk Miller over against St. Clement's Church in the Strand, Bookseller. What will be the issue I cannot tell. Mrs Downing continued March 17,[172] 1734–5.

[*Monday*] 9. Sir Jo. Gonson reports that Mr Rivington is a Non-Juror. I sent for him. He tells me he has often taken the Oath of Allegiance but has had some scruples about some words in the Abjuration Oath. I sent him a letter on this head and my father's printed one which I hope will satisfy him. If not I cannot in conscience be for a man who won't give the present government all the security they desire, especially at a time when Popery is daily gaining ground and so great a disaffection reigning amongst the Common People against the present Administration.

[*Friday*] 20. At the Society [173] in the Mews. Sir John Phillips has promised to ask Sir Robert Walpole for Dr. Maddox's City Living of Foster Lane if he is made a Bishop.

SUNDAY 22. Preached at Stretham for Mr Bullock Morning and Afternoon. Dined with Mr Waldo. Came home in his coach

---

[172] "Upon reading a petition from Mrs Dowding desiring to be continued in her late husband's business as Bookseller and Printer to the Society and receiving a message from Mr. Woodgate her son in law in her behalf . . . agreed that the Society come to a resolution about this business, that Mrs Dowding be allowed to continue to serve the society as her late husband used to do" (S.P.C.K. Minutes, 10 Sept. 1734. Mr Wilson in the chair).

This was the beginning of a friendship between Wilson and Rivington and over the next few years Wilson seems to have used Rivington's house as a *pied-à-terre* in London. In March 1739–40, however, Rivington accused Wilson of putting it about that he had printed a clandestine edition of Bishop Wilson's Works.

[173] At this meeting it was reported that "the charges of transporting 25 Grown Men from Rotterdam to Georgia amounting to £707. 9. 2 including for the provision of as many women and children as may make the number 40 excepting articles of freight and maintainance of them" (S.P.C.K. Minutes).

with Mr Baker, lady and daughter, a wine merchant in Lawrence Pountney Lane.

Tuesday 24. At the Society.[174] 54 Saltsburghers coming over to Gravesend and our Society are at the whole expense of the embarkation and maintaining them there. They desire me to take care of them there.

Wednesday 25. Paid the Bishop of Winchester's lady a visit and received very kindly.

Friday 27. At the Society. Dined with Sir John. Yesterday he asked my Lady Walpole and her son to beg Sir Robt. the living in Foster Lane if Maddox be made a bishop and they promised to use their interest.

SUNDAY 30. Preached in the morning for Mr Smith at Aldgate and in the afternoon a Charity Sermon at Sir G. Wheeler's Chappel in Spittal Yard. Dined with Dr. Tylliard.

OCTOBER 1734

Tuesday 2. At the Society. Sent to Mrs Hoadley to know how my Lord did who has not been ill as reported in the news.

[Wednesday] 3. A letter from H. Patten about Mrs Tollet's sister and his brother's illness.

[Friday] 5. At the Society. Dined at father Patten's in the afternoon. Went to see Sir Hans Sloane's fine collection of rarities with Dr. Guerdes and my wife. Saw his Chinese Golden Fishes, very pretty.

SUNDAY 7. Preached and administered the sacrament at Horsey for Mr. Carthwright. One Mr Towers of Christ Coll. Camb. his curate.

[Monday] 8. Went with Dr. Guerdes to Mr Calamy in Carpenter's Hall, to Dr. Harris, Mr Chaloner in Ayloff Street near Goodmans Fields to recommend the Saltsburghers. Mr Chaloner

---

174 "Agreed that Mr Wilson and Mr Butjenter be desired to go down to Gravesend to visit the Saltsburghers on notice of their arrival there and to inform themselves of the condition of the emigrants and what may be wanting to make their voyage comfortable" (S.P.C.K. Minutes).

proposed that we should choose some of them of our Society and then they did not doubt of large collections. I answered that we were but single members and did not know how to venture proposing what was entirely new but that I hoped whether that could be done according to our rules or no. I hoped it would not be made an objection or Barr to our present undertaking. Civil reply but I am afraid there it will hang.

[Break in the Diary until 8 Jan. 1734-5.]

JANUARY 1734-5

[*Wednesday*] *8.* One of the greatest storms that have been known for many years. It began here about 1 in the morning. Its greatest violence between 3 and 4 in the afternoon. Thermometer below stormy 2 degrees. Lightning and Thunder during the night of the storm.

[Break in the Diary until 18 March 1734-5.]

MARCH 1734-5

[*Tuesday*] *18.* This morning about 6 my dear wife began to be in labour. I went immediately for Dr. Bamber to be present at the labour and he came at 8. At 14 minutes after eleven she was delivered by Mrs Gates of Gower Street of a fine boy, with very little pain. God be praised for all his mercies. The Dr. was afraid some of the skirts of the After Burthen was left behind by the Midwife's being so very quick, and pulling it with the child away at the same time, which is a very wrong practice. In the afternoon I wrote to Mr Thoresby to give me leave to baptise my child privately, afraid of any mischance, intending, God willing, to present him publickly in the Church. Baptised him by the name of Thomas.

[*Wednesday*] *19.* My wife much better and the child in a fair way to do well.

[*Thursday*] *20.* Dr. Bamber came here and found all very well.

[*Friday*] *21.* At the Society for Propagating the Gospel in Forreign Parts. The Bishop of London was pleased to approve of the *Circular Letter* that I drew up for our Society in Bartlett's Buildings and desired that it might be published. I measured my boy and he was 27 inches long. My dear wife tried to suckle her little one but her nipples were so sore and so small that the child could not get hold of them and so, I hope, it will be pardoned for I know that it is every woman's duty to nurse her own child.

[*Saturday*] *22.* We still continue well, God be praised. Wrote to Cousin Patten to desire his wife to stand Godmother for my child.

[SUNDAY] 23. A letter from my father dated the 11th.

[*Monday*] *24.* My dear wife taken with a disorder like the Stranguary. I am afraid she got cold by having her room washed this morning.

[*Tuesday*] *25.* My Molly made water freer but had a great forcing afterwards. I am afraid her midwife did her some injury. She drunk Emulsion.

[*Wednesday*] *26.* Still the same disorder, weak, restless, no stomack, drinks Emulsion. I cut my finger to the bone.

[*Thursday*] *27.* The same disorder, tho' a little better.

[*Friday*] *28.* I would have sent for Dr. Bamber, but she did not care for it.

[*Saturday*] *29.* A great forcing after making water.

[SUNDAY] 30. *Sunday.* Sent for Dr. Bamber to see my Dear Molly. He ordered her a Stoupe of warm spices and white wine twice a day and a spermatic tea draught every six hours. I pray God give a blessing to all our efforts and endeavours for her recovery.

[*Monday*] *31.* A letter from Dr. Smith that the Bishop of London had applied for me to the Queen and that he hoped I should soon have preferment. A kind letter from Cousin T. Patten of Warrington in which he says that his wife willingly embraces the opportunity of being Godmother to my little boy and has ordered me 3 Guineas. My dear wife no better.

APRIL 1735

[*Tuesday*] *1*. My wife a little feaverish. Sent for Dr. Bamber. He ordered her 25 Gr. of Gascoin's Powder and 25 Gr. of Crabbs Eyes every 6 hours.

[*Wednesday*] *2*. No better.

[*Thursday*] *3*. A little cooler and so continues upon the mending hand the 4th and 5th.

[SUNDAY] 6. The fever gone pretty much off.

[*Monday*] *7*. Dr. Bamber came here again and thinks her pretty well. The Spermacetea Draught and the Gascoin's Powder every 8 hours.

[*Tuesday*] *8*. My finger very much enflamed.

[*Friday*] *18*. My dear Boy was received in Newington Church by Mr. Thoresby. Father Patten stood himself. Mr Hayward for my father and Aunt Jackson for Cousin Tho. Patten's Wife.

SUNDAY 21. Preached for one Mr Bedford in the morning at Aske's Hospital near Hoxton Square (Coloss. iii.1). In the afternoon I preached at the request of Mr Waldo for the Charity Children of Cordwainers and Bread Street Wards at Aldermary Church. A beautiful church but a very thin congregation owing in some measure to the non residence of the Incumbent (Dr. Walker).[175] Shall I have grace constantly to reside upon my preferment and cure if it please God I ever have one. My little Boy much disturbed with wind. Gave him Crabbs Eyes. 5 Gr. and 2 of Salt of Wormwood *bis in die* and twice a Night Gascoin's Powder 5 Gr. and Rhubarb every 4th Night.

[*Monday*] *22*. My little Boy something better I thank God.

[175] Dr John Walker was also chaplain to the King and to the Archbishop of Canterbury, Dean of Bocking, Rector of Great Easton, Essex, Chancellor of St David's, Archdeacon of Hereford and vicar of St Thos. the Apostle, City of London. Was of great service to Dr Bentley of Trinity Camb. in collating MSS. at Paris and Brussels and elsewhere.

[*Monday*] *12*.   Monday. Went in a chariot and met my dear father at St. Albans and brought him here in good health, thank God.

[*Tuesday*] *13*.   My father Patten met my father. We dined at home.

[*Wednesday*] *14*.   Went in the morning to Sir John Phillips who promised to do all in his power.

[*Thursday*] *15*.   Waited upon the Bishop of London. Not at home. Saw the Bishop of Llandaff at White Hall. Waited upon my Lord Ashburnham in Germain Street near St. James's Street. Offered to introduce us at Court. My father was presented by the Duke of Manchester, Lord of the Bedchamber in Waiting and had the honour to kiss his Majesty's hand. He afterwards went to the Queen's side, who immediately came up to him and promised she would be kind to me. She afterwards told a lady that stood by her that no body envyd this honest man his bishopreck upon which my father said that neither did he *envy anybody or desire their bishoprecks* upon which she said *I believe you, you are a very Honest Man.*

[*Friday*] *16*.   Went to the Society for Propagating the Gospel in Forreign Parts. Saw the Bishop of London who told my father that we must no longer rest in generals and desired he would come and talk with him at Fulham next Thursday. Dined with Sir John Phillipps who promised to go with us next Thursday to Sir Robert Walpole's.

[*Saturday*] *17*.   At home.

[SUNDAY] 18.   *Sunday.* My father preached for Dr. Knight[176] at St. Sepulchre's. We afterwards visited him who I think cannot live many dayes.

[*Monday*] *19*.   My father, Molly and I went to see my Lord Burlington's fine house and gardens at Chiswick and dined with

[176] Dr James Knight, vicar of St Sepulchre's Holborn 1716–35. Died 26 May 1735 and buried in St Sepulchre's.

his steward Mr Brown. N.B. Mr Miller of Chelsea has a perpetual ticket from my Lord.

[*Tuesday*] *20*. At the Society. Dined with Sir John Philipps.

[*Thursday*] *22*. Waited upon Sir Robert Walpole at St. James's Square. Very kindly received and he promised to do anything for me in his power and advised to consult with the Bishop of London what was fit to be asked. Went from thence to Sir Richard Ellis' in Bolton Street. Set forward to Fulham. Dined with the Bishop of London who told us to come to White Hall Monday next at 9 a clock to talk to him further upon the affair.

[*Friday*] *23*. Waited upon the Duke of Atholl (in Dale Street). Very glad to see us. Called upon Lady Shannon. Invited to dine next Sunday. Dined with the Bishop of Durham. Promised to be kind to me and set me down in his book 4th. Saw the Bishop of Winchester—*coole*.

[*Saturday*] *24*. At Home.

[SUNDAY] *25*. *Sunday*. Went to Court at Kensington. My father was introduced by my Lord Baltimore to the Prince. To the Duke by Mr Poyntz. To the Princess by Lady Bell Finch and met with a very gratious reception. He dined with Lady Shannon. I preached in the afternoon at the Temple Church. Went afterwards to Lady Shannon's and brought my father home.

[*Monday*] *26*. Went to the Bishop of London at White Hall who advised my father to present a Memorial to the Queen begging her Majesty would give me the promise of the Canonry at Christ Church, or a Prebend of Canterbury, which shall first become vacant. He told him that Windsor and Westminster were deeply engaged. That Gregory and one Chamberlain had made interest for Christ Church, but he did not know whether they had any promises. That he believed Canterbury was disengaged. He was very friendly and I believe he is in earnest.

[*Tuesday*] *27*. At the Society. My father dined with Sir John. He afterwards waited upon Sir John Cheshire (in Essex Street). He gave my father £20 towards the Vicarage Houses of the Isle of Man. Promised to dine with him at Thistleworth.

[*Wednesday*] *28*. I carryed a Memorial to the Bishop of

London at Fulham who approved of it and desired we would get it presented to the Queen as soon as possible.

[*Thursday*] *29*. Waited upon My Lord Ashburnham who promised to deliver my father's letter to the Queen this day and accordingly he wrote to my father that he had done so and that her Majesty had received it very gratiously.

[*Friday*] *30*. Dined at father Patten's.

[*Saturday*] *31*. My father and I went to the Court at Kensington. The Queen was pleased to promise us the first of the above preferments when they would become vacant, which my father acquainted the Bishop of London with, as her Majesty ordered him to do. Dined with Dr. Tyrwit, Dr. Holcome, Prebend of Canterbury, at the Chaplain's Table.

JUNE 1735

[SUNDAY] 1. Preached at Hackney 2 sermons for the Charity of Georgia.

SUNDAY 8. Preached before the Lord Mayor, Aldermen and Judges (First Sunday in Trinity Term) at St. Paules. Dined with the Lord Mayor, Sir Edward Bellamy.

[*Friday*] *20*. My father administered the Sacrament to Auditor Harley [177] in Lincolns Inn. Very devout. His modesty was so great that he did not think himself qualified for partaking in that Holy Mystery, tho' his whole life has been one Preparation for Futurity. We dined with his son in law Mr Verney, Chief Justice of Chester, Mr Edward and Mr Robert Harley. At the Society at the Mews. The Bishop of London told my father that Sir Robert Walpole had consented that the Queen's promise should be made

---

[177] Mr Auditor Harley (Edward Harley) was the second son of Sir Edward Harley, K.B., and brother of the Earl of Oxford. M.P. for Leominster, also Recorder. Auditor of the Impost from 1702 until his death. Particularly devoted to the work of Christian Knowledge he was Chairman of the Trustees of the Charity Schools of London from 1725 and the author of *An Abstract of the Historical Parts of the Old Testament with Reference to the Other Parts of Scripture* (1730) and *The Harmony Between the Psalms and the Other Parts of Scripture* (1732). (Nichols *Literary Anecdotes*, i, p. 431.)

good to me and bid him rest contented with a certain prospect of succeeding.

[*Saturday*] *21.*   At home.

SUNDAY 22.   My father preached at Newington.

Monday 23.   My father went a horseback to Dr. Hales at Teddington.

Tuesday 24.   I paid Jasper Walters a visit. He told me that Mr Holden and Mr Buck had pressed Sir Robt. last session for the Repeal of the Test Act. His answer was that it was drawing near the end of the Sessions and not proper but that if they would apply next sessions he would not oppose them by which Mr W. there sees what will be in the other house before this time. Mem. He did oppose them in it.

Wednesday 25.   Dined with Sir John Cheshire in Essex Street in the Strand. My father. Justice Cook. Jas. Cook and his brother, Justices. Lady and daughter. Lady Dolins and her daughter.

Thursday 26.   At home.

Friday 27.   Mr Seers dined with me.

Saturday 28.   Breakfasted with Mr Biscowe and visited Mrs Garnet in King's Square near Soho Square. Dined with Lord Oxford in Dover St. Lady. Duke of Leeds. Lord Duplin. Mr Edward and Mr. Robert Harley, sons of the Auditor whom we visited in the evening and found him in a languishing condition.

SUNDAY 29.   At Newington.

JULY 1735

Tuesday 1.   At the Society. In the afternoon visited Cousin Murrey and his family in Surrey Street.

Wednesday 2.   Went to town. Met Mr Heath of Rotherhith and the Rainbow Coffee House near the Change. He gave me £2 14. 0. from his aunt, the widow Christian in the Isle of Man, which I gave my father.

Thursday 3.   We visited Mr Husbands of Tottenham

Friday 4.   Cousin Murrey, son and 2 daughters, Sir John Phillips and Mr Thorold dined with us. Mrs Kennett and her grand daughter Miss How in Carteret Street near the Broad Way, Westminster.

Saturday 5. We dined with Mr Rowe.

SUNDAY 6. I preached for Mr Thoresby at Newington,

Monday 7. My father taken with a fit of the gout. Waited upon the Bishop of London. He assured by father that he would do all that was in his power that I might have some preferment and would speak to the Queen again next week. Lady Blount's [178] sister of Twickenham Mrs Butler [179] waited upon my father in the Market.

Tuesday 8. I waited with Sir John Phillips upon Sir Robert at James's Square. Assured me that upon the Bishop of London's recommendation he would do all that lay in his power for me.

Thursday 10. I went to Kensington introduced by Mr Sumner (Preceptor to the Duke) to Mr Morel (Page of the Back Stairs to the Queen) who was very civil. Advised me to send my paper to her Majesty by way of Lord Grantham which I did; the following:

The Bishop of Man being confined to his Bedd humbly begs leave to introduce to the Queen's Most Excellent Majesty That a Canonry of Christ Church in Oxford is like to become vacant very soon and hopes your Majesty will have the goodness to remember his son.

Friday 11. At home.

SUNDAY 13. In the afternoon preached at Newington.

Tuesday 15. Dined with Sir John Phillips.

Friday 18. Waited upon the Bishop of London at White Hall. He told me that the first Canonry of Christ Church was engaged to Gregory. That one Chamberlain, Chaplain to the King, puts in to be Canon.

Saturday 19. At the Society for Propagating the Gospel in Forreign Parts.

Tuesday 22. At the Society in Bartlett's Buildings. Dined with Sir John. Had some words with him about Mrs Drummond the Quaker Lady. The attempts by Wesley a literal translation left all

[178] Martha Blount (1690–1762) Pope's friend to whom he bequeathed all his household possessions, the contents of his grotto and made his residuary legatee.

[179] Mrs Grace Butler, a great benefactress to the Church in Man.

the passages relating to Popery. Sir John very angry about its being recommended to the Society.

Wednesday 23. My father took leave of the Queen at Kensington. Her Majesty said she had spoke in relation to me to the Bishop of London. I am afraid she will not be so much a friend as I could wish. Duke of Newcastle very complaisant to me. I wonder at it. We dined at Mr Lorenzi's in Kensington Square. Very civilly entertained. Mr Sumner, Sub-Preceptor to the Duke, told us that the reason of the break between Spain and Portugal is upon the double Match,[180] the King of Spain promised to abdicate in favour of the Prince of Asturias but the Queen having some great designs to carry on for Don Carlos in Italy which she could not do without the name of her husband and this affair has been in the King of Portugal's mind ever since. Prince of Wales to be married, 'tis thought the King's Birth Day, to one of the family of Sax Gotha.

Thursday 24. Dined with the Archbishop of York at Edmunton. He gave me his option to the Rectory of Rothbury in the bishopric of Durham. Mr Sharp the present Rector. Worth £350 pr. ann. It is in trust to Mr Hayward for me and the Deeds are drawn up.

Friday 25. At home.

SUNDAY 27. My father preached at Newington for Mr Thoresby.

Monday 28. My dear father left us in his Journey to the North. We went with him as far as Rick's End and dined there and took leave of him. Found my little boy very ill of a Looseness.

Tuesday 29. My little boy rather worse. Took Rheubarb. God

[180] On the death of Augustus, Elector of Saxony, in 1732/3 the succession to the throne of Poland of his heir Frederic Augustus was disputed by Stanislaus Leczinsky. Louis XV favoured Stanislaus and after the election of Frederic invaded the Emperor's dominions. George II wanted to intervene on his behalf but was restrained by Walpole. He then negotiated for an alliance between Spain and the Emperor in which the Emperor should marry the second archduchess to a Spanish prince, but Walpole warned Queen Caroline that if England got involved in the foreign imbroglio "her crown would at last as surely come to be fought for as the Crown of Poland". As Lord Harvey put it, "the shadow of the Pretender beat the whole germanic body".

grant it may do him good. At the Society. Dined at Mr Rivington's.

Wednesday 30. Wrote to my father. My little boy still ill.

Thursday 31. My child, I thank God, better. The Lord be praised for all his Mercies.

AUGUST 1735

Friday 1. This day month etc. I waited upon the Bishop of London. He was busy. To dine with him a Thursday next. Went to Court with Mr Hansard, Secretary to the Irish Protestant Schools. Dined with Mr Eccleshall, Clerk to the Kitchen, at his Lodgings at Mr Giles, Clerk of the Works. His lady a very sensible woman, relation to the Bishop of Oxford. Returned home with Mr Briscowe and Dr. Lavington.[181] Talked about the Bishop of Winchester's book.[182] He had not explained himself in any point so clear as against the satisfaction of Christ. Carried below the Arian. Makes Christ only a Protomartyr. Dying to testify to the Truth of the Gospel etc. London said that if he had printed this before he would never have been Bishop of Winchester. The Bishops would have in a body remonstrated. Foster a good answer to Stebbing upon his present plan. Must lay it wider and bring in the Fathers or else he will be too hard for him. The Bishop of London says the Bishop of Oxford intends to answer Winchester's book. Mem. I am to preach next Sunday fortnight for Dr. Baker at St. Paul's in the afternoon and for Dr. Lavington Sunday 5 weeks. A letter from my father.

Saturday 2. At home.

SUNDAY 3. Preached for Mr Dubourden at Hackney in the afternoon on Contentment. Drunk tea with Mr Chester.

Monday 4. A letter from my father.

Tuesday 5. At the Society.

[181] George Lavington, canon of St Paul's 1747–62. Bishop of Exeter where, according to his epitaph in Exeter Cathedral "an Indulgent Candour sweetened his Government". He was "a determined enemy to Idolatry and Persecution and a successful Exposer of Pretence and Enthusiasm".

[182] *A Plain Account of the Nature and End of the Lord's Supper.*

Wednesday 6. At home. A letter from my dear father complaining of an exceeding bad and wearisome journey.[183] At Park Gate the 3rd inst. Feavorish etc. I pray God restore to him his health.

Thursday 7. Went by water to Fulham. Dined with the Bishop of London. Remarked upon Hoadley's Book. Spoke to me a good deal about Clandestine Marriages. Chancellor Henchman said that there were 4000 every year in the Fleet. That a Scotch Duke was married there a few years ago. The Parliament never in earnest against them unless the Fleet entirely put down. A Change in Act of Parliament [184] making the consent of Parents necessary to children under age, made in last session but one. Came home in the evening with Dr. Vernon who spoke very much against the Proceedings of the Commissioners of the 50 New Churches.[185]

Friday 8. At home.

Saturday 9. Paid a visit to Mr Crewe at my Lord Archbishop of York's at Edmunton. My Lord Chancellor, nephew to the Archbishop, there.

SUNDAY 10. Preached at dined with Mr Briscowe over against South Sea House. In the afternoon I preached at St. Paules for Dr. Baker Residentary. Drank tea with Mr Ryder.

Monday 11. Received a letter from my father that he is a little better God be thanked. At the Committee at Warwick Court.

Tuesday 12. At the Society in Bartlett's Buildings. Sir John looked coole. I don't know at what.

Wednesday 13. At home.

---

[183] The Bishop's journey to his diocese was certainly exhausting. It lasted six weeks and included a tour in the Archdiocese of York for Archbishop Blackburn where he confirmed upwards of 15,000 people (Keble, ii, p. 767).

[184] This did not come to pass until 1753. Lord Hardwicke's Marriage Act.

[185] The Act which set up a Commission to build 50 new churches in London to be paid for by a tax on coal, was passed in 1711. But only twelve Churches were built and the Commission terminated in 1733. Six of the 12 Churches (St Anne, Limehouse, St George, Wapping, St Mary, Woolnoth, St George's, Bloomsbury, St Michael's, Cornhill, and Christ Church, Spitalfields) were by Hawksmoor who was the principal Surveyor to the Commission throughout the whole period of its existence (Colvin, *Dictionary of British Architects*, pp. 273, 277, 751).

Thursday 14. The Revd. Mr Wilson, Prebend of St. Patrick's Dublin and his brother a Packer in Rhode Lane came to visit me and I have promised to dine with them next Tuesday.

Friday 15. At the Society in the Mews.

Saturday 16. At home.

SUNDAY 17. Preached for Mr Thoresby at Newington in the morning. Mr Williams came to me and brought me 2 of his bookes.

Monday 18. At home.

Tuesday 19. At the Society. Proposals about letting the Trustees of Georgia have £1000 etc. Met Mr Oglethorpe at Cheap Side Coffee house. Talked about the Affair of Gin etc. Told me that a certain member of Parliament in the Minority had received £5000 from the Distillers to oppose any Act that should be brought against it next sessions. I go with him to the Master of the Rolls next Tuesday. Dined with Mr Wilson a Packer of Rhode Lane, his 2 Brothers.

Wednesday 20. At home.

Thursday 21. Mr Hayward went to Epsom. Lord Tylney sent me half a buck. I sent the neck to Mr Rowe, the Haunch to the Archbishop of York at Edmunton, who received it very kindly. Wrote to my father in answer to his of 13th.

Saturday 23. At home finished the Presentment against Gin.

SUNDAY 24. I was this day 32 years old. God grant I may grow wiser and better.

Monday 25. Mr Hayward returned. A letter from my father.

Tuesday 26. Mr Oglethorpe carried me to the Master of the Rolls at Bell Bar. Mr O. would have it proposed to the Queen to give the Isle of Man in Reversion to the Duke of Cumberland. Mem. To think of this and draw up such a paper as may be delivered to her Majesty. The Master of the Rolls and his lady received us very kindly. Took the presentment I had drawn up against Gin and promised to correct it. Gave me a letter to Counseler Lane in Boswell Court or at Hampstead to desire him to extract the Lawes now in force against Gin. I mean the power of the Justices of the Peace now of preventing and suppressing. I find the Master intends to bring in a bill next sessions and I believe it will be by laying on a greater duty. The Master no friend to present State Politicks. Told me a great deal about Mr Quincey's Imprudences.[186]

Wednesday 27. Went to town. Found Mr Lane, Chairman at the sessions at Hicks Hall and invited me to dine with him and the Justices which I did. Promised to go with me to the Master of the Rolls next week to Bell Bar and he call upon me here. Went afterwards to Mr Oglethorpe in Palace Yard. Mr Burton dined with him. Mr Heathcote and Mr Vernon came in. Talked of the Saltsburghers Comp. of having fallen on very barren ground. Promised to give them the land lying below the Hill where Ebenezer stands not desiring to draw 'em to Presbit. having an interest there himself and later he would sell. This is forbid in Georgia. Waited upon Auditor Harley. He was very low spirited and wanted the inward comfort, tho' nobody has lived so useful or so innocent a life. Desired to know whether he could serve me in anything. Mem. I am to go with Mr Lane to the Master of the Rolls next Friday fortnight at 8 a clock in the morning.

Thursday 28. This evening I saw that Dr. Brampston, Prebendary of Worcester and Rector of St. Christopher's and Vicar of Mortlak died at Worcester. Aged 80. Last Monday night.

Friday 29. This morning I waited upon the Bishop of London at White Hall and modestly asked for St. Christopher's, tho' I have little hopes of it. I at the same time moved the Bishop to speak to Sir Robt. for Worcester. This I am afraid is promised however I think it not amiss to remind them now and then of their promises. The Bishop not at home. I left a letter for his Lordship.

Saturday 30. At home.

SUNDAY 31. Preached in the morning a sermon for our Charity Children. Collected £13. 14. 3. more than there ever was in the morning. In the afternoon Mr Carter, curate to Mr Seers preached. £6. 2. 6. Spent an hour after prayers with Mr Green the Treasurer. Mr Thoresby. Mr Seers. Mr Carter. Mr Crisp. Mr Rowe. Mr Ferrers. Mr Hayward.

[186] See entry for 21 October 1735.

SEPTEMBER 1735

Monday 1. Waited upon the Bishop of London at White Hall. Told me that Stillingfleet was to have one of the vacant Prebends of Worcester and the other lay between Meadowcourt and one Wilson of Newark supported by the interest of Lady Sundon.

Tuesday 2. Waited upon Sir Robert. Not at home. Having had a letter from Bath that Dr. Terry was much worse I applyed for the Canonry of Christ Church to the Bishop of London.

Wednesday 3. At home.

Thursday 4. Went to Sir Robt. again. Too late. Went to Court.

Friday 5. Went with Mr Lane to see the Master of the Rolls at Bell Bar. Gave me further directions about the Presentment of Gin etc and wrote a letter to be shewn to Sir John Barnard.

Saturday 6. Shewed Sir John Barnard the Master's letter. He is against Gin but not very forward for the suppressing of Spirituous Liquors. This I take to be his fear of the Distillers in the next election for Members of Parliament. Poor Reason!

[Break in the Diary until 5 October.]

OCTOBER 1735

SUNDAY 5. Waited upon the Bishop of Salisbury at the Temple. Kindly received. Promised to speak for me to the Queen.

Monday 6. Visited Mr Oglethorpe.

Tuesday 7. Dined with Sir John Phillips and Sir Robt. W's niece.

Wednesday 8. At home.

Thursday 9. At home. Mr Rivington and his wife. Mr Miller of Chelsea, dined with me.

Friday 10. Waited upon the Bishop of Durham and dined with him and his lady at Grosvenor Square. Dr. Sharp not well at Bath—Rothbury.

Saturday 11. At home.

DR SAMUEL CLARKE

1684-1750

ROCKS AT TUNBRIDGE WELLS

From a watercolour by Paul Sandby (1725-1809)

SUNDAY 12. At Kensington. Took leave of Mr Oglethorpe. Mr Wesley presented her Majesty with his father's book on Job.[187] The Queen said my father was her christian Bishop. Sir Robt. W. told Mr Oglethorpe that I stood as fair as any man in England for preferment in the Church. Mr O. gave me a letter of recommendation to Mr Hill of the Custom House. Dined at the chaplain's table. Dr. Regis and Mr. Medlicott in waiting (who lives at Bolton Street, Pick a dilly). There were besides Dr. Naylor, Dean of Winchester, Maddox, Dean of Wells, Dr. Lilly a Physitian. Mr Medlicott talked of the Pretender's being often seen with the Queen Ann at St. James. Seen once riding to Windsor. If my Lord Derwentwater had spoken out in this affair he might have pardoned that this might have fallen upon Lord Oxford. The reliableness of Lord Derwentwater's [188] case spoke of as mentioned by Genl. Wills to Medlicott.

Monday 13. At home.

Tuesday 14. At Sir R.W.'s Levee.

Friday 17. At the Society for Propagating the Gospel. Dined with Mr Medlicott in Bolton Street. Dr. Wilson of Dublin, his son and nephew and daughter in law. Mr. Medlicott married Genl. Pepper's widow for his first wife and a 2nd Widow for second. By both he had fine fortunes. He told me that the Duke of Grafton sent his own relations and himself to the Bishop of London before he would make them chaplains.

SUNDAY 19. Preached at the Trinity Chappell in Conduit Street for Mr Medlicott. Went to Court. Dr. Maddox, Dean of Wells, desired me to preach for Dr. Gilbert on the 5th Nov. before

---

[187] The Rev. Samuel Wesley died in April 1735. John Wesley saw his father's book through the press and presented it to the Queen the Sunday before he embarked for Georgia on 14 October 1735 (V. H. H. Green, op. cit., pp. 254–5).

[188] James Radclyffe, third Earl of Derwentwater (1689–1716) was brought up at the Court of St Germains as a companion to Prince James Edward. He joined the Rising of 1715, for which he was examined before the Privy Council on 10 Jan. 1716, impeached on 19 Jan., and executed on 24 Feb. His brother Charles (1693–1746) settled in Rome, was for a time secretary to Prince Charles Edward, and was executed on Tower Hill on 8 Dec. 1746, having been captured off the Dogger Bank in Nov. 1745 by the frigate *Sheerness* on board a French ship sailing from Dunkirk to Montrose with arms and supplies for the Chevalier.

the King, which I promised to do. Dr. Holmes preached a most admirable sermon before the Queen. The Prince of Modena was introduced to his first audience of the Royal Family. I dined with the Chaplains. Dr. Briggs, Dr. Holmes, Dr. Egerton, Dr. Maddox and Dr. Naylor. Came home with Mr Hayward, Mr Rider and Mr Baker.

Monday 20. At home,

Tuesday 21. At the Society. Dined with Sir John. Mr Vernon proposed [189] the discharging of Mr Quincey [190] from Savannah for many reasons that he then gave, his taking a maid contrary to Mr O's advice, who ran out of doors the first night saying he attempted to lye with her.

Thursday 23. At home. About my sermon.

Saturday 25. At the Society. Was at the Archbishop's. Walked in the Park with Dr. Hayter. Met the Bishop of London. Hayter told me that Mr Fynch [191] was very ill and that Dr. Sharp was in a declining state of health at Bath.

SUNDAY 26. The King passed the exchange from Harwich in an open chaise with the Marquis de la Foret. He was very gratious to the people as he passed. He set out from Hanover [192] a Tuesday night and was at Helvetslews Friday and was at anchor off Harwich Saturday evening, lay aboard all night.

Monday 27. At home. Justice Cook and his lady paid me and my wife a visit.

[189] Not in the Society's Minutes.

[190] On his first visit to Georgia, Oglethorpe took Henry Herbert, son of Lord Herbert of Cherbury, as chaplain. On his death the Rev. Samuel Quincey was appointed. On his dismissal John Wesley was appointed as his successor (V. H. H. Green, op. cit., pp. 253–4).

[191] Edward Finch, 5th son of Heneage Baron Finch, Earl of Nottingham. Prebendary of Canterbury as well as holding the rich livings of Kirkby-in-Cleveland and Wigan. Chaplain to the King. Also prebendary of York. Died 14 Feb. 1737–8 and buried at York.

[192] It was on this excursion to Hanover that George II became acquainted with Amelia Sophia, wife of Count Von Walmoden, who became his mistress. He confessed the same to Queen Caroline with the words "you must love the Walmoden for she loves me". It was at this time also that the marriage of the Prince of Wales with the Princess Augusta of Saxe-Gotha was arranged, which took place on 27 April 1736.

Tuesday 28. At the Society. A proposal for emplying the children of the Charity Schooles. I dined with Justice Lane in Boswell Court near Lincolns Inn. He shewed me the Bishop of Bristol's Letter to his clergy and a No. of Queries about the No. of Papists in his diocese. The three last queries relate to the No. of Dissenters which has given some offence to that Body of Men and indeed I think they should not be mentioned so close to the papists who upon many accounts do not merit Toleration. They can give no Security of their Duty or Allegiance, but when the Pope can dispense with and often has done so much the most solemn Engagements and Oaths.

Wednesday 29. At home.

Thursday 30. At St. James (The King's Birth Day). Dined with the Chaplains, Dr. Egerton, Dr. Bundy, Dr. Thomas Hayter, Dr. Pearce. Returned home.

Friday 31. At home.

NOVEMBER 1735

Saturday 1. At the Society.

SUNDAY 2. At Newington Church.

Monday 3. At home.

Tuesday 4. At the Society. Sir John desired me earnestly to preach the Reformation Sermon,[193] but I could not think of doing it as having no Preferment may make myself a great many enemies, if I speak plain, and if I do not, better to decline preaching at all. In town in the afternoon with Dr. Davis. Mr Shepherd the Popish Priest there. Waited upon Lord Ashburnham.

Wednesday 5. I preached at St. James's Chappel. Neither the King or the Queen there. Dined with the Chaplains Dr. Egerton and Dr. Bundy and Captain Hodgson. Talked of Mr Wesley's having a more than ordinary call to go to Georgia [194] which Dr. Egerton called Enthusiasm. A good deal of talk about it and other things. I take him to be a warm man, says abundance of things

---

[193] I.e. for the Society for the Reformation of Manners.
[194] V. H. H. Green, op. cit., pp. 251–2.

which he does not seem to weigh much. Seems to understand the affairs of the world well and the business of a Justice of the Peace as well if not better than that of a divine. Returned home in the evening.

Thursday 6. Went to town. Waited at Sir Robert Walpole's Levee. There was a Board of Treasury so he saw no company. Went to Court. Dr. Bundy and I prevailed with the Dean of Wells to preach the sermon Before the Reformation of Manners and dined with Sir Joseph Jekyl Master of the Rolls at the Rolls, his lady, 2 others and Mr Hamilton, a lawyer belongs to the South Sea House and a Director. Very good Mathematician. Defended Sir Isaac Newton's opinion against Dean Berkeley about the Terms Nascent and Evanescent Motion. Went afterwards to Sir John Phillips. Mr Thorold, Mr La Serre and Mr Griffith Jones. Talked about annexing and Abstract of the Lawes against Swearing, Gaming, Gin-Shoppes etc. to the next Reformation Sermon. At. Mr. Rivington's. Supped with him and lay there all night.

Friday 7. Waited this morning upon the Bishop of London at White Hall. Kindly received. He told me that he had spoken to Sir R. W. about my succeeding Mr Finch at Canterbury, that Sir Robt. told him the Duke of Newcastle was pressing for Dr. Burrell, his and the King's Chaplain. That he the Bishop had some warm words with the Duke about his pushing for preferments and perhaps sometimes for undeserving persons. That as matters were now carried 'twas all a scramble, an interest thought the least sometimes carried it. That he did not think the Queen would forget what had passed between my father her Majesty and himself upon a former occasion and that he would not fail putting her in mind of it. He expressed his fears of the great Mischief that is done by *The Plain Account of the Sacrament* etc. and spoke very much in commendation of Dr. Watts' learning and piety. Recommended his book upon The Strength and Weakness of Human Reason as an excellent one. That he had many from him but never saw him. Told his Lordship of Mr. Hansard's Imprudence in speaking in praise of the *Plain Account* and his speaking of the Bishops were of a different opinion about Dr. Rundle's [195] character. The Bishop took it very well and I think it was only my duty to let his Lordship know of anything that I thought reflected upon him. Tho I hope he will not name me to H. for this may make ill blood. I wrote this afternoon to the Bishop of Salisbury at Thertfield near Royston in Hertfordshire offering my service at the Temple during his Lordship's absence. He has been very much out of order of late.

Saturday 8. At home.

SUNDAY 9. I was at St. Paules in the morning. In the afternoon I preached at Mercer's Chappell, nominated by one of the Wardens at Hackney (Mr Barrow) (20s). Returned home at night in Mr Hayward's coach. Father Patten told me of an ugly affair of the Grocers Company and the Lord Mayor (Sir Jno. Williams). I think there were faults on both sides however 'tis dangerous shewing the populace the way of insulting magistrates. They are too apt to do this when they are enflamed, very hard to be bought off. Langley Hill the Grocers Clerk a very proud sawcy fellow, loves mischief.

M. 10, T. 11, Wed. 12, Th. 13, F. 14, Sa. 15. At home. Read the Strength and Weakness of Human Reason wrote by Dr. Watts [196] and recommended to me by the Bishop of London.

SUNDAY 16. This afternoon I went to town. Lay at Mr Rivington's.

Monday 17. Set out with Wm Belitha Esq next house to the Turn Pike this side of Kingston. Kindly treated. From thence to Thames Ditton, called upon Dr. Young curate of the place. Left Mr Rivington there and proceeded a mile further to the Speaker

[195] It was over the suggested appointment of Dr Rundle, prebendary of Durham, to the See of Gloucester that Walpole fell out with "the Whig Pope" Bishop Gibson of London. Dr Rundle's appointment was opposed by Gibson on the grounds of heresy but he was strongly supported by Queen Caroline. In the end Gibson prevailed but Dr Rundle was later promoted to the Bishopric of Derry (J. H. Plumb, *Sir Robert Walpole, the King's Minister,* p. 299; Sykes, *Bishop Gibson,* p. 414).

[196] Isaac Watts resided at Stoke Newington from 1712 until his death in 1748 and was the Diarist's near neighbour and they became very friendly. Watts had been at the Dissenting Academy at Stoke Newington 1690–94.

of the House of Commons Arthur Onslow Esq. We talked before dinner of the Isle of Man. My father's Law suite etc.—how much it had injured him in his circumstances etc. Dr. Hales came in. We dined, his lady and one Entwick a clergyman from Kingston. Talked of Mathematical Experiments. Imateriality of the Soul. Began upon the Gin Affair. Heartily for suppression. All spirituous liquors the highest calamity there are before a nation but difficulties will lye in that way. To forbid spirits being imported from abroad will give umbrage to our neighbours and to suppress the Distillery at home will raise great clamour from that set of men and the Country Gentlemen upon account of its taking Barley. He desired I would enquire and find out the decrease of the Brewery and the increase of the Distillery since the Repeal of the Gin Act and compare them together. Then to shew the loss may be equal to any farmer, especially if it be considered the more fewer cloths are worn and much less coarse meat eat than formerly. Increase of Poors Rate. Immoralities. Weakness. To enquire whether more children have not died of late years under 2 years old than formerly. To enquire about Havock Rum etc. makes in the West Indes. Talked about Charities in London. Considered their management. Approved of work being added to the Charity Schooles. Spoke of the Riot at the House of Commons at the time of the Excise Bill. His advice was to have sent for the Sheriffs of London and ordered them to keep the peace and disperse the Mob and after that some time to have given up the Bill but not before, that it might not be said they were bullied out of it. Spoke of the danger Sir Robt. W. was in that night and himself too tho' all the Constables of Westminster were there. Commended *Neal's Last Vol. of the History of the Puritans* for its moderation etc. and blamed him for still insisting upon the genuineness of and independent character in Lord Clarendon's History which the Speaker does not think genuine. But he says the Oxford men should tell the world what is become of the MSS. from whence they printed it. That he had seen a MSS. in Lord Clarendon's own hand writing at the Bodleian Library at Oxford in which the character was inserted and another in the hands of a private gentleman where it was in the margin in the same hand—a material alteration tho' in his character of Hampden (as he thought) added in a Parenthesis by the editors—just before the words—*In Defence of Liberties etc. of his Country* which very much alters and is contrary to the sense of my Lord Clarendon at that time, in relation to Ship Money. That Archbishop Laud died a martyr for the Church of England, very wrong says the Speaker because the Articles exhibited against him were not for keeping up but exceeding and going beyond and contrary to the Rules of the Established Church and well proved against him by Neal. Took leave of the Speaker who very kindly invited me to see him in town which I intend to do. Went thro' Molesy Water, which was very deep and dangerous. Got safe to Dr. Hales at Teddington at night. Lay there.

Tuesday 18. We went this morning to Twickenham and waited upon Lady Blount and her 2 sisters. Mrs Butler. One of which is the unknown benefactress [197] to which my father dedicated his book on the Sacrament. Lady B. has a fine closet of Rarities and a well chosen study of pious bookes. A fine collection of Shells and Egyptian and English Pebbles. Took leave of Dr. Hales. Told the ladies of my father's persecution and my own shipwreck etc. Set out for London. Dined at the King of Bohemia's Head at Turnham Green. Called upon Vertue in Brownlow Street, just begin my father's picture. Too late to return home. Very ill of the cholick. Took Rheubarb and went to bed etc. Thank God rested pretty well.

Wednesday 19. Walked home to Newington. Found my wife and child very well.

Thursday 20. At home.

Friday 21. At the Society for Propagating the Gospel. Moved for some German Prayer Books for the Saltsburghers at Georgia. Referred to the Committee [198] when I intend to attend. Objected by the Bishop of London as it is not exactly the same with the

[197] *Bishop Wilson's Journal*, June 1735: "Dr Hales sent me £20 from an unknown lady to buy Bibles etc."
[198] Not referred to in the Minutes.

English Prayer Book. Saw the King's fine Dun Mouse coloured horses from Hannover. Really very pretty. Came to Bartlett's Buildings with Sir John Phillips. Read him and Mr Griffith Jones Mr Pen's letter of Jamaica. Dined with Mr Waldo in Bread Street. Came home.

Saturday 22. At home.

SUNDAY 23. At Stoke Newington. Master Hayward's Birth Day. Father Patten at dinner. Mr Davis and his family here in the afternoon.

Tuesday 25. Mr Thoresby and Mr Davies payed me a visit. Talked about the Bishop of Winchester's Book.

SUNDAY 30. At Newington.

DECEMBER 1735

Tuesday 2. At the Society.

SUNDAY 7. At Court (Princess Louisa's Birth Day) (12 years old). Dined with Mr Eckersal Clerk of the kitchen, Dr. Hutton, son and Mrs Poole. Dr. Cobden preached before the King and commended The Societies for Propagating the Gospel and that for the Reformation of Manners.

Monday 8. At the Society about making Charity Working schooles. The Trustees for St. Andrew's School there. We gave them our proposal to think of and report their resolution for we should be glad to begin with one of the largest schooles and the rest would probably follow their example.

Tuesday 9. I recommend Mr Blackburn of Oxford for a Corresponding member of the Society. Dr. Hutton and I dined together. We concluded to bye 100 New South Sea Annuities which cost £109. 10s. which stands in our names for the use of Widows and orphans of poor clergymen in the Isle of Man. I presented the Countess of Harold [199] with my father's books by Dr. Hales.

Wednesday 10. Dined with Father Patten. My wife and child. We had a narrow escape of our lives in the coach by a brewer's

[199] Quite clearly *Harold* in MS. Possibly a mistake for Errol.

cart running against us. A letter from my father dated the 22 last month.

Thursday 11. Waited upon the Master of the Rolls. That he had seen the Queen who seemed to be an hearty enemy to distilled and spirituous liquors. Said she had seen a great deal of Bestialities and Indecencies as she has gone by in the streets. He proposed to her Majesty that the King should mention something of it in his speech. The Master took the opportunity of recommending me strongly for preferment. Met Dr. Hales at the South Sea House and accepted of the Stock and Mr Lamb paid me 100 and the 40 I laid down out of money I had of him. The Dr. and I waited upon Mr Hicks in Bristol Street near Bloomsbury Square. Talked about the Gin Affair. Proposes to have a private meeting of the Brewers to subscribe towards the expense of printing etc. Since the drinking of Gin less Milk is sold and the farmers about Islington have decreased their stocks of Corn. That all kinds of labourers do less. That a farmer instead of having good drink out of his own malt, buyes spirits and abundance of Gin Punch is made. I am to meet Mr Hicks at Briton's a Tuesday.

Friday 12. This day I had a letter from Mr Dewe telling me that the Bishop of St. Asaph was at the point of death.

Saturday 13. I waited upon the Bishop of London who promised to speak to Sir R. Walpole that I may succeed to the Canonry of Christ Church. Told me that Gregory was not secure. After went to my Lord Ashburnham. He told me his speaking would do harm because he must work by Newcastle who is against us in this affair. He told me that the Bishop of London could do anything. I waited upon the Bishop of Durham. Kindly received. He is against our Society's medling with things forreign to their proper business. Went to Court. Dined with Dr. Pearce and Dr. Cobden. Waited upon the Bishop of Salisbury at the Temple. He promised me his assistance in this affair and to speak to the Queen. Lay at Mr Rivington's.

SUNDAY 14. At the Rolls Chapel. Mr Trebeck preached for the Dean of Carlisle. Dined with the Master. Lord Chief Justice Hardwicke and his lady there. He desired me to see whether the

Governors of the Hospitals would not come to some resolution about not admitting patients that are given to the drinking of Gin. Very kindly received. Came home at night.

Monday 15. I waited upon the Bishop of London. He told me that he believed the Duke of Newcastle would push hard for Gregory and perhaps not be denied, which I believe too. Lay at Mr Rivington's. Spent the evening with Dr. Robinson and him at the Queens Head Tavern.

Tuesday 16. I waited upon Sir Robt. W. Told him that the Bishop of St. Asaph [200] died Sunday night between 8 and 9 and he told me that he would do what he could for me which I take to be a civil ministerial denial; as I found it an hour afterwards at the Bishop of London, who tells me that the matter is settled and Gregory to have it. One Chamberlain, King's Chaplain, is putting up for a canonry and has been recommended the Bishop tells me to Sir R. W. The Bishop has promised again to desire Sir R. W. to put the Queen in the mind of her promise. I afterwards waited upon the Bishop of Salisbury who had been so kind as to speak to Sir R. W. and the Queen this very day and found the thing settled for Gregory. He told me that the Queen said she had spoke to Sir R. W. and the two Secretarys.

Tuesday 30. At the Society. Dine with Sir John. Mr Lowther a clergyman from Yorkshire. Mr Thorold, 2 sons. Came home.

Wednesday 31. Visited Dr. I. Watts. He owned himself the author of *The Strength and Weakness of Human Reason* and gave me a copy of the 2nd. Edit. with Amendments and Corrections. Is to publish a book in dialogue about the *Attonement of our Saviour* and the Influence of the Holy Spirit. Not with his name to it. Commends my father's book upon the Sacrament,[201] especially the last section in the page of evening prayer for a family beginning with the words *Vouchsafe to us Interest etc.*

[200] Thomas Tanner.
[201] Bishop Wilson's *Instruction for the Lord's Supper*, which, together with his *Sacra Privata*, was one of the most popular of his devotional works.

Thursday 1. New Year's Day. Visited the Bishop of Salisbury at the Temple. The Bishop of London at White Hall. He asked me whether I would be contented with a City Living from the Crown. I left it entirely to his Lordship. By which I guess if Dr. Maddox is made a Bishop he intends to ask Foster Lane for me. I went afterwards to Lord Ashburnham who was ill of the gout. Lord Tylney not at home. Bishop of Durham not at home. Waited upon Sir Robt. Walpole at his Levee and his Grace the Lord Archbishop of York. To Court afterwards. I dined with Lord Tylney in Hanover Square and so came home. My dear little boy has not been well these last 2 or 3 dayes. I pray God restore him to his health. God grant that this may be the beginning of a new life to me.

Friday 2. At home. Wrote to the Bishop of London.

Saturday 3. At Home.

SUNDAY 4. At Court.

Monday 5. Dined at the 3 Crowns.

Tuesday 6. At the Society. Went with Dr. Denne to White Hall.

Wednesday 7. Mr Davis and his family dined with me.

Thursday 8. At home.

Saturday 10. Waited upon the Bishop of London. He told me that he had asked the living of Foster Lane for me of the Queen and had a promise of it if Dr. Maddox was made a Bishop.

SUNDAY 11. I heard the Bishop of London preach an admirable sermon at St. Matthew's Friday Street. Charity Sermon. I dined with Mr Guidot of the Temple. No. 3 the left hand Kings Bench Walks. I preached in the afternoon at the Temple Church. Came home.

Monday 12. The very learned and pious Dr. Isaac Watts made me this day a present of his book enttled *The Redeemer and The Sacrificer or The Sacrifice of Christ and The Operations of The Spirit*

Vindicated. This book is designed as an Animadversion upon Dr. Hoadley's *Plain Account of the Lord's Supper*.[202]

Tuesday 13. At the Society. Dined with Sir John, son. He himself is still much out of order with the Cholick. Dr. Williams of Dartmouth Street and I had a good deal of talk about the Gin Affair which I have inserted in my little Tract. I waited upon the Bishop of Llandaff[203] who is not yet resolved whether he will accept of St. Asaph which makes my having Foster Lane a little uncertain.

Wednesday 14. Dined with Father Patten. Cousin Jonathan there.

Thursday 15. I was at the House of Lords. Introduced very kindly by my Lord Bishop of Durham. Heard the King's Speech. Dined with Mr Pyke at a little house near Westminster Hall.

Friday 16. At the Society in the Mews. They agreed to allow the Salary formerly given to Mr Quincey at Savannah to Mr Jno. Wesley.[204] Gave Mr Vernon a copy of my *Gin Book* in MSS to peruse. I afterwards left one of them at the Porter's Lodge for the Honble. the Master of the Rolls for his opinion. Met Capt. Hopley in the morning at John's Coffee House, St. Martin's Lane Charing Cross from whom I heard calamaties done to the landed interest by the Distillery and had another observation or two from him.

Saturday 17. At home.

SUNDAY 18. My dear little Boy had his Gums lanced by Mr Gill the Surgeon, New Broad Street, who did it dexterously. Cousin Martha and Father Patten dined with me.

Monday 19. Went to town. The Reformation Sermon at Bow. Dr. Cobden preached. Waited upon the Master of the Rolls. He had read my Tract against Spirituous Liquors and approved it in

---

[202] It was during a discussion on this book between Queen Caroline and Lord Hervey that George II burst out against Hoadley "as a canting hypocritical knave crying *My Kingdom is not of this world* at the same time as he, as Christ's ambassador, receives £6000 or £7000 a year" (*Lord Hervey's Memoirs*, Ed. Sidgwick, London 1952, pp. 160–1).

[203] John Harris, Bishop of Llandaff 1729–38.

[204] Not in Minutes.

the Maine. Only desired that its Moral Reflections might be kept to the last and not intermixt in the Body of the Treatise. He told me that he desired I would make him Debtor to the whole charge I have been or shall be at. Accordingly I agreed with Mr Rivington to print me 100 in large paper and stitch in Marble Covers and 900 in small paper in blue covers for £20. Dined with Mr Smith of Aldgate at Dolbyes.

Tuesday 20. The Princes Birth Day. At Court. The Bishop of Durham very civil. Invited by Dr. Galby to dine with the Chaplains. Too late. Dr. Maddox told me he would not keep me a day out of Foster Lane when he was confirmed Bishop. A letter from Ja. Vernon Esq with my MSS against Gin and his entire approbation of it. Sent it to the Press.

Wednesday 21. At home. Corrected the first sheet and amended it.

Thursday 22. My wife and I and little lad dined with Mr Rivington. Mr Dewe of Oxford and Billy. Came home. God be thanked without any mischance.

Friday 23. In town in the morning. Sent one sheet and $\frac{1}{2}$ more to the Press. Dined at home. A letter from Dr. Hales telling me that he should be glad to see me a Tuesday morning in the City.

Saturday 24. A letter from my father dated St. Stephen's Day in which he tells me that he has been much out of order but I thank God much better. That there have been lights in the air coming as it were out of the Earth or Sea and for a few seconds as light as day.

FEBRUARY 1735-6

Tuesday 3. This day I waited upon the Duke of Atholl who told me that he had an express this day before of Lord Derby's death. That now he was Lord of Man. That he should take my father's advice about the affairs relating to the Isle. That he should go down there himself this summer. By all which I cannot see that he intends to sell it to the Crown. I wrote this afternoon an account of the matter to my father.

Wednesday 4. My Dear Molly's Birth Day and my wedding

day. God Grant that we may live long happy together. 2 Years.

Thursday 5. I went to town and presented the following gentlemen with my bookes *Upon Distilled Spirituous Liquors*

Sir John Phillips.	Bishop of Peterborough.
Bishop of Salisbury.	Bishop of Litchfield and Coventry.
Master of the Rolls. 6.	Erasmus Phillips Esq.,
Speaker of the House of Commons,	Robert Hicks Esq.,
Ja. Vernon Esq.,	Lord Shaftesbury.
Bishop of Durham.	Bishop of Oxford.
Bishop of Winchester.	Mr Thorold.
Bishop of Bristol.	Lord Egremont.
Lord Ashburnham.	Lord Chancellor.
Bishop of London.	Mr Talbot.
Archbishop of York.	Bishop of Gloucester.
Mr Hayter.	Dr. Williams.

Dined with the Archbishop of York. Sir John Phillips said he intended me £20 towards the above design. I find Dr. Thomas,[205] Chaplain at the Factory at Hamburgh, is putting in for St. Vedast Foster Lane. God's will be done. I expect nothing but disappointments in the world, especially from the court. No faith in these sort of people. I gave the Archbishop the Option of Rothbury that he had presented me with so that I have no prospects of any preferment in the Church.

Friday 6. Went to town. Saw the Duke of Atholl at the House of Lords. Told me he would not be hasty in making New Offices in the Isle of Man or doing anything till he had heard from my father. Told me I should be very welcome to be his chaplain and desired me to bring him an Instrument and he would sign it. Dined with Sir John Phillips. He gave me £20 for my book against Gin. The Master of the Rolls told me that he had left the Bill with the Lords of the Treasury for their approbation and he is drawing up another for imploying the Poor of the Nation. An excellent design. Came home.

Saturday 7. Went to town with Molly. Returned to dinner.

[205] John Thomas, D.D. (1696–1757), prebendary of St Paul's 1731, rector of St Benet's and St Peter's Paul's Wharf 1733–57, royal chaplain. Finally Bishop of Peterborough 1747–57.

Tuesday 10. Went to town. Complained to the Bishop of London and Salisbury who tells me that Dr. Thomas of Hamburgh had the Living of St. Vedast upon a promise made to him when the King was last at Hannover. No dependance upon anything.

SUNDAY 15. At the Rolls. The Master told me that he would have the gentlemen concerned know that he would have the Petition from Hicks Hall brought in on Wednesday and that I would acquaint Mr Talbot which I accordingly did. He tells me that Mr. Scrope is against it but he does not doubt carrying it. In the afternoon I preached at the Temple (Jo. 7.24). Drank tea with Mr Rider at Amen Corner. Dr. Baker there. Advised me to say nothing of my disappointment and that I need not doubt of success at another time, tho' I doubt it very much.

Monday 16. At home.

Tuesday 17. At the Court. Dr. Madox complained much [206] he was belyed and abused by those who talked so warmly of liberty. That they raked in Private Families to hurt him.

Wednesday 18. Dined with Father Patten. The House of Commons adjourned upon Account of the Entertainment given at Somerset House by Count Rinski upon the marriage of the Duke of Lorrain with the eldest Archduchess. A Masquerade at night. The King and all the Royal Family there.

Thursday 19. At home.

Friday 20. This day the petition of the Justices of the Peace at Hicks Hall against the Geneva Shopps was presented to the House by Sir Francis Child, The Master of the Rolls, Mr Heathcote, Mr Sands for a total suppression of all Distilled Spirituous Liquors. Mr Peckham spoke well on the same side. Mr Pultney for the Distillers as they were a large body of men that had a Charter, served their times to a trade. Referred to a Committee of the whole House on Monday.

SUNDAY 21. At Newington. In the afternoon drunk tea with Mr Davis.

[206] But Dr Maddox got his bishopric. St Asaph 1736, translated to Worcester 1743.

Monday 23. Went with Mr Hayward to Dr. Meads. Afterwards to the House of Commons. The House resolved itself into a Committee with Sir Charles Turner in the chair. The Master of the Rolls began with a speech setting forth the abominable Practices carried on in the Geneva Shopps, mentioned the heinous custom of murdering children even in the womb, and afterwards by giving it them weakening them, making Parish Nurses giving it children to quiet them which it effectively did and ended with his heart's wishes that an entire suppression may be put to it. Afterwards Dr. Coales the Physitian took notice of the Malignant Effects it had upon Human Bodies. Mr Sands was for a total suppression and laying such a duty as would amount almost to a Prohibition. Mr Lockwood and Alderman Perry were for letting the Distillers have the Management and alleged that the laying of a high duty upon our home spirits would encourage the importation of forreign and smuggling etc. However the Master got all his four Motions past the House which are the leading strokes for a Bill. Sir Robt. closed the debate by showing that the Revenue by the Suppression of Spirits would be a Loss to the Crown of near £292,000 pr. ann. That it was no trifle to give up. That he was for restraining Gin Shoppes, but not losing the whole Revenue. That he never found the Malt Tax or that upon Hopps to be lessened in any Proportion to the Increase of the Distillery. That the Brewery was more or less according to the good or bad cropps of corn in the Kingdom. That if the House went at the present methods, no doubt they intended it as a total Prohibition and then he hoped they would seriously consider of replacing this Duty in some other way, no visible one yet appearing to him. Answer was made by Sir John Barnard that his Majesty's Duty on Wines would be increased if Punch was left off and that he was for including it in the Act now going to be made. The Master of the Rolls declared no one would be more against the lessening of the Public Revenues than himself and none readier of coming to some method of replacing it but that he hoped the Honourable Gentlemen would not oppose the putting an end to a Practice big with so many mischiefs for any Collateral Consequences that may for the present accrue from such a Prohibition. In short the 4 Motions were almost unanimously carried and the Report ordered to be made tomorrow morning.

Thursday 26. At the House of Lords. Bill for Repeal of Act against Witchcraft [207] passed with some Amendments.

SUNDAY 29. At Court. Dined with Mr Harrison.

MARCH 1735-6

Monday 1. The Queen's Birth Day. The Duke of Atholl gave me an Instrument making me his chaplain which was the first Act as Lord of Man and the Isle. A very full Court but plain. They keep their fine clothes for the Princess' Wedding.

Tuesday 2. Dined at Mr Davis'. My poor boy got a very ill cold.

Wednesday 3. My poor lad much worse. Gave him a purge. Coughed exceedingly. Mr Gill lanced his teeth.

Thursday 4. He was at the worst. I was afraid we should have lost him. My wife and I sat up with him all night. Put him on a Blister and I hope is a little better.

Friday 5. He still continues very short breath'd and hoarse. The Lord preserve him and restore him to us.

Saturday 6. We gave him a vomit which agreed very much with him and he is much easier and hope has got over the worst.

SUNDAY 7. I preached and administered the Sacrament for Mr Thoresby. My little boy (God be praised for all his Mercies) is much better and I hope the danger is now over.

Tuesday 9. At the Duke of Atholls. He shewed me a letter he had received from my father which he was much pleased with as having brought the Island to submit to him a rightful Sovereign. I had a letter at the same time which I communicated to his Grace. I hope every thing will be made easy in that place especially to my father. With the Bishop of London. Maddox not to be a Bishop at last.[208]

[207] The last trial for witchcraft took place in England in 1712 and in Scotland in 1732.

[208] See note 206.

Friday 12. At the House of Commons. Two more resolutions against Gin.

SUNDAY 14. At the King's Chappel. Bishop of Durham preached an Admirable sermon. I afterwards dined with him. He told me that the Master of the Rolls had recommened me very heartily to him and said if he had £500 a year he would give it me. His Lordship repeated his Assurances of serving me. Came home.

Monday 15. At home. Mr Rivington and Mr Smith drunk tea with me.

Tuesday 16. My 2nd. Edition of *Distilled Spirituous Liquors the Bane of the Nation* was printed off. I sent them this evening to each of the chief Members of the House of Commons. The debate upon this head coming up tomorrow. I dined with Lord Ashburnham, Dr. Hales, his brother Mr Ashburnham, my Lord St. Asaph, his eldest son. Very kindly received. Liked my pamphlet very well. Heard that the affair went on very well in the House today. Down with it at all Adventures.

Wednesday 17. Dined with Lord A. not yesterday. I received £40 from Dr. Hales, the benefaction of Mrs Dionysia Long and another lady towards the expenses of printing and dispersing the 2nd. Edit. of my little Tract.

Thursday 18. The Anniversary of the Meeting of the Trustees of Georgia. Mr Watts preached at Lincolns Inn. Gave them (they say) an Ingenious sermon. I made him a present of my pamphlet. This is my dear little boy's Birth Day. God send him many of them to his glory and the good of his own soul. Father Patten dined with us.

Friday 19. Dined with Sir John Phillips. Mr Hayward. Mr Warham. The House of Commons agreed to their report last wednesday. Think that the Duties arising from spirits should be paid into the Aggregate Fund and that Annuity pay with from these Duties to be paid out of the Sinking Fund.

Saturday 20. Mr Verney, Chief Justice of Chester, sent for me and told me that he was a near relation of the Countesse of Derbyes and concerned for her. That he desired me to write to my father. To send him word whether there are any traces before or since the Act of James I of any Widow Countess haveing Dower in the Isle of Man. Whether the late Lord had any estate in the Island of his own purchasing and Lawes and Customs of the Island relating to Widows in general. He told me that the Countess was in manner kept a prisoner, not allowed above a room or two and about £100 a year for her maintenance. That she has now the whole estate absolutely her own to dispose of and 2 or 3 very good Livings and that she will have Dower of my Lord's estates in Lancashire. I with him, his lady and one Miss Charleton. I intend to write to the Countess. The Chief Justice told me that the present Earl of D. designs to sue for the Island, that the Duke has an absolute right by the Act of James I a copy of which he has promised me. Came home.

SUNDAY 21. At home. Mr Dacier came to see me to desire my interest with Father Patten for one Mr Vaux to be under Beadle to the Grocers' Company.

[Break in the Diary until June 1736. During this time the Diarist was ill of the Small Pox. Also his child died.[209]]

[209]   *Upon the Loss of a Child*

            1   4
O Mornings Gay and Shining   A Child of whom kind Heaven
    The Dayes or Joys declare   Not only Hope bestowes
At Evening no repining   But has already given
    And Nights all void of care.   Him all our Hopes propose.

            2   5
A fond transported Mother   The happy Sires possessing
    Was often heard to say   His share in such a Boy
O where is such another   Adds still a greater blessing
    So Blessed of heaven as I.   To all my other Joy.

            3   6
A Child at first was wanting   But Ah! This shiny weather
    Now such a son is sent   Becomes too hot to last
As Parents most lamenting   Black clouds begin to gather
    In him would find content.   And all the Sky o'ercast.

Thursday 3. I was chosen Corresponding Member of the Society for Propagating the Gospel in Scotland.

Monday 21. Dr Guerdes came to see me. Told me that the Bishop of Durham sent me a very kind message that he would have me go to Court once in 3 weeks or a month. From him I found that the Bishop was betrayed in the last consultation about the Quakers and the Mortmain Acts. The reason for the Bishop of London's disgrace is that his saying in Rundle's Case [210] that the Clergy were the fittest persons to recommend to Bishoprecks, his refusal to have anything to do in the Quakers Bill tho' desired by Sir Robt. Walpole. This was the Dean of Durham Dr. Bland. A friend of his carrying odd stories to Sir Robt. However I find the Bishop seems resolved to have no more to do with recommendations to Court in Ecclesiastical affairs. They say that Salisbury, Chichester or Oxford are to take his place. Molly's face was opened by Mr Gill and found nothing bad in it.

Tuesday 22. In Town visited A. Byfield. Molly's face was dressed.

Wednesday 23. A letter from the Master of the Rolls in which he tells me that he will take the first opportunity of speaking to the Queen in my favour. A letter from the Bishop of Durham.

Thursday 24. Waited upon the Duke of Newcastle. Asked him

<table>
<tr><td>7</td><td>8</td></tr>
</table>

So Fierce a Fever rages
  We all lie drown'd in Tears
And Dismal Sad Presages
  Come thundering in our ears.

The doubts that made us languish
  Did Worse, far Worse, than kill
Yet Oh! with all our Anguish
  Would we had doubted still.

9
But why so much Digression
This Fatal Loss to shew
Alas! There's no Expression
To tell a Parents Woe.

May 1736.

[210] See Note for 6 Nov. 1735.

for the Chaplainship of the Tower vacant by the death of Mr Hawkins.[211] His Grace told me that my Lord Leicester, Constable of the Tower had desired it for a friend of his and he could not as a relation refuse doing him what service he could and that another person pretended a prior right so that it was improper forme to come at it. He told me that he would be glad to serve me for my father's sake and my own and the recommendation of the Master of the Rolls. These are words of course and I don't mind them much. I went afterwards to Kensington to Court. The Queen spoke much in praise of Dr. Butler's Book (The Analogy) *Of Religion Revealed in the Course of Nature*. Said it was very intelligible. That she had read it and understood it easily. That it was a scheme a Midway between Woolston and Dr. Clark.[212] That he was a little too severe. Expected too much perfection in the world. This discourse with my Lord Hay who said he would read it and give his opinion of it. The Queen said she had heard it was metaphysical and dry but found it otherwise but says it may appear to your fine genius in another light.

Friday 26. Waited upon the Bishop of London. Too late. The Court had lost the clergy. That there was a misunderstanding between him and the Ministry about the Quakers Bill but he the Bishop had wrote to my father about writing directly to the Queen in my affair. That she could not well get off her promise to me of preferment. Seemed very civil though I have no great confidence of any profession, they so often having failed me even made in the strongest terms.

Saturday 27. Visited Dr. Watts. He objects to Dr. Butler's book that he rather answers the objection made in relation to the Soules of Brutes under authority. That reason. Mem. To ask his further opinion realating to it when I see him next.

SUNDAY 28. At Newington.

[211] William Hawkins, minister of St Peter ad Vincula and prebendary of St Paul's 1707–36. His father, Francis Hawkins, D.D., Dean of Chichester 1688–99, had been also the Chaplain to the Tower.

[212] Dr Samuel Clarke, rector of St James's, Piccadilly. His most important work at the time of the Arian Controversy in the early part of the eighteenth century was *The Scripture Doctrine of the Trinity*.

Tuesday 30. At the Society at Bartlett's Buildings. Dined at the Sun Tavern, Ludgate Street.

Thursday 1. Waited upon the Master of the Rolls. Told me he intended to wait upon the Queen and speak himself in my favour tomorrow. That the Bishop of Oxford had now the disposal of Ecclesiastical Preferments. That whoever knew the Chancery knew likewise that there was absolute necessity for passing the Mortmain Act. To prevent attoning for sin, by mercy given at our death from the right heir, which is a great crime because it is giving what is anothers on a person's demise. That he was against the Quakers Bill unless it could be more universal and extend for the Benefit of the Clergy giving them their just Dues. Mentioned the Bishop of Salisbury's little Pamphlet with some applause and a little thing called *A Letter to the Quakers upon the Loss of their Tyth Bill.* Spoke of the true Nature of Parties. A Country Party will not do because their opposition to the Ministry will be carried on at all adventures whether with reason or against it. Witness the Craftsman's Behaviour about the late Gin Act etc. His personal view about the King about the time of Franklin's Tryal [213] which lost him a good deal of popularity. The true party must be this. Every Person independent in the House of Commons making the Publick Welfare his chief concern and study which makes him always a good friend to the King, even when he opposes his Ministers who are only pro tempore whilst the King's vertues reach out to posterity. Who if he can make things go easy and run on during his time does not come in with confusion they be left to his successor. That every member then independent of any

[213] On 27 Jan. 1727 *The Craftsman* published a satire of Walpole—"The Vision of Camilick"—for which the editor and the printer, Franklin, were arrested but the evidence against them proved insufficient. On 13 Jan. 1731 *The Craftsman* published a letter, purporting to come from The Hague, exposing Walpole's secret negotiations with the Imperial Court concerning the Treaty of Seville which had been discovered by Bolingbroke. The offices of *The Craftsman* were raided and Franklin imprisoned on a charge of sedition (J. H. Plumb, *Sir Robert Walpole, the King's Minister,* pp. 142, 151, 228).

Party should speak out according to the Dictates of his Conscience. That a sort of man so acting may be called Patriot and no other. Wished somebody would write a little thing on this head. Spoke against the Bishops voting always one way. Their writing Circular Letters upon the late occasions to their clergy. Against addressing at Sion College etc. Put a stop to by the Bishop of Salisbury. The Bishop owned in the House of Lords that the Mortmain Act did not affect the Church of England. The Duke of A.[tholl] too severe, did service to the cause he was speaking against.

Friday 2. Dined with Mr Verney, Chief Justice of Chester. Told me that the clergy of the Isle of Man must sue my Lord Derby as a Counter Security for the Rectoryes in the Island. Told me that any person may leave what sum he will to Corporation or otherwise and leave it either to his honour whether they will lay it out in land in perpetuum or no, but nothing of that must be mentioned in the Deed or Will of Bequest. This must be the method of Lady Hastings etc. is to take. Did not say anything of my preferment which I wonder at.

N.B. When I was with the Master of the Rolls on Thursday he told me that the Bishops went in a body to consult the Abp. of York about the Quakers Bill and he said in a very serious manner *It is now time to ring the Larum Bell*—an odd expression for one who has not exercised Episcopal Jurisdiction in his diocese for many years and whose character has not stood in the fairest light. Perhaps he or some other Bishops at the meeting betrayed their Bretheren too. The Bishop of Durham told Dr. Guerdes that everything he had said upon this occasion was told again at Court perhaps very disadvantageously.

Saturday 3. Wrote a letter to the Bishop of Oxford. Dr. Rye. Dr. Smith Provost of Queens to speak to his Lordship to put the Queen in mind of her promise to me. Wrote to Lord Ashburnham to recommend me to the Duke of Newcastle. Whether any of these letters be to much purpose I dare not say only that I ought not to omit any proper opportunity of addressing those Great Men that are supposed to be in my favour.

SUNDAY 4. At home.

Monday 5. At the Master of the Rolls. He told me that he had yesterday waited upon the Queen and in the strongest manner recommended me to her Majesty. Told her that I was the strongest friend to their Majestyes and a sincere enemy to the present factious spirit that is now reigning amongst the clergy (which seemed to strike the Queen very much). Who is studying how to quiet it. Bishop of Durham spoke for the Mortmain Act. Gloucester [214] and Norwich [215] went below the stairs to avoid voting at all. The Master against Pluralities and Non-Residence. As to the Chaplainship of the Tower the Constable and the Secretary of War both pretend to a right of nominating to it. Burton not a good character. Could have wished I had it. Advises me to write to the Bishop of Oxford and tell him what the Queen had said viz. *That she would certainly prefer me.* Soon she may find an opportunity if she pleases but whether she is in earnest or no I dare not say. The Master thinks she is.

Tuesday 6. At the Treasury. They do not make any difficulty about paying the Clergyes Annuity of £100 out of the Exchequer. Wrote to my father acquainting him with this. That he would write to the Bishop of Oxford and Sir Joseph Jekyl thanking him for his civilityes.

Wednesday 7. Wrote to the Bishop of Oxford. Dr. Rye etc.

Thursday 8. At home.

Friday 9. With the Bishop of London. He has not received any letter from my father in answer to his last in which he advised him to apply again to her Majesty for me. With the Master of the Rolls. Told him that I had received a message from the Bishop of Oxford, but a coole one. He told me that he would speak to Lord Hardwicke to interest himself for me at Court.

Saturday 10. At home.

SUNDAY 11. Dr. Crowe preached here twice.

Monday 12. Waited upon the Master of the Rolls. Gave me a copy of Abp. Tillotson's Letter[216] to the Earl of Shrewsbury

---

[214] Martin Benson, Bishop of Gloucester 1735–52.
[215] Robert Butts, Bishop of Norwich 1733. Translated to Ely 1738.
[216] The letter is as follows:

Copy of a Letter written by Dr Tillotson, Dean and afterwards Archbishop of Canterbury, to the Earl of Shrewsbury.

My Lord,

It was a great satisfaction to me to be in any wayes instrumental in the gaining of your Lordship to our Religion, which I am really persuaded to be the Truth. But I am and always was more concerned that your Lordship should continue a virtuous and a good man, than become a Protestant; being assured that the *Ignorance* and *Errors* of Men's *Understanding* will find much easier forgiveness with God than the *Faults of the Will*. I remember that your Lordship once told me that you would endeavour to justify the sincerity of your change by a conscientious regard to all other Parts and Actions of your life. I am sure you cannot more effectually condemn your own act than by being a Worse Man after your Profession of having embraced a better Religion. I shall certainly be one of the last to believe anything of your Lordship that is not good; but I always feared that I should be the first that should hear it. The time I first waited upon your Lordship I had something which afflicted me very sensibly, but I hoped it was not true and was therefore loath to trouble your Lordship about it. But having received the same from those, who, I believe, bear no ill will to your Lordship I now think it my duty to acquaint you with it. To speak plainly I have been told that your Lordship is of late fallen into a Conversation dangerous both to your *Reputation* and *Vertue*. Two of the *Tenderest* and *Dearest* things in the world. I believe your Lordship to have a great *Command* of yourself. But I am very sensible of Human Frailty and of the dangerous Temptations to which youth are exposed in this dissolute age. Therefore I earnestly beseech your Lordship to consider, besides the High Provocation of Almighty God and the Hazard of your Soul, whenever you engage in a bad course what a Blemish you will bring upon a *Fair* and *Unspotted* Reputation. What uneasiness and Trouble you will create for yourself from the severe Reflections of a guilty Conscience, and how great a Violence you will offer to your good Principles, your Nature, your Education, to a mind the best made for virtuous and worthy things. And do not imagine you can stop when you please. Experience shows us the contrary and that nothing is more vain than for Men to think they can set Bounds for themselves in anything that is bad. I hope in God no Temptation has yet prevailed upon your Lordship so far as to be guilty of any lewd Act. If it has as you love your soul let it not proceed into a Habit. The Retreat is as yet easy and open, but will every day become more difficult and obstinate. God is mercyful but upon the Repentance and Resolution of Amendment. He is not only ready to forgive what is past, but to assist us by His Grace to do better for the future. But I need not Inforce these Considerations upon a Mind so acceptable and easy to good counsel. I shall only desire that your Lordship to think again and again how great a point of wisdom it is in all actions to consult the peace of our minds and to have no quarrel with the consistent conversation of our life. If others displease us we may quit their company. But he that is displeased at himself is unavoidably unhappy, because he has no way to get ridd of himself.

My Lord. For God's sake and your own think of being Happy and resolve by all means to preserve yourself from this Untoward Generation. Determine rather which he desired I would print. Assured me of serving me to the utmost of his Power.

Tuesday 13. At home.

Wednesday 14. Set out for Tunbridge. God grant we may return home safe. In Brown's Coach and 4. Breakfast at Lewisham with Mr Lewis over against the Rookery—dyed soon after of the Palsey—To Bromley. Farnborough. Dined at the Crown at Sevenoke. Pestered with Barbers, Butchers etc from the Wells for our custom. Which is called *Touting* from a French Word *tout*— one and all. From Sevenoke to the Wells but an indifferent road. At Sevenoke there are just beyond the town fine stone Buildings— Hospitals. Came to the Wells about 7 a clock. Plagued there again with touters. Agreed for Lodging at £1 5. 0. per week at one Knights at the front of Mount Sion.

Thursday 15. Begun drinking the waters. 3 Glasses ½ Pints the first morning. A great deal of Company coming in every day.

People of Quality

Duke and Dutchess of Richmond.
Duke and Dutchess of Norfolk.
Dutchess of Northumberland.
Dutchess of Richmond. 2 Daughters.
Duke of Dorset's Daughter.
Lady Betty Germain.
Lord and Lady Tylney. Sir Robt. Long and Lady. Lady Dorothy.
Lord Castlemain.
Lord and Lady Augustus Fitzroy.
Lady Di and Lady Dorothy Greyes, Lord Stanford's daughters.
Lady Mollineux.

upon a speedy change of your condition than to gratify the inclinations of youth in any way but what is lawful and honourable; and let me have the satisfaction to be assured from your Lordship either that there has been no ground for this Report or that there shall be none for the future; which will be the welcomest Newes to me in all the world. I have only to beg of your Lordship to believe I have not done this to satisfy the *Formality of your Profession* but that it proceeds from the truest affection and good will that one man can possibly have for another. I pray God every day for your Lordship with the same Constancy and Fervour as for myself and do now earnestly beg that this Counsel may be acceptable and effective.

I am, My Lord, etc.

Lord James Cavendish.
Lord J. Beauclerk.
Lord William Manners.
Lord Southwell.
Lord Ashburnham.
Baron Spence.
Lord and Lady Litchfield and daughter.
Sir James Whitchcote.
Lady Leighton and Daughter and Grand Daughter.
Lady Murson.
Sir Jo. Buckworth.
Sir Charles Hardy.
Lord Rockingham.
Lord Paisley.
Lord Onslow.
Lord and Lady Westmoreland.
Lord Vane.
Lord Stanhope and Lady Lucy his sister.
The Honble. Stephen Poyntz and his Lady. Miss Mordaunt. Little boy.
William Poyntz Esq. Commissioner of the Excise and Lady Frederick.
Sir Thomas Frederick and his brother and 2 sisters.
Richard Grenville Esq. Lord Cobham's Nephew and Heir.
Sir Thomas Frankland.
Sir Robert Austen.
Sir Jo. Kelly, his lady, sister to the Duke of Newcastle and daughter.
Sir S. Smythe.
Mrs Titchbourne. Dresser to the Queen.
Mr Debouverie. A Gentleman of Vast Estate.
Sir Jo. Stanley.
Mr Jackson. Formerly Envoy to Sweden.
Col. Churchill.
Col. Handasyde.
Col. Cope.
Mr Frankland. Member of Parliament.
Pearce A Court Esq. Member of Parliament.
Solomon Ashley. Member of Parliament.
Lord Euston. Duke of Grafton's Eldest son.
Mr Onslow. Son of my Lord.

Friday 16. I think the waters have in some measure taken off the Heats that I was troubled with on Nights.
Saturday 17. Drunk tea with Mrs Lethurier at Moylayes Coffee

House. Mem. To subscribe at Upton's Coffee House (Whigg) if ever I should go to Tonbridge again.

SUNDAY 18. Mr Elton [217] the curate of the Chapel here preached twice. He has married a good fortune and has a pretty estate in the country. A gentleman who understands worldly affairs very well. Of no great Depth, reckoned an honest man because very blunt, when a little more civility might not be improper, tho' he knows, or his wife better, how to condescend and I think even to fawn upon those from whom they expect something. For most, if not all, their income arises from voluntary contributions of the Gentlemen and Ladies that drink the waters. Those that have families give a Guineas and single persons Half a Guinea so it sometimes amounts to £200 pr. ann. There is a Chapel built by the Contributions about 70 years ago and improved since by the addition of a very fine ceiling in stocher work. It is maintained and repaired, as well as education given to 50 boys, by a Collection made the 1st. Sunday in August. 2 Charity Sermons being generally preached on this day by some clergyman who happens to be there.

Monday 19. Miss Skerrett, Sir Robt. W's supposed Miss, came down with her companion Mistris Floyd and Mrs [gap in text]. She seems to be very ill.

Tuesday 20. Mr Elton spoke to me to preach for him which I promised to do when I was a little more able.

Wednesday 21. The waters purging me a little occasioned I believe by the sudden chillyness. I drank the first glass warm. They have a method of doing it without losing much of its vertue by keeping some of it boiling in a tea kettle on a fire at the well and putting some of it to a glass just taken up.

Thursday 22. More company come in daily and the weather is very inviting. All the inconvenience is that in a dry season it is prodigous dusty and the houses are so thin and badly fitted up that they are not at all made for windy or rainy weather. But a month

[217] John Elton, Jesus College, Cambridge, Vicar of St Charles the Martyr, Tonbridge Wells 1723–44, rector of Speldhurst 1727–8 and rector of Trottiscliffe from 1744 until his death in 1747.

ago a sudden flood the Houses below the Hills were overflowed near 4 foot in the lower rooms.

Friday 23. This evening it is confidently reported that Sir R. W. came here to see Miss Skerrett. This I had from one that pretends to have seen him. This seems to have been more common compliment in a Prime Minister; more say the married ladies than he would probably have done for his lady. Then State Affairs, Counsil Day, the Commands of the Queen Etc. and 100 other excuses would have detained him at home. They say he has a daughter [218] by this lady 15 years old which he keeps a coach and 6 for and lives in great splendour in St. James Square.

Saturday 24. Miss Brett, Daughter of Col. Brett by Lady Macclesfield, came to the Wells. She is supposed Mistress of the late King. Has £800 a year allowed her. It is said here that she was too grave to have gained much on that Monarch's Affections if he had come over again. She behaves here very discreetly. People avoid her company when the same persons are proud of being seen with Miss Skerrett. The Miss of the reigning Minister is to be feared when that of a Dead Lyon may safely be neglected. Tho' in a Gay World one would think the latter should be preferred as being more honourably wicked. Unlike to both these are the 2 Miss Berties, Natural Daughters of the Countess of Coventryes, who brazen it in publick places with an uncommon assurance, keep company with all the Gamesters and Rakes and seem to live by gaming. And what is very strange, very grave in other respects. Prudent Ladies will converse with and suffer their daughters to being familiar with them. This seems very unaccountable since their behaviour and character is so well known and they themselves take no pains to conceal it. They say my Lord Coventry is very fond of them and suffers them to live with his own children.

SUNDAY 25. The President of St. John's, Dr. Holmes, preached a most excellent sermon. A Learned discourse but being a few minutes about 20 the ladies were out of all patience and the gentlemen began to follow their example. I dare say they will

[218] Walpole's daughter Maria by Miss Skerrett. Born 1725.

not be so rationally entertained this season. 'Tis plain this is an Entertainment they do not at all Relish and indeed it is almost impossible that anything grave, solid or serious should be good for Minds so long weakened, softened and depraved by a Round of Impertinence, Buffoonery, Noise and Nonsense. Mr Miller Author of The Man of Trust preached a very indifferent sermon in the afternoon.

Monday 26. Sir R. W. returned to London. There was a sneering paragraph in one of the papers last week. Viz: We hear from Tunbridge that Miss Skerrett is upon the Mending Hand. That Sir R. W. returned such a day from T. and immediately waited upon his Majesty at Kensington and *met with a most gratious reception.*

Tuesday 27. Walked up to Mount Ephraim. Very handsome lodgings there at the Castle etc. and cheaper than nearer to Wells. And for those that keep coaches preferable in every respect. Too far to walk. On the other side of this Hill are the Fish Ponds, a very retired entertaining House but extravagantly dear.

Wednesday 28. Mrs Lethurier carried us in her coach and 6 to the Rocks a Mile and ½. Prodigious Large Stones growing by the side of one another about 70 or 80 foot perpendicular in this form:

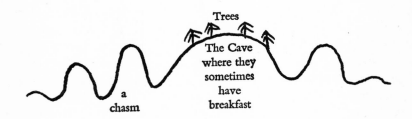

An old woman lives under these, sells cakes and makes wine. They are seated in a low valley and are worth seeing for once. As we came home we looked from a steep hill into the Cold Bath where they sometimes bath in the summer time. There they drink the Waters which must certainly be very good for weak nerves.

Thursday 29. The President of St. John's told me some Memories of *Mr Nash*'s Life who has been so famous at Bath for many years and which he had from good hands Viz:

That he was a Welchman, entered Servitor of Jesus in Oxon. but beat the Proctor Mr Wynne (now Bishop of Bath and Wells) and was expelled for it upon which he merrily said that they had hindered him from being a Bishop as well as Wynne. He afterwards went to sea before the Mast and was cast away upon the Coast of Ireland, Where he is supposed to have turned Papist and afterwards he went into the French Service and was Captain of a little Man of War and employed against the Protestants. He was broke for some Misbehaviour and came over into England. Turned Gamester and having a good stock of assurance set up for Director General at Bath where he won a vast estate of Lord Howard and the Duke of Bedford and generously gave it up again upon condition that he should have a Rent Charge out of these estates £1300 pr. ann. for life. Upon which he set up his Chariot and 6 and keeps up the same Equipage and has a fine house at Bath and another in town, complemented by the Mayor and is in reality the Governor of the Place. At Tunbridge he does not assume so much Authority. He was formerly Rude and Saucy to strangers and especially Country Ladies that had not secrets to keep, no Intrigues to fear the Discovery of. At present he is much civiler. He playes with a good deal of Sedateness and Fairness. Is a man of tolerable good sense and well fitted for the station he is in. A trifling idle life. Looks now younger than he did about 20 years ago. Gets up at 4 a clock in the morning, drinks little wine. He once danced both at Bath and Tunbridge the same day for a Piece of Galantry; from 4 a clock in the morning to 10 at night. Rode 15 horses.[219]

Friday 30. Drank 4 Glasses in a morning and agrees well with me.

---

[219] The story of Nash's beating the Proctor and of his wager are not told by Goldsmith in *The Life of Richard Nash Esq.*, but he speaks of him arriving in Tunbridge "in a post chariot and six greys, with out-riders, footmen, French Horns, and every other appendage of expensive parade".

AUGUST 1736

SUNDAY 1. This week end reckoned the chief Sunday in Tunbridge. I preached in the Morning (Set your affections on things above). Read prayers in the afternoon for Mr Elton who preached.

Monday 2. Took a Walk to Mount Pleasant House. A fine house belonging to the Earl of Egmont [220] but now let to a tenant who setts it out at Lodgings. The Princess Amelia lodgd there. Lord and Lady Litchefield this year. It is a very good house, excellent rooms and well furnished.

Tuesday 3. Dined with Mr Rogers (at Dusmore's Mount Ephraim). Kindly entertained by him and his brother. Mr Ladds a Wine Merchant in Tower Street. This The Prophet's House as they call him. A man of a strange turn. Pretends he has intercourse with God by the Angel Gabriel, who assures him that he shall never die or feel pain. Whether he puts this on to amuse and make the people stare, or whether his resignation is so strong as to believe these Whimsies I will not take upon me to say. In wordly affairs he is very shrewd. Has £400 or £500 a year and letts lodgings and so does Mrs Ruck a very rich woman. Jeffrey's very good lodgings and so are Woods and Brothers upon the top of Mount Sion near the Bowling Green. A very handsome house.

Wednesday 4. Petitioned Mr Rice, one of the executors of Mr Wright's will who died lately at Newington for some part of the Charity left by him to the widows of Dissenting Ministers, for Mrs Humphreys whom we left at home in our house in our absence. A very good woman. Lives in Plaisterers' Hall Addle Street, near Aldermanbury.

Thursday 5. Drank 5 Glasses in the morning. Agrees well with me. But speaking the next day to Dr. Batey he told me that drinking too large a quantity was of ill consequence to the Con-

---

[220] John Percival, 1st Earl of Egmont (1683–1758). Actively interested in Georgia, keeping *A Journal of the Transactions of the Trustees* and publishing *An Impartial Enquiry into the State and Utility of the Province of Georgia* (1741) and *A Brief Account of the Causes that have Retarded the Progress of the Colony of Georgia in America* (1743).

stitution, that it widened too much the passages of the kidneys and occasioned Gravel etc. They tell me that at Spaw in Germany it is common to drink 8 or 10½ pint glasses in a morning.

Friday 6. People still continue to come in very fast and is the finest season that has been known for many years.

SUNDAY 8. A Charity Sermon was preached by Harteswell of Greenwich and another in the afternoon at both was collected over £50 for repairs to the Chapel, the education of 50 poor boys and the repair of the Walks and Wells etc.

Monday 9. This seems to be the height of the season and there seems to be about 900 Gentlemen and Ladies. There is some private Gaming of a Sunday evening but it is amongst the profligate and loose.

Tuesday 10. Received a letter from Erasmus Philipps in which he tells me that he had spoke to Lady Walpole in my favour who told him that Sir R. said he really thought I was already provided for, which was a ministerial answer indeed and just meant nothing.

Wednesday 11. I applyed again to the Trustees of Mr Wright's will for the widow of Mr Humphreys a Dissenting Minister and hope to get money for her.

Thursday 12. The company that came at the beginning of July are dropping off every day.

SUNDAY 15. Mr Harteswell preached a sermon that set all the congregation a smiling. Upon the text—*As his Name is, so is he, Nabal is his name and Folly is with him.*

Monday 16. I asked Mr Chaloner, the Dissenting Minister, his opinion of Dr. Butler's Book. He said it was very well in the Main. That he liked his Chapter on the Mediator the worst. Upon the whole he said that he had demonstrated *That A Deist must be a Fool.* In conversation he jested and said that the Dissenters furnish us all with Bishops, meaning Secker and Madox and Butler that it to be. Mem. They were all brought up at the same Academy [221] with him. Gives me but a mean account of *The Cure of Deism.*

[221] At the Nonconformist Academy at Tewkesbury.

SUNDAY 22. I preached at the Chappel upon Praise and Thanksgiving for which I was mightily complimented.

Tuesday 24. My Birth Day. Now 33 years old. Ah! Quot Dies Perdidi. For all is Loss and Folly but serving God. May I retrieve the time I have spent in Idleness by a more Active, studious and pious life.

Wednesday 25, Thursday 26, Friday 27, Saturday 28. I set out this day in my return home in company with Mr Vincent, a Stationer in Ludgate Hill and Mr Shaw, Fellow of Queens Coll. Cambridge. We breakfasted at Sevenoke. Dined at the George at Farnborough, things but indifferent, bad wine and very imposing. We arrived home about 8 a clock and found everything in good order and safe, praised be God for all His mercies.

SUNDAY 29. At Newington.

Monday 30. Father Patten came to see us.

Tuesday 31. We dined with Father Patten.

SEPTEMBER 1736

Wednesday 1. Received a letter from my father with one for the Queen and one for Sir R. W. enclosed.[222]

[222] Copy of my father's letter to Sir Robt. Walpole. Aug. 8. 1736.

May it please your Honr.

My Agents meeting with some difficulty in receiving the Royal Bounty of 100 a year to the poor clergy of this diocese, my residence in this remote place constraineth me to apply to your Honr. in this way.

About 36 years ago I received a Power from the Trustees named in The Letters Patent by which I have ever since received and faithfully paid the said Bounty of which I have discharges by me.

Now the difficulty of sending for New Powers upon the death of many Trustees would be very great as well as chargeable to this poor people and therefore I hope it may be dispensed with and the Money paid as formerly. Our New and Noble Lord has already given a Check to one very evil and common practice of stopping Tobacco and Other Debenture Goods into the Running Wherryes.

I must omit not this occasion of acknowledging with the greatest gratitude your Honr's marks of kindness to me, when I had the honour to wait upon you in London and I hope to see even yet the good effects of her Majesty's Promise to my son and your honour's good offices upon that occasion. In the Mean Time I am and ever shall be your Honr's most obliged and humble servant.   T.S.M.

Copy of My father's letter to the Queen. Sent me Aug. 8. 1736.

Thursday 2. Waited upon Sir R. W. Gave him my father's letter. Said nothing.

Friday 3. At home.

Saturday 4. My wife taken very ill after eating Pidgeon Pie and was extreamly out of order with Purging and Vomiting which made us stay at home all day. I thank God she is a little better.

Monday 6. I hope my wife's disorder is passing off.

Tuesday 7. She was well enough to meet Mr Hayward upon his return from Scarborough at Waltham Cross. I was on appointment to wait upon Sir R. W. with Mr Phillips. He did not say anything to purpose.

Wednesday 9. At home. Paid Dr. Watts a visit. Talked about the Analogy, Dr. Butler's Book. As much against as for.

Thursday 10. I waited upon the Duke of Newcastle who promised to give my father's letter to the Queen which I saw him do in the Drawing Room. She put it up in her pocket. I dined with Mr Bronsal of Bedfordshire at the New Tavern in Kensington.

Friday 11. Waited upon the Bishop of London at White Hall. He said the person that was now consulted with about Ecclesiastical Preferment was the Bishop of Oxford who had the certain promise of the Archbishopric of Canterbury. That the Queen would take the disposal of Church Preferments into her own hands. I went with Mr Bronsal to Court. Sent in a message to the Queen by my Lord Grantham who said nothing. Dr. Butler very civil to me.

Saturday 12. At home.

SUNDAY 13. Dined at Mr Rivington's. Preached in the

May it please your M.

The Bishop of Man would be utterly unworthy of the great regard your Majesty has had for him if he did not after the most sincere manner rejoice with the rest of your Majesty's faithful subjects on Account of the Disposal of your son The Prince of Wales to a Princess of an Illustrious Family, that with the Protestant Interest has not had many superior patrons. May the Virtues of your Majesty's and her Royal Highness Ancestors be very long continued in your Majesty's Posterity that we may be blessed with a Succession of Princes, fearing God and following His Holy Religion, which has been and shall be the Prayer of your Majesty's etc. . . .

afternoon for Mr. Jackson, the lecturer at St. Austin's and St. Faith's.

[*September 14. 1736.* Inserted on loose leaf at a later date. 1 May 1737.]

Speaking of My Lord Macclesfield's Death Dr Pearce of St. Martin's who was with him an hour before he died gave me a different account of him. That he was a sincere Christian. That he met death with a strange composure. Died of a suppression of urine. No Pain. Called his son the afternoon before he died. Gave him excellent advice. Told him he was going to be a lord, that he should not value himself upon his title, but the advantage would give him of serving his country and doing more good. Denyes the story of his son's former marriage or that there ever was such an Italian Lady in England. That he did keep a woman, but that a friend of his got an officer to keep her afterwards so that she could have been proved to have been a woman of a very bad character. That as to Mandevil my Lord had often dumbfounded himself in defence of the Christian Religion the arguments of which no man has been better capable of managing. In short what I observe is that Dr. Pearce had a great obligation to Lord Macclesfield and perhaps Cunnibear might have been ill used so that the truth perhaps lies between both of them. Mem. I have heard say that in the Earl's Tryal it will appear that money was paid for the Living of St. Martin's.

Monday 14. I set out to pay the Master of the Rolls [223] a visit. Breakfasted with Mr Holmes a soapboiler at Southgate. A very serious pious man. Went across the Chace to Bell Bar. Found Dr. Pearce at the Master's who had been there from saturday. Dined with the Master. He is a very exact man in his family.

[223] The Master of the Rolls who has appeared so often in the Diary already was Sir Joseph Jekyl (1668–1738). An ardent Whig of whom Pope wrote:

Jekyll, or some old Whig
Who never changed his Principles or wig.

Strong supporter of Walpole. Country estate at Brookman's (Bell Bar) Herts., near North Mimms. Married Elizabeth, daughter of Lord Somers.

10 Minutes before Eight he has Family Prayers from Dr. Patrick's Devotions.[224] He gets up always at 6. Breakfast after prayers. A little before 12 he walks out in the Woods and comes in before 1 and the dinner is upon the table. Walks out in the afternoon an hour. Supps at 8 and 10 before 10 has Family Prayers and then all go to bed. He shewed me Lady Sundon's [225] letter. Who tells him that she had read his letter to the Queen and that her Majesty was pleased to say she had a very good opinion of me. That she laughed and said it was well that the Master's friend Mr. Wilson was not in Westminster Hall when he was like to have been blown up. The Master intends to write to her when he knows that she will be in waiting. That he will speak again to the Queen, Bishop of Salisbury etc. He told me that Sir Robt. Walpole was afraid to use rigorous methods against the Rioters and that he prevented a pardon being offered to the informers in the Last Proclamation, afraid it should be known who were the authors. These Lenitives may produce greater and more terrible Disturbances. Witness the late Audacious Insult last Tuesday at Edinburgh. The Mob rising and taking Capt. Porteous [226] out of prison and hanging him in contempt of the Queen's Reprieve. A Fact hardly paralleled in these later ages. And if there been example made we may expect Insults offered even to the Persons of our Princes. The Queen asked Lady Sundon how Queen Ann came by such a character of Piety etc. She answered. *Madam.*

[224] Dr Simon Patrick (1625–1707), Bishop of Ely, Old Testament commentator and controversial writer; also the writer of many devotional works among which one of the most popular was *The Devout Christian Instructed how to Pray* (1672).

[225] Mrs Clayton, afterwards Viscountess Sundon, Mistress of the Robes.

[226] John Porteous, Captain of the Edinburgh City Guard who, at the time of the execution on 14 April 1736 of Andrew Wilton, an Edinburgh merchant sentenced to death for robbing the Custom House at Pittenweem, ordered his men to fire on the Mob, the Riot Act not having been read. Porteous was brought to trial and sentenced to death but a reprieve was granted at the intercession of General Wade. A body of men, whose identity has never been proved, broke into the prison, captured Porteous and murdered him. A Bill was introduced in the Lords for the punishment of the Provost of Edinburgh, later modified in the Commons to degrading the Provost from holding any other office and levying a fine of £2000 on the City for Porteous' widow. The plot in Scott's *Heart of Midlothian* is based on the circumstances of the Porteous Riots.

The Queen Ann went constantly to prayers herself and when there behaved with the greatest Seriousness and Devotion.

Tuesday 15. We dined with Mr Sambroke at Gubbins. ¼ of a mile from the Master's. Very elegantly entertained. A Batchelor. His sister keeps house. A very understanding Lady and skilled in the Mathematicks. Fine walks in the woods 2 miles about, laid out in a very elegant Tast. A round Wood the prettiest I believe in England. He has lost 1 eye and is almost blind of another and yet very chearful. The Master earnestly invited me to stay longer with him but I took leave with him. The Master married Lord Somers sister by whom he had Bell Bar and a large fortune. Her niece married Lord Chancellor Hardwicke. He has nephews of his own. Mr Terrick is his chaplain.

Wednesday 16. Set out from Bell Bar by Heywood Hill, Hendon and Hampstead. Dined with Father Patten (His Birth Day. 67 years old). Molly and Mrs Hayward. Came home.

Things forgot at Bell Bar.

The Master told me that the late King, at the time he quarrelled with his son was once resolved to go to the Parliament House, and ordered the horses to the Coach, to desire they would withdraw the Annuity settled upon him, which would have been of fatal consequence to them both.

Thursday 17. At Home.

Friday 18. At the Society for Propagating the Gospel. Promised Dr. Moore that I would vote for his brother to be our Agent in Barbadoes for our estates there. Mr Hayward told me that Mr Wm. and Sam. Baker had a Bill drawn for £500 by Mr Oglethorpe upon the Trustees of Georgia, which they had refused to pay, so it was protested, which will blast his credit in Carolina, where they are already sufficiently exasperated. The Spaniards are sending Shipps and Troopes against the Portuguese to Buenos Aires, 'tis well if they don't fall upon and swallow up Georgia in the way. And then Mr Oglethorpe will have reason to reflect upon poor Sir Walter Raleigh's unhappy case when he was betrayed and given up to the Spaniards. Wrote to Dr. Hunter about this. Dined with Dr. Rider in Amen Corner.

Dr. Baker. W. Baker. Mr Hayward and one South of Staffordshire.

Tuesday 21. At the Society.[227] Received a letter from Dr. Hales in which he tells me that 2 Men one at Kingston and the other at Chiswick are setting up Brandy Shopps, upon pretence of having been bred Apothecaries, as a manifest evasion of the late act. But advises not to mention any Amendments of the Act yet awhile, but we should lose rather than gain.

Wednesday 23. Mr Hayward set out for Bath. Mr Smith of Aldgate came to visit me. He told me that Mr Whiston told him the Queen had said lately that Dr. Herring [228] should be a Bishop. Proposed going with him to Kensington to visit Dr. Heylin at Kensington Thursday fortnight and to call upon him in the morning at his house near the Church, London Wall. This is to get the Dr. to let the Trustees of Georgia have a sermon this winter at his church. I am to meet Mr Whiston at his house to get him to speak to the Queen in my favour in order to put her often in mind of her promise to me and my father.

Thursday 23. In town. Called upon Mrs Titchbourn. Gone to her country house in Oxfordshire for 3 or 4 dayes. Went to Sir R. Walpole's Levy, desired that he would remember. Promised that he would. Called upon the Archbishop of York. Not at home. Lady Leighton comes home in a fortnight or less. Dined at Dolly's and drank a glass of wine and saw the fine set of Plate made for the Czarina by Mr. Robt. Dingley. More £1400 worth.

Friday 24. At home.

Saturday 26. Wrote to Dr. Watts to desire a New Edition of his Strength and Weakness of Human Reason for Mr Rivington to print. An answer from him. Lady Sundon goes into waiting at Court about 3 months hence.

Wednesday 29. This is the day the Act to restrain the retailing of Spirits is to take place and the Populace having shown lately a very great disposition to be riotous and commit disorders the

[227] At this Meeting "the Rev. Mr Geo. Whitefield of Pembroke College in Oxford was recommended to the Society as a Corresponding Member" (S.P.C.K. Minutes).

[228] Thomas Herring, Bishop of Bangor 1738, Archbishop of York 1743, Canterbury 1747.

Government very wisely ordered several Regiments of Horse and Foot to approach the City and patrol in common Gardens Lincolns Inn Fields, by which precaution the Peace of the City was kept and no Riots, except some little Quarrels occasioned by those that drunk too much of the bewitching Liquor. The Gin Shoppes now sell a liquor made of Raison Wine and Currant Wines which they make very strong with Ginger and other hot spices. But the poor wretches say it makes them sick and not drunk which their beloved Gin did. I hope the next Generation will drink Ale as their Forefathers did, who worked as hard and lived longer.

Thursday 30. Lady Abney [229] and Dr. Watts made me a visit. The Dr. has promised under certain conditions to let Mr Rivington print a 2nd. Edition of The Strength and Weakness of Human Reason.

OCTOBER 1736

Friday 1. Received a letter from Mr Douglass living with Lord Jno. Murray which I answer tomorrow. I am told that Jonny Murray is either to be Governor or Comptroller of the Island.

Saturday 2. At home. A letter from Cousin Goulborn about Wakefield Estate at Leigh which I answered and wrote again to Wm. Peters upon the same account.

SUNDAY 3. At Newington Church. Mr Thoresby. Mr Carter in the afternoon. When I was last with the Master of the Rolls he told me that he thought *Popery ought to be tolerated in England.* I objected in the common manner, that they ought not, not upon their religious differences, but because they owned a foreign juris-diction and could give no proper security to a Government for their Duty and Allegiance, but they have and probably will always be dispensed with. He replyed that this is not the case. The Papists in France own no such power in the Pope. The Papists in Holland are tolerated by the State and have great Privileges and yet it has never been known that they made any ill use of it. Nay so far from that they have intrusted them with the Command of

[229] Mary, wife of Sir Thomas Abney, Lord Mayor of London, who inherited the Manor of Stoke Newington on the death of her brother John Grimston.

Troopes and they have proved the Best Friends. For all this I cannot agree with the Master. Most of our English Papists are under the Management of the Jesuites, who are grasping at powers not only here, but wherever they are allowed to have any ground.

Monday 4. Dr. Watts giving me the liberty to print a 2nd. Edition of The Strength and Weakness of Human Reason I gave it to Mr. Rivington.

Wednesday 6. Visited the Bishop of London. Asked him how it stood in relation to a Prebend of Worcester. He told me he believed Mr Stillingfleet [230] would have it.

Friday 8. I went on horseback to Bell Bar. The Master received me very kindly, gave me a letter to Lady Sundon and one to Lord Chancellor Hardwicke at Carshalton intreating very earnestly their favour for me in the vacant prebend at Worcester. I went with a message for him to the Rolls. Came home in the evening.

Saturday 9. Went this morning to Lady Sundon's. Not at home. Dined with Father Patten. Sent a porter with a letter to Lord Hardwick. In answer he excusing himself from intermedling at this time because he has an application for some Church Preferment for a relation of his own. Went between 6 and 7 (the windiest night and the greatest storm of rain I ever was out in) to Lady Sundon's in Cleveland Row, St. James's. Her Ladyship told me very frankly that Lord Sundon had a friend for Worcester and Bishop Hare, Mr Herbert. Mr Bathurst pressed hard for Mr Stillingfleet who in all probability would have it. Told me that the Queen was well affected to me at a proper Juncture, but when will this be if so many great men interfere in everything that dropps? Came back to Mr Rivington's about 9. The wind then at its worst and blew a rank storm. Wrote to the Master word of the unsuccessfulness of my pursuit and sent him a letter from Lady Sundon to the purpose above. Wrote to my

[230] Edward Stillingfleet, Merton College, prebendary of Worcester from 1737 until his death in 1777. Son of James Stillingfleet, rector of Hartlebury and Dean of Worcester. Grandson of Bishop Stillingfleet of Worcester and first cousin to Benjamin Stillingfleet who was renowned for wearing blue stockings in the company of learned ladies, this being the origin of the well-known phrase "Benjamin Stillingfleet" by R. W. Ketton-Cremer in *Norfolk Portraits* (1944).

Lord Chief Justice hoping that his Lordship would be so good as to mention the Master's Request to the Queen but I am afraid he will not. Lay at Mr Rivington's. Lady Sundon of the opinion that Spirits should not have been suppressed all at once, but by degrees. I disagreed exceedingly with her Ladyship. I am afraid there will be alterations in the Act. Lay at Rivington's.

SUNDAY 10. At home. Came home in the morning from London.

Monday 11. Mr Rivington and I hired a Chariot and went together to Kensington. Mrs Titchbourn told me very kindly that she would acquaint her Majesty with my request to succeed Mr Downes [231] in the Prebend of Worcester. Sir Robert Walpole told me that it was hardly possible for me to succeed. Mr Stillingfleet and Lord Godolphin's friend had made so great an interest. Called upon the Bishop of Durham who is lately returned from his diocese. Prevailed with him to go to Kensington with me tomorrow sennight about 12 to speak to the Queen in my favour. Told me that he believed the Bishop of London would come in again this winter which I much question. Came home at night.

Tuesday 12. At the Society. Wrote to the Master of the Rolls acquainting him with his friends refusal to speak to the Queen in this instance. Put into the papers a paragraph that whereas there used to be Court Meetings twice a week for the Punishment of Vices and Consequences of drinking Gin, there had not been one since the Act took place and there is a visible alteration in the behaviour of the lower kind of people as I am informed from the Constables and Watch Men. Dined with Mr Rivington. Mr Broughton. Came home.

Wednesday 13. At home. Mr Seers came to desire I would preach for him here for the Benefit of the Trustees of Georgia, which I excused myself from, being engaged so much in affairs of my own.

Thursday 14. At home. Visited Mr Reyner. A letter from the Master of the Rolls in which he tells me he had wrote a letter in

[231] John Downes of Painswick, Glos. Pembroke College, Oxon. Vicar of Painswick 1701, rector of Segebarrow, Worcs., and canon of Worcester 1727-36.

my favour to the Queen and sent it this very day by his Secretary to Kensington.

Friday 15. At the Society for Propagating the Gospel. Dined at the George in Ironmonger Lane by myself. Mr Rivington told me that he was the night before with Dr. Webster who assured him that the Bishop of London was lately closetted with Sir Robt. Walpole an hour, in order to propose his coming in again. This I doubt. Came home.

Saturday 16. Mr Richardson sent me word that Dr. Blechyndon,[232] Head of Worcester was dead. That he was one of the Prebends of Gloucester in the King's Gift. A mistake it is in the Lord Chancellor's. At Home.

SUNDAY 17. A letter from Mr Dewe that Mr Knipe, Canon of Christ Church, was dead. Wrote to Lady Sundon about it and to Mr Phillips to speak to Sir Robt. W. At home.

Monday 18. At home. Wrote to Mr Dewe.

Tuesday 19. Went this morning to the Bishop of Durham who carried me to Court and spoke to the Queen in my behalf, who told him that it was impossible for me to come in at Worcester. He then spoke for the next that fell and mentioned Christ Church which she was pleased to lend a favourable ear to as I had been bred up there etc. The Queen said that I had a good Remembrancer in the Master of the Rolls. The Bishop replied that her Majesty might be so good as to make me my own remembrancer by having me be one of the King's Chaplains, which she readily agreed to and ordered him to tell the Duke of Grafton so, which he promised to do and as he can now serve him in his son's election at Coventry he will make the serving me a point with his grace. Dr. Guerdes dined at the Bishop's and walked with me to Bishopsgate Street. Came home. Mr Hayward came home this morning from Bath with a little touch of the Gout. Saw Majr. Stevenson at Brook Street Coffee House who had been in the Isle of Man. The Bishop told the Queen that this was the first

---

[232] Richard Blechyndon, D.C.L., last Principal of Gloucester Hall (1712) and first Master of Worcester College, Oxon. (1714), canon of Gloucester from 1711 and of Rochester from 1710.

Ecclesiastical Preferment he had asked for for any clergyman since he was a Bishop and hoped it would be the more readily complyed with.

N.B. The Bishop of Oxford is made a Privy Councillor. We may be sure that he will be the Prime Minister in Ecclesiastical affairs and not till then 'tis rather thought that the Bishop of London will come in again as the most proper man for the office as any upon the Bench.

Thursday 21. At home. Visited Mr Carter the schoolmaster. This afternoon I received a letter from Dr. Rye telling me that the Bishop of Oxford would be at his old home in Old Palace Yard next Tuesday evening. Mem. That I pay my duty to him on wednesday.

Friday 22. Princess of Orange's birthday. Went to town. Dined with Mr Rivington. Returned home.

Saturday 23. Received a letter from Mr Quincey upon an extraordinary occasion. Answered it.

SUNDAY 24. Preached at St. Paules. Dined with my Lord Mayor. Sir John Williams. Had a long conversation with him. He says that by his management and the character he is in with the people has kept things pretty quiet, but that it will not be so long. That people are generally uneasy and dissatisfied with the administration of affairs, especially with the King's long stay in his forreign dominions at a time when both Scotland and England are ripe for a Rebellion. That the Papists increase prodigiously. That there are 45,000 men of that persuasion ready and able to take arms and always disposed to join with those that would do mischief. That he had told Sir R. W. this and intends to speak very plainly to his Majesty concerning the present evil dispositions and the occasion of them. Came home at night. 40s. in silver in the private drawer of the right hand and 10 Guineas besides and 5s. and a Guinea Piece.

Monday 25. Waited upon the Bishop of London. Knipe, Canon of Christ Church, certainly dead. Fanshawe [233] puts

---

[233] John Fanshawe, D.D., 1696–1763. Ch. Ch., rector of Cotenbach, Worcs., 1727–63, Staverton, Northants, 1739–41, Regius Professor of Greek 1735–47, Regius Professor of Divinity 1741–63, canon of Ch. Ch. 1741.

in for it by the Duke of Newcastle's interest. Sure this man is voratous. The Bishop thinks they will make a Canon of Windsor or Westminster that are Oxford men change for a Canonry of Christ Church. Give one of them to Dr. Hutton. The Master of the Rolls came this day from Bell Bar to his house in Chancery Lane. I waited upon him and dined with him. He asked me who had been for me with the Queen. I told him the Bishop of Durham which he was very glad of and said he would thank him when he saw him. That he would speak to the Queen himself very soon about the Canonry for me. That My Lord Hardwicke had a clergyman who married his sister that he is ingaged for some preferment for him from the Court. Spoke of the great and general uneasiness that the people are under.

Tuesday 26. Went with Mr Rivington to Court. Called upon the Bishop of Durham. Not at home. Dined with Dr. Briggs and Mr. Medlicott, Chaplains. Came home in the latter's coach. In the evening at the Coffee House with Mr Rivington next door. Lay at Rivington's.

Wednesday 27. Went to the Master of the Rolls. Promised to speak to the Queen a saturday for the Canonry of Christ Church. Went to Westminster Hall. The Recorder of Oxford, Sergt. Skinner asked me whether there was any hopes of making a Push for a Whig to succeed member of the University in the room of Dr. Clark, I told him I should be very forward to push such a thing. Mr Trevor proposed by the Whigges. Went to the Bishop of Oxford. Not at home. Went to the Bishop of Durham. Decided I would not mention the hand he has had in my affairs to any body. Dined with Mr Jones of New Bond Street at the Crown Tavern in New Palace Yard. Went afterwards to the Bishop of Oxford. Gone out but left word for me with his secretary that he knew my business and would certainly take care of it. Spent the evening with Mr Rivington at the Queen's Head Tavern. Lay at Mr. Rivington's.

Thursday 28. Came home to dinner. Wrote to Lady Betty Hastings.

Friday 29. At home. Gave half a Guinea to the collection for Georgia.

Saturday 30. The King's Birth Day. Mr. Phillips spoke to the Bishop of Oxford in my favour who assured him that he would be very ready to serve me. Asked him whether the Bishop of London had ever really done anything to purpose for me to the Queen. This looks as if he thought him not sincerely my friend. Went to Court. A great many people but no new clothes. The Master of the Rolls spoke to the Queen for me. Her Majesty said that there were 1000 for Christ Church canonry but that there would soon be a Living vacant in the City and that I should certainly have it. We shall soon see whether this is serious or no. The Master advised me not to go so often to Court. I suppose that the Butler had told him that the Chaplains perhaps were jealous of my coming so much there. Alass! Their Leavings would satisfy me. Dined at the Crown Tavern over against the Rolls, Chancery Lane, by myself. Went afterwards to the Master of the Rolls who told me as above and that he should go in 3 or 4 days to Kensington and talk further to the Queen about my affair. They talk of a coolness between the Queen and the Prince. The people will be ready enough to take advantage of any such unhappy misunderstanding. And indeed the Nation itself in general are too ripe for a change without knowing what scheme would make them easier and more free. Angry with the Prime Minister and yet no other better offered to succeed him. In short, as the Bishop of Durham told me the other day, we wanted a war to take off a No. of Idle Hands that wanted imployment at home and therefore grumbled. That in times of peace we should imitate the Romans who sent Colonies to the most distant parts of their Dominions. How much better would this be than purchasing Negroes which Trade carried on with so many temptations to those poor people to fight one another in order to sell those vanquished as slaves to us that in all probability *draws down God's severe Judgments upon our American Islands Etc.*

SUNDAY 31. At Newington Church.

NOVEMBER 1736

Monday 1. At home. Wrote to my father and sent him the accounts between us since the beginning. Ballance due to him 25. 9. 6. Wrote to Dr. Hales excusing myself from medling any further in supporting the Gin Bill unless I am sure of being reimbursed, besides the Hazard I am of my life or being abused by a Mob.

N.B. Last Saturday at Court the Bishop of Oxford himself spoke very kindly to me. Told me when ever anything droppt to come to him and he would certainly serve me with the Queen. That there are many schemes in relation to Christ Church and that he was afraid it would be too difficult for me to come in. But that if the Queen mentioned me to him among the rest he would be sure to do me Justice. Mem. That I wait upon his Lordship some morning to see whether the Queen has mentioned me since the Master of the Rolls spoke to her.

Tuesday 2. At home. Fine frosty morning.

Thursday 4. At the Society's Committee for Propagating Christian Knowledge in Scotland which meets 4 times a year at the Scots Hall in Black Fryars to receive Benefactions or to consult about furthering the designs of the Society which are principally erecting and maintaining English Protestant Schooles in the Highlands of Scotland, sending 3 Missionaries to the Borders of our Colonies in the West Indes, by an estate left them by the late Dr. Williams. I was in the Chair for the first time. Nothing remarkable done. I proposed the Society's making an abstract from all their printed Accounts and Books of the Rise and Progress and Designs in order to raise larger subscriptions and to show the credulous world that there are such things as *Truly Disinterested Charitable Corporations.* Dined at Father Patten's. Came home.

Friday 5. Went to town. Waited upon the Bishop of Oxford at his house. He told me that there was no such thing as succeeding to the canonry at Christ Church. That there was no promotion going forwards at present. When there was if I would learn what was proper to apply for he would very readily do it. And that the Master of the Rolls might acquaint the Queen that I was well known to his Lordship. Came to the Rolls. Sat half an hour with Mr Terrick,[234] preacher there, who is to be the Speaker's Chaplain next sessions but one. He is a pretty ingenious young man, was scholar to my old Master Mr Clark at Kirkleatham. Dined with the Master. After dinner he was pleased to tell me that he had last wednesday spoke to the Queen in my favour who promised that I should have the next good living in the King's gift that I should ask for. My Lord Chief Justice was pleased to tell her Majesty that I deserved her notice and that if she was pleased to prefer me it would be agreeable to their Majesty's friends. Dr. Bentley is going to publish a New Edition of his Philoburtheia Lippensis with Additions which the Master said was the best work he had ever performed. Mem. That I desire Mr Terrick to lend me his Ecton's *Valor*[235] with the Patrons of the several Livings in England. The Bishop of Derry, Dr. Rundle, not a very good preacher said the Master. Wrote to Dr. Hales.

Saturday 6. Received a letter from Lady Hastings with one enclosed to the Bishop of Oxford in my favour which I sent by the Penny Post. Wrote to my father about Dr. Hales paying me the £25 put into his hands for Charitable Purposes in the Isle of Man etc. Wrote to Dr. Pelling about Mr Kippax's brother's reasons why the Indentures for him were not yet executed. They

---

[234] Richard Terrick, Bishop of Peterborough 1757, London 1764–1777. The Diarist had been for a short time at the Grammar School at Kirk Leatham near Redcar.

[235] *Thesaurus Rerum Ecclesiasticarum*, published by John Ecton, receiver general of First Fruits for Queen Anne's Bounty, under the title of *Liber Valorum* in 1711; being a reproduction of the MS. returns of Henry VIII's Commissioners in 1535 concerning the names, condition and values of all churches and benefices in the country. In 1742, after Ecton's death, there was a new edition giving "the names of the saints to whom the churches and chapels are dedicated . . . for which the editors are obliged to the learned and communicative antiquary Browne Willis Esq". In 1786 John Bacon, who like Ecton was a receiver for First Fruits for Q.A.B., reissued the book under the title of *Liber Regis* under his own name, suppressing those of Ecton and Willis.

say Thistlewaite is to resign his Prebend of Westminster in favour of Dr. Hutton and he is to be Canon of Christ Church, or a change made with a Canon of Windsor.

SUNDAY 7. At home.

Monday 8. Hearing that Mr Jackson, Lecturer of St. Faith's and St. Austin's was dangerously ill several of my friends interested themselves for me to succeed him. Staid in town. Spent the evening with Mr Rivington at the Queen's Head Tavern Pater Noster Row. Lay at Mr Rivington's.

Tuesday 9. Waited upon Mr Salvin. He promised me his interest and vote for the Lecture if vacant. Lay at Rivington's. Dined with Mr Dewe.

Wednesday 10. My wife and I dined at Mr Rivington's. I went to the Speaker's. Promised me to use his interest further with Salvin. Went in a chair to Mr Vernon's and Mr Hicks. Supped with Mr Rivington. Lay there.

Thursday 11. Returned home. The Bishop of London wrote to Dr. Cobden for his interest in the Lecture.

Friday 12. Mr Dewe and his nephew Baker dined with me.

Saturday 13. At home.

SUNDAY 14. At Newington Church.

Monday 15. This evening hearing that Mr Jackson was relapsed I walked to town. Saw several of my friends. Spent the evening with Mr Rivington at the Queen's Head Tavern Pater Noster Row. Mr Jackson better. A letter from Dr. Cobden. Excuses himself because he had a prior Ingagement for his curate Mr Kay, Lay at Rivington's.

Tuesday 16. Dined at Father Patten's. Visited Mrs Titchbourn and the Bishop of Salisbury. The former told me that she had heard a great many good things said of me to the Queen and did not doubt that I would be very soon taken care of. Sat with Mr Terrick and the Rolls. Sunday fortnight I am to preach at the Rolls Chappell. At home at night.

Wednesday 17. At home. Mr Jackson I hear is relapsed and in a very dangerous way.

Thursday 18. Went to town. Dined with Mr Rogers. The

King's absence has given unusual Distrust to his subjects. Came home.

Friday 19. The Princess' Birth Day. 18 years old. I went to Court which was very splendid which have made some amends to the Tradesmen for the loss that they sustained by the Baulk in the King's Birth Day not being kept. It is now doubted whether the Princess of Orange be with child or no. This day I saw in the Newes Papers that Mr G. Sale [236] was dead. A man of universal learning and great probity and yet neglected by the world, kept low, and I am afraid by various disappointments his life was in some degrees if not shortened made very disagreeable. Visited Mrs Humphreys, a poor woman widow to a Dissenting Minister, at Plaisterer's Hall near Wood Street. Gave her 5s. If I had more I hope my heart would be inlarged towards objects of Misery. If not *Riches, Preferments* etc. would be rather a curse than a blessing.

Saturday 20. This day I read in the Newes that the Princess of Orange is brought to bed of a Prince but this wants confirmation. I wish it may be so but I am afraid she is not breeding.

SUNDAY 21. I went to London. To Sergt. Skinner's, Recorder of Oxford. Preached at Sergeant's Inn in Chancery Lane for Sergt. Orling, Deputy Recorder of the City. There were there Judge Denton, Judge Probyn. Judge Page and Sergeants. The Sergeants take it in turn to provide Preachers in Term Time and to give 2 Guineas and a Handsome in the Hall. Sergt. Skinner told me that there was a meeting of the Whig Heads at the Dean of Christ Church's in order to put up a Member in the room of Dr. Clark, but could not come to any positive resolution and he thinks as I do that Bromley will certainly carry it. There has been no call taken since the breaking up of the Constitution Club of keeping up any spirit in Oxford. The Whigs have not been taken notice of as they deserved and new converts put over their heads

[236] George Sale, 1697–1736, orientalist. Chiefly memorable for his translation of the Koran, 1734. Previous to this date he regularly attended meetings of the S.P.C.K. but the Society did not approve of this work and suspected his orthodoxy.

which have chagrined the others. However it may be thought that they will scheme the end of the Ministry they will certainly fail him in the day of Trial and recur as fast to their former principles as ever they left them. Dr. Thomas is come over from Hamburgh, not very well satisfied with Foster Lane which would have pleased me. He intends, they say, to stay here this winter and then return to his chaplainship till he can get something better from the Government which he may wait long enough for if I am not mistaken. Came home in the evening.

Wednesday 24. I went to town. Dined with Mr Rivington. They have a mind to make a Party Business of the Lectureship by which means I shall lose it and perhaps it will be better to give it up. I visited Mr Sedgwick Common Counsel Man in Watling Street, St. Faith's Parish, who has promised me his interest for the Lecture if Mr Jackson should die, who is dangerously ill. I received a letter from my dear father whom I thank God for and may His Providence long continue him a blessing and a comfort to that Poor Place. I answered it this evening and sent him an Oxford Almanack.

Thursday 25. Went to Town. Came home.

Monday 29. In town. Mr Jackson dyed this night of a mortification in his Bladder. Lay at home.

DECEMBER 1736

Tuesday 30 [Nov.] Wednesday 1, Thursday 2, Friday 3, Saturday 4. In town. Lay at Mr Rivington's. Canvassing for the Lecture.

SUNDAY 5. Preached at Mr Warneford's Church in Bread Street in the morning and at Foster Lane in the afternoon.

Monday 6, Tuesday 7, Wednesday 8, Thursday 9, Friday 10, Saturday 11. Canvassing in town most of these days.

SUNDAY 12. Preached in the afternoon at St. Austin's for the Lectureship.

Monday 13. I waited upon most of the parishioners in both parishes but without any probability of success. However my friends all force me to stand it out.

Tuesday 14. The Election came on. Mr Tipping was thrown out by hands and Mr Kay and I stood the Ballot. He had 142 and I had 49 so that is an end of a very troublesome affair and I hope I shall never be tempted to ingage again in popular elections in the city where none but a Jacobite can have the least view of succeeding. Dr. Cobden was very rude to me. Came to me in a violent manner and would have pulled me from the place where the Churchwarden desired me to sit; told me that I had no business to supervise the Election, nor sit down etc. Strange usage and very unbecoming either a Clergyman or a Gentleman. He had much better take care of the soules of the people committed to his care and there is most shameful neglect of this kind all over town. *Not less than 22 Non Resident City Rectors at this time.* Lay at Mr Rivington's.

Wednesday 15. Thanked my friends that voted for me and told them of Dr. Cobden's usage of me which they were very much surprised at.

SUNDAY 19. Preached at the Rolls. Dined with the Master. He told me he had lately been with the Duke of Newcastle who assured that a Minute should be taken of the Queen's Promise to me. That there was now a little Living vacant in Essex which he did not know but Mr Hussey would accept of and then there was an open passage for me, by which I find that gentleman is first to be thought of. His honour promised that he would put the Queen in mind of me again a Tuesday. My Lord Chief Justice his lady and 3 sons. Dined there and one Mr Gibbon. The Master said that the Bishop of London did not intend to trouble the House of Lords much this next session unless affairs of moment brought him there. Preached in the afternoon at Mercer's Chappell upon the nomination of Mr Ruck one of the Wardens. 20s. Came home late.

Friday 24. Dr. Watts made me a visit. Approved very much of Rivington's edition of his book entitled *The Strength and Weakness of Human Reason.* He told me that most of the arguments for reason were taken from Jackson's Pleas tho' he did not mention it, not being willing to bring controversy upon himself. That he had made the Bishop of London a present of his book [237] upon the *Love of God* which his Lordship thanked him very heartily for and told him that ever since he had it it had been part of his Sunday Meditations which the Dr. took as a very great compliment.

Saturday 25. Went to town. Dined at Mr Rivington's. Preached Xmas Day at Bow a Charity Sermon for 80 Boys and Girls of Corwainers and Bread Street Wards by the desire of Mr Waldo. Mr Webb Treasurer.

SUNDAY 26. At home. Not well.

Tuesday 28. Waited upon the Duke of Atholl in Dover Street. He is removing to Savil Row, Burlington Gardens.

Thursday 30. At home. Dr. Thomas, Rector of Foster Lane, Mr Rivington and his wife and Mrs Humphreys dined with me.

JANUARY 1736-7

Saturday 1. New Years's Day. Presented the Bishops of Salisbury, London, and Durham. Archdeacon Hayter, Mrs Titchbourn, with Dr. Watts book of the Strength and Weakness of Human Reason. At Court. Came home in the evening. The Bishop of Durham told me that the Duke of Grafton sent him

[237] Copy of Dr Watts letter to the Bishop of London sent with copy of his book.

'Twas your goodness my Lord and your professed admiration for this little book which gave me the first access to the honour of your Lordship's acquaintance. 'Tis by the earnest desire of the Rev. Mr T. Wilson and I presume with your Lordship's approbation that I have now reissued it a second time unto the world. The additions and Improvements are scattered abroad tho' the papers and perhaps may amount to 1 sheet in the whole. I feared it would be a piece of rudeness if not injustice to withold the light of it from your Lordship whose recommendation hath so much encouraged the sale of the first impression.

Since the season of the year leads me to it I flatter myself your Lordship will accept it as a little New Year's Gift and since your Lordship hath conceived so good an opinion of it I hope it may have some further tendency to discourage and suppress the Spirit of Infidelity which is gone thro' the Nation. May our Good God abolish it in his time. With all sincere wishes of success to your vigilance and pious care for your care of the Church of Christ I send your Lordship the Compliments of the Season and am My Lord your humble and obedient servant

I. WATTS.

word that if he had any interest I should be chaplain to the King soon and that he believed there would be 2 or 3 vacancies very soon and I should have one and he believed he had enough interest for it.

Tuesday 4. A great fire in the Temple. At the kitchen. Burnt 33 Chambers.

Wednesday 5. Went to town. At Court. The Duke of Newcastle could not present my father's letter to the Queen. I heard the Queen say that the King was in great danger in the last storm and that Sir Ch. Wager had shewed the greatest skill and Courage and affection for his Majesty's Person and Government. Waited upon the Bishop of Salisbury. Oxford told me again that he would be ready to give the Queen and Ministry a good character of me etc. Lay at Mr Rivington's.

Monday 6. One of the Brothers of St. Catherines vacant. In the gift of the Queen. I do not think it worth my asking for, but £20 pr. ann. and 4 Months hard duty. This day the Duke of Atholl presented my father's letter to the Queen who gratiously received it and assured his Grace that upon the next vacancy I should be thought of. I heard the Queen say to day in the Drawing Room that she was very averse to the Quakers' Bill and told the Speaker she was very glad it had not passed the House of Lords. That she hoped to have things continue in the old way and would have no alterations if she could help it. Spoke very much of the King's absence and could take no pleasure 'till he arrived. Spent the evening and lay at Mr Rivington's.

Friday 7. Wrote to the Master of the Rolls about writing to the Queen. Was with Mr Stone at Cock Pitt. He assured me that my name stood in the Duke's bookes for the next living. That Mr Hussey was now provided for and that the Duke of Newcastle was sincerely my friend. Told me that Mr Trevor would make a very pretty show for Member in Oxford. I was this morning with the Bishop of Durham. He told me inter alia that the Bishop of Oxford would have very little interest at Court and that the Ministry were resolved that no Bishop should have much hereafter. Came home at night.

SUNDAY 9. Preached at Newington Church for Mr Dacier. Prov. 12.6. in the afternoon.

Monday 10. Spent the day and dined at the Fountain Tavern near the Temple with Mr Moreton and Mr Gibson of the Temple, a lawyer. Talked about the election of Member of Parliament for Oxford. A letter from Mr Skinner which I answered the same day.

Thursday 13. This afternoon with Dr. Bamber. Got a violent cold by coming home late at night.

Friday 14. Very ill of my cold. Running at the nose, sore eyes.

Saturday 15. Rather worse. Pains in my stomack and back.

SUNDAY 16. Staid at home.

Monday 17. This day Dr. Wake, Archbishop of Canterbury, died in his Palace of Lambeth, aged 79 years and 4 months and odd dayes. He was a celebrated preacher in King William's time and one of the chief writers in the Popish Controversy. Wrote an excellent book about the Rights of Convocation in answer to Dr. Atterbury which is a Treasure of that sort of learning as the Master of the Rolls tells me. He kept a large correspondence with the forreign Protestant Divines. For the last six years of his life he declined very much, left the management of his affairs to Dr. Lynch his son in law, who by heaping up to himself a multitude of preferments brought down odium in general upon the clergy and may be the occasion of drawing down some severe act of Parliament upon them. Indeed the many pluralities of late and Non Residence of the higher clergy and the ill usage of some of them to their curates, gives a handle to some that wish well to the clergy to make some regulation. But whether in the heat of such an affair the enemies to all religion may not take advantage to mulch the clergy too much I can't say but I am afraid.

Tuesday 18. Dined at home. Father Patten.

Wednesday 19. Went to town. Dined with Mr Skinner in Chancery Lane. He says I ought by all means to go down to vote at Oxford in the next election.

Thursday 20. Very ill of a cold. See the account that should be placed here from Thursday 13 to Sunday 16.

Friday 21, Saturday 22, SUNDAY 23   Ill of a cold.

Monday 24.   This day the Archbishop of Canterbury died. See above 18th.[238]

Tuesday 25.   Dined at home. Father Patten.

Wednesday 26.   Went to town. Saw the Bishop of Oxford. He told me that what was not done might not be but that he believed he should be Archbishop of Canterbury. He is the only Bishop that has not been translated these 21 years. He filled the Divinity Chair with great sufficiency for many years. He wrote well against Tindal. Saw Mr Oglethorpe. He told me a great deal of the Imprudence of Mr Von Rock and of the great Imprudence of Mr Quincey. That he ought not to be suffered to come to our Society after having been charged with so many false steps. That the Saltsburghers were very honest sort of people but weak and irresolute. At Court. Dined with Mrs Titchbourn, one of the Women of the Bedchamber to the Queen. There were Lord Berekeley [239] (just come of age weak and I am afraid not very well inclined to virtue), Col. Town, a sweet tempered man, her brother Capt. Molesworth and her 2 daughters. Very civilly entertained. Came to St. Poules Church Yard. Supped and spent the evening at the Castle Tavern with Mr Rivington.

Thursday 27.   Went very early in the morning to Mr Oglethorpe's. From thence to the Bishop of Durham, who told me that he had been twice at the Duke of Grafton's about my being chaplain to the King. That he wrote him a pretty pointed letter which the Duke answered by saying that there were 3 vacant and that I should have one of them if he had any interest. Complained that the Bishop was too short with him. His Lordship thinks that if I have patience I may expect to have one of the three tho' I very much question it. Waited upon Mr Erasmus Phillips who received me very kindly. Dined at Mr Rivington's. Came home in the evening.

[238] 24 January 1736/7 was the correct date (Sykes, *Archbishop Wake*, Vol. II, p. 256). The confusion with 17 January is due no doubt to the diarist's making up his journal some days after the event had taken place.

[239] Augustus, only son of James 3rd Earl of Berkeley. Succeeded his father as 4th Earl in 1736.

Friday 28. Waited upon Mr Stone at the Duke of Newcastle's in Lincoln's Inn Fields at 11. Told him of another person that might be got to vote for Mr Trevor. Desired him to speak to the Duke that I might have the Bishop of Oxford's commendam of Newington near Oxford. Went to the Master who wrote a very kind letter to the Duke upon that head which I enclosed in one to Mr Stone. I wrote also to Mrs Titchbourn upon the same account. I question whether it be not disposed of when droppt from the Bishop of Oxford. Dined at the Devil Tavern by myself, Temple Barr. Spent the evening at Rivington's with his wife. Lay there. This day I waited upon the Bishop of Salisbury who told me that he hoped to see the Queen this evening and would mention Newington to her Majesty. I trust it will not be too late.

Saturday 29. At home.

Monday 31. At London.

FEBRUARY 1736-7

Tuesday 1. At home.

Thursday 3. Set out for Oxford. Lay at Stoken Church Hill.

Friday 4. Came to Oxford. Found the University in a good deal of heat upon account of the approaching election in which Mr Trevor puts up upon the Court interest against Mr Bromley a Tory. By which I find the latter will carry it by a great majority.

Saturday 5. Waited upon the Dean. Dr. Cockman. Sat an hour with Dr. Smith Provost of Queens. He seemed to think that this opposition would do a great deal of mischief to the University. That the Court did not heartily espouse it. That the Bishop of Oxford was cool. That they had him engaged at Queens a long time by the Commands of Mr Mitchell a gentleman who has promised to leave them a great sum of money. That he had taken care to make all things easy with the Queen which I question.

SUNDAY 6. Dined with the Dean, his lady, a good sort of woman. Received very civilly by them both and invited to come down to Oxford with my wife and be at their house. This will be too great a freedom.

Monday 7. Dined with Mr Moreton at the High Table at Corpus Christi.

Tuesday 8. Visited Dr. Cockman at University. Thinks the opposition very bad.

Wednesday 9. The Election came on. Mr Bromley carried it by 315 to 126. Great Triumphs on the occasion.

Thursday 10. Dined with Dr. Pardo, Principal of Jesus Coll.

Friday 11. Set out for Newington with Mr Dewe. Lay at Stoken Church.

Saturday 12. Came home. God be thanked very safe.

SUNDAY 13. At Newington Church.

Monday 14. At home.

Tuesday 15. Went to town. Dr. Potter, Lord Bishop of Oxford was nominated to the See of Canterbury. Congé delire went down accordingly.

Wednesday 16. The King was much better. There is talk of moving in the House of Commons for an Appenage to the Prince out of the Civil List of 100,000 pr. ann. and the King should be addressed to do it. This seems to be an affront to the King and distress to the Ministry. Yesterday morning died of an Inflamation in his lungs The Lord Talbot Baron of Honsol, Lord Chancellor of England. He was eldest son of the late Lord Bishop of Durham. Made Chancellor Nov. 29. 1733. Married Cecil, daughter and heir of Ch. Matthews of Glamorganshire Esq. by whom he had 3 sons now living, William, John, George. As soon as his Lordship's death was known there approached an uncommon concern amongst all Ranks and Orders of men. No man served his friends more readily and none lived more esteemed and died more lamented. He had an uncommon share of eloquence and the clearest and most discerning head for business and if he did not find Justice in any cause almost at the first hearing it remained so to all that were concerned in it. Few of his decrees were reversed and the late Lord Chancellor being very dilatory and having a confused head in the latter part of his time a much greater load came upon Lord Talbot's share and he went thro' more than any man of his time. The lawyers often complaining that he would kill them. He grew (as they say) somewhat averse to the Ministry in the latter part of his life and the Ministry had some hopes that he would have resigned his post but this I am not assured of from good hands. I know he would not proceed with Mr Willis being made Lord Chief Justice of the Common Pleas. He was a friend to the Privileges of the Clergy and many think they have had a loss of him, not remembering how earnest he was for the promotion of Dr. Rundle and how much he promoted the Interest of Arianism etc. His Lordship is to be succeeded by my Lord Hardwicke which I hope may be of some advantage to me by the recommendation of the Master of the Rolls.

Thursday 17. On Tuesday My Lord Egmont's son was married to the 2nd. sister of the Earl of Salisbury.

Friday 18. There was a proposal made by Mr Littleton and recommended by Mr Pulteney and others that the Prince should have 100,000 out of the Civil List and a Jointure for the Princess and that his Majesty should be addressed accordingly. It was opposed by Sir Robt. as no way belonging to the House to meddle in—being unprecedented.

SUNDAY 20. At Newington.

Monday 21. At home. The Prince's affairs debated in the House of Lords. Carried in the negative 144 to 43.

Friday 25. I waited upon the Archbishop. He told me that he believed Dr. Lisle [240] would be Bishop of Oxford. That he had given up Northall which was in the Lord Chancellor's gift but that he had spoke to the Master of the Rolls to speak to his Lordship for it which he promised to do.

SUNDAY 27. I waited upon the Master of the Rolls.

MARCH 1736-7

Tuesday 1. The Queen's Birth Day. I was at Court. A most splendid one. The King seemed very well recovered and the Prince was there and seemed pleased so that it is to be hoped differences which might otherwise have ended ill are now made up.

[240] Samuel Lisle, Bishop of St Asaph 1744, Norwich 1748-9.

[*Wednesday*] *2*, [*Thursday*] *3*, [*Friday*] *4*. At home. Not very well.

SUNDAY 6. Dined with the Master of the Rolls. He told me he had spoke to the Lord Chancellor about North Hall. That his Lordship promised it to Dr. Lavington, Residentary of St. Paules, but that he would give up his late living in Basinghall Street and would I undertake it. That the Dean and Chapter of St. Paules should present whoever the Lord Chancellor should appoint and that his Lordship desires I should have it.

Monday 7. The Archbishop told me the same and that he looked upon it to be an unreasonable request.

Wednesday 9. I now hear that Dr. Lisle since he is not able to keep both in commendam has declined the Bishopreck so that all my views are at an end.

Tuesday 15. At the Society in Bartlett's Buildings. Yesterday the Duke of Atholl got his case in the House of Lords and is to take his seat as Baron Strange.

Wednesday 16. I went to compliment his Grace upon his late successs.

Monday 21. A proposal made by Sir John Bernard in preference of paying the debts of the nation to reduce National Interest to 3 per cent. This scheme will fall hard upon those who have all their moneys in the Funds, upon those Orphans whose Trustees can neither be paid the Capital or sell out.

Tuesday 22. It was brought into the House of Commons to be further considered a friday.

Wednesday 23. I spoke upon this head to the Master of the Rolls who seems to be entirely for it in order to take off the great Load of Taxes and pay off our debts but I am afraid the Ministry will never consent to this at present at least.

Thursday 24. It was debated and 2 or 3 resolutions carried almost unanimously in the House. Viz. That the King should borrow money at 3 per cent in order to pay off the annuitants etc.

Friday 25. The whole city was in the greatest alarm upon it. Stocks fell 7 per cent and a clamour almost as great as at the Excise time.

Saturday 26. It continues worse than ever.

SUNDAY 27. At Newington.

Monday 28. A Bill ordered to be brought in persuance of the above Resolution and Mr Wortley and the Master of the Rolls and Sir John Bernard to bring it in which I am told cannot be finished until after the Holy Dayes. This scheme is intended by the Master (whatever end Sir John may have in it) to pay the Publick Debts of the Nation, to reduce Luxury, to take off in a few years the Taxes that lye so heavy upon the Industrious part of the Nation. But the Ministry will hardly come into this, especially a Ministry that has justly or unjustly (no matter) incurred the odium of the people. They must be supported by a Majority in the House, and how can it be secured but by the Multitude of Officers and Dependants that govern in elections, and how are those Members to be attached but by Pensions paid out of our own money. If this scheme takes place it will fall in a few years upon the Landed Men, for people can't afford by a 3rd at least to expend the commodities of the Kingdom, so that the Farmers must either fall, their prices or else their demand will be less, either way they will be losers and consequently the Landlords must fall their rents or get no Tenants. For at present it is a great complaint that rents are not paid. Many estates are thrown upon the Gentlemen's hands and there is a kind of combination to destroy the Landlords more, or oblige them to make great abatements, and will not the case be much more depressed if Interest of Money be more reduced. It has been so in a remarkable manner since the Reduction from 5 to 4 per cent and must be much more now. If all the Taxes will be taken off I should say there was some reason for the thing, but if the Prime Minister has power enough in the House to put a Negative to any Proposal of this nature he will have much more favour, when he will have the entire management of 5 or 6 Millions in a year. And what makes one distrust the present great men is that their own Favourite Child, the Sinking Fund, for 13 years has not paid off 3 Millions. This gives me but little encouragement to trust such a vast concern in a man's hands who will have still more power to stop any Enquiries of that Nature. I made use of this argument to the Master and I hope the Temper he saw the House is in has made him cooler than he was towards this scheme, expecially at this Juncture. Sir Robert assures his friends that he is against it but I am sure he would be glad it could be brought in and carried by the Ministry who might have the blame. This was the reason that when it came into the House the other day he divided against it and his brothers and his friends staid in. The Master told me that the Queen told Lady Jekyl that she was not of the same opinion with her husband in this affair and thought the reduction very bad. The Master thought this very Unpolitick since the design was at least to pay off the Publick Debts which she ought to have appealed for. The Merchants were resolved to shew that they were averse to this scheme and drew out their money from the Bank to shew that they would prevent the Bank agreeing with or assisting the Government to redeem Interest by having so great a sum in their hands. This gave a General Fright and brought for 6 days a great run on the Bank in which time they paid off their Notes to the Amount of 1,000,000 or more.

[*Tuesday*] *29*, [*Wednesday*] *30*, [*Thursday*] *31*. The Run on the Bank continued.

APRIL 1737

Friday 1.   At home.

SUNDAY 3.   Preached at Hackney for the curate. Drunk tea with old Mr Newcombe the Vicar. He is still very hearty of his age. Parliament adjourned. Preached at St. Michael's a Charity sermon.

Thursday 7.   At home. Passion Week.

Easter Day 10.   At Newington.

Monday 11.   Visited Mr Seers,

[*Tuesday*] *12*, [*Wednesday*] *13*, [*Thursday*] *14*.   The Run at the Bank was over upon a Supposition that the 3 per cent Bill would be dropt and Stocks Rose 4 or 5 per cent. I can't see a reason for this suggestion. If the Ministry pushed it hard the Government can't but come into it. I mean as much of it as will serve their turn. Yet as for taking off the Taxes till the thing takes is not reasonable and even to admit of a debate which should first be taken off would be dangerous for the Prime Minister and got without doing of either and Patriots would not trust the Minister with so much money as would be raised by the Reduction. However the Master may lead it is very hard upon Widows and Orphans and those who have their all in the Funds. It will send them down to cheaper countries and as it will lessen London so the demand for Meat etc. will be less. What I mean is that the people cannot afford to pay so great a price which will reduce the farmers and so fall heavy upon the Landlords, especially at a time when the farmers all over England are breaking or leaving their farms. Whether this is owing to their or their Landlords' luxury. This Bill, if it passes, can in no way amend the matter. It will certainly make it worse. I am told that all sorts of people begin to see this and are very Clamorous and tho' I am far from encouraging such a spirit yet upon some occasions Vox Populi est Vox Dei.

Friday 15. At the Society for Propagating the Gospel. The Archbishop told me he was afraid Dr. Gooch [241] would prevail to keep his living so that there will be no vacancy for me. His Grace assured me that I was never out of his mind and that he would assist me all that lay in his power. I question at least if anything will come of this long pursuit. Went with Dr. Guerdes and dined with the Bishop of Durham. Talking of the *Egyptian Idolotry* he said it was his opinion that this last Bill was this. Each city had a beast or a vegetable displayed in their standards and as they were victorious under them in time they worshipped their animals as Gods, that they fought under. He told me that the Archbishop would have no more to do with recommending for Church preferments. That the Ministry would just suffer and that not for a very long time either. Salisbury is the chief person in favour with the Queen. The Bishop of Durham tho' not concerned in the Funds is not a very great enemy to the 3 per cent. scheme. Rev. Mr Stillingfleet and one Mr Knatchbull, a clergyman, dined with the Bishop. Qu: Whether he is not one of the Bishop's chaplains—

[241] Sir Thomas Gooch, Master of Caius College, Cambridge. Bishop of Bristol 1737, Norwich 1738, Ely 1748–54.

an acquaintance of Mr Colebrook's. Dr. Gully came in after dinner. Mem. to write to the Bishop once more to put the Duke of Grafton in mind of the Chaplainship.

Saturday 16. At Newington and on Monday 18 dined with the gentlemen of the town and neighbourhood at the 3 Crowns. All mightily averse to the 3 per cent scheme.

Tuesday 19. At the Rehearsal of the Musick for the Sons of the Clergy.

Friday 22. At the Parliament House. A great debate occasioned by a Clause in the Land Tax Bill to discharge the Prince from paying it upon the money that shall be allowed him from the King. This was put in by the Committee without any instruction from the House or knowledge even of the Speaker. A thing of Dangerous Consequence if permitted to go in other cases. Mr Pultney, Shippon, Sands, Sir W. Windham spoke warmly and fully against Sir Robt. W. and were answered by Sir R. W. Mr Pelham, Mr Winnington. That the Royal Family were of course exempted from the Land Tax and the reason why the Prince's Name was not inserted before was because his allowance was monthly and so not subject to the Land Tax but that now it was yearly. Sir John Bernard brought up his 3 per cent. Bill. It seems to be artfully drawn up. It was read the first time. Sir R. W. said it was of vast consequence altering at once the properties of so many 1000's and therefore ought to pass with great deliberation, desired a Coppy of it and time to consider of it. It was ordered to be read a 2nd. time a Friday next when it is generally thought a motion will be made that it be committed to a Committee of the whole House and that it will pass in the Negative and so the Bill for this year will be dropt but will certainly be taken up next. Lay at Mr Rivington's. A Letter from my father.

Saturday 23. Was with Mr Oglethorpe. Is of opinion that something very warm will be done in relation to Pluralities etc. next session. Is afraid that the Spaniards will attack Carolina if so Georgia will certainly be in danger, the Ministry remiss, he having given them full notice of this design long since. Was with the Master of the Rolls. Says it is a shame that Bishops should keep

Cures of Souls in Commendam. That Pluralists are little better than Robbers, taking that money originally intended and left to those that do the Duty. Promises to speak again to the Queen for me.

SUNDAY 24. At home.

Monday 25. With the Archbishop. He told me that Dr. Gooch would keep his living and so the Bishop of Salisbury said, so I am fairly off between them. In short 'tis a shame for Bishops to keep Cures of Souls in commendam. They know their duty calls them strongly to another place and so leave their parish the greatest part of the year to a curate. Dined with the Trustees of Cordwainer's School.

Tuesday 26. At the Society. Dr. Denne showed me some exceptional places in my Father's Catechism which they desire may be altered in another impression, but as he designed the book for his own diocese and the Doctrines objected to perhaps true they shall remain as they are for me. I went afterwards with Dr. Guerdes and dined at the Cyder House near Westminster Hall. To the House of Lords. Heard the debates about the Irregularity of the Lords Justiciaries in Scotland concerning Capt. Porteous. Lord Carteret, Lord Bathurst, Lord Winchelsea, Bishop of Salisbury against the Judges. Lord Funlater, Lord Ismay, Duke of Newcastle, Lord Chancellor for them. Viz. That they acted according to the Lawes of Scotland. This debate adjourned to friday and the Scotch Judges to attend the House. They all seem determined to punish the Magistrates of Edinburgh for their connivance at the Riot and Murder of Porteous and if they do not they may expect much greater mischief. That Country ever since the Union has paid only a forct obedience to the King of England.

Friday 29. At the Parliament House. The 3 per cent. Bill was read a 2nd time. Sir John Bernard moved for the Commitment of it and was seconded by Wortley Montague and the Master of the Rolls. Sir Robt. Walpole opposed it in along speech of above a Hour and a half setting forth the Hardships of so sudden and a great change in the properties of 1000's. The difficulties it would bring Nos. into. Declared that it was against Parliamentary Faith and the Customs of Parliament ever since these Funds were first established. Viz. Not to lower the Interest without the desire of the Proprietors at a General Court which should always be a first step taken in such a Momentous affair. Concluded against the Motion. He was answered by Sir John Bernard.

Speakers for and against it

For Committing it.	Against Committing it.
Sir John Bernard.	Sir Robert Walpole.
Mr How of Gloucestershire.	Col. Bladon.
Lord Baltimore.	Mr Knight.
Sir William Saunderson.	Alderman Heathcote.
Mr Sands.	Mr. Sloper.
Sir William Windham.	Mr. Oglethorpe.
Mr Gibbons.	Mr Winnington.
Wortley Montague Esq.	Sir Wm. Young.
Sir Jos. Jekyl.	

Pulteney did not speak, tho' he divided with Sir John Barnard.

249 against committing and for rejecting it.
134 for committing it.

———

Majority 115. In all 383.

———

Upon this all the Stocks rose 3 per cent and are likely to be much higher. People in general are mightily pleased and Sir Robert could not have done a more popular thing. Sir John Barnard's scheme will very likely thro' him out of a seat in Parliament for the City of London for whatever future ages might have reaped from such a reduction 'tis plainly against the present interest of the City, the Married Men and Traders.

MAY 1737

SUNDAY 30.   Went to town. Dined at home.
Monday 1.   At Newington.
Saturday 7.   In town. Dined at home.
SUNDAY 8.   At Newington Church.

Monday 9. Waited upon the Archbishop in the Cloysters at Westminster.

Tuesday 10. Hearing that Dr. Watson of St. Stephen's Walbrook was very ill I ventured to ask the Master of the Rolls to beg that living of my Lord Chancellor for me which he was so kind as to promise that he would do accordingly.

Friday 13. He wrote a very kind and pressing letter in my favour accordingly.

Saturday 14. I waited upon his Lordship who told me that he had the greatest regard to whatever the Master should ask of him but that he had made it a settled rule with him that he would never give a positive promise before the living was vacant. But says "I will preserve his Honour's letter that I may not be surprised into any other engagement."

SUNDAY 15. I preached at the Rolls Chappell and dined with the Master. In the afternoon at St. Dunstan's Church. Mr. Batty preached.

Friday 20. My wife not very well. Consulted Dr. Bamber. Advises Tunbridge waters.

SUNDAY 21. This afternoon the Master wrote to me word that my Lord Chancellor was so kind as to offer me the rectory of St. George's Southwark with £120 vacant by the death of Dr. Nathaniel Hough.[242] I went to see St. George's parish. Met with Mr Wilson the curate who was very earnest with me to accept of it. There is no house for the minister nor one in the parish fit for him to live in. A large No. of people. Not the easiest managed. The Rules of the King's Bench subjects to great Irregularities and Marriages without Licences [243] commonly practised by 2 bad

---

[242] Nathaniel Hough, D.D., Jesus College, Cambridge, incorp. at Oxford 1717. Rector of St George's Southwark 1715 and Newington, Surrey, 1731 until his death.

[243] The Rules of the King's Bench and the Marshalsea were in the parish of St George's, Southwark. Hence the voluminous Registers which Little Dorrit made her pillow in the vestry of St George's. Clergymen who officiated at such marriages were liable to lose their benefices but a clergyman within the Rules of the Prison had no benefice to lose! This abuse brought to an end by Lord Hardwicke's Marriage Act 1753.

clergymen in the parish. Various clergy induced me not to accept of this Living.

Monday 23. At Court. Dined with Dr. Lavington at the Chaplain's table. Waited upon the Bishop of Durham. He told me that the Duke of Grafton had renewed his promise that I should be King's Chaplain this vacancy. Came home in the evening. Promised to preach for Dr. Lavington the 12 June at St. Paules in the afternoon.

Tuesday 24. At Court. It was whispered that the King intended to go over this summer. Waited upon Betty Hastings in Conduit Street. She is going to Kent. The King going to his German Dominions. His friends hope he will not and dread the consequences of it. Dined at the Chaplain's table with Dr. Holcombe,[244] the King's Chaplain and Prebendary of Canterbury. This evening I wrote a letter to the Master of the Rolls giving him my reasons why I begged to decline St. George's but still with the hopes that it should not deprive me of some marks of his Lordship's future benevolence.

Wednesday 25. I waited 4 hours with Mr Terrick to see the Master but he was so busy that I had not that satisfaction. Dined by myself at the Rumour Tavern in Bishops Gate Street. Came home early in the afternoon.

Thursday 26. My wife and I dined with Dr. Bamber at his house in Mincing Lane. Very civilly entertained. In the evening went to the Master's. Not at home. Walked cross the fields home.

Friday 27. At the Rolls. The Master owned that my reasons were good ones and was sure my Lord Chancellor thought them so and seemed pretty sure that I should soon be provided for by his Lordship. Told me with some pleasure that the Bill to restrain Play Houses was carried by a great majority. Was extreamly and agreeably surprised to find so many good and religious things said upon this and the occasion of inforcing the Gin Bill in the House

---

[244] Samuel Holcombe, D.D., Fellow of Pembroke College, Cambridge. Royal Chaplain and Prebendary of Canterbury as well as holding St Benet, Gracechurch St., Christ Church, Old Southgate, and several country parishes. Died at Canterbury in 1761 aged 95 and buried in the Cathedral.

of Commons. Was very much surprised at Mr Pulteney's violent opposition to the Play House Bill. Goes to Bell Bar tomorrow for a fortnight. Came home in the evening. Found my wife much better.

JUNE 1737

Wednesday 1. Went to town. Waited upon the Archbishop. Told me that Bishop Cecil [245] of Bangor died a sunday of the Gout in the Head. Asked me whether I should like a living that might become vacant 150 miles off. I desired to be excused going so far hoping to be settled nearer London. Waited upon the Bishop of Durham. Was in the evening with Mr Idle my Lord Chancellor's Clerk of the Presentations, at Lincolns Inn. Lay at Mr Rivington's.

Thursday 2. Mr Idle told me that he had shewn my letter to the Lord Chancellor. That he was very well pleased with my declining the living of St. George's and that he did not doubt that I stood very fair for something good in his Lordship's Gift, especially since I had so good a friend in the Master of the Rolls. Went to the House of Lords who passed the Play House Bill, limiting them to Westminster of where the King resided during his residence only and that no Play should be acted without being firstly censored by the Lord Chamberlain. It was opposed in a wily speech by Lord Chesterfield who said that whilst Religion and Modesty was attacked the Stage went unpunished but now that the Minister was attempted to be abused all was in a flame. It seems the occasion of this Bill was a design of acting a most Scandalous Farce in which the Queen and Sir Robt. were most abominably ridiculed. Lord Walpole very imprudently defied Lord Chesterfield to prove any Innuendoes against his father. My Lord said he meant none in particular and the whole House thought W. was weak in taking notice of it and which his father did not thank him for. Came home in the evening. The Duke of Grafton assured me before the Duke of Atholl that he

[245] Charles Cecil, Bishop of Bangor 1734-7.

was bound in conscience and honour to make me King's Chaplain. I believe it will not be the first as he solemnly promised the Bishop of Durham.

Friday 3. At home.

Saturday 4. In town. Went to visit the Bishop of St. Asaph and Mr. Oglethorpe. Both out of the way. Called upon Mrs Titchbourn (one of the Queen's Bedchamber women) at Somerset House. She told me that when she was in waiting she had mentioned me to the Queen who expressed a design of serving me but that it often happened that she was frustrated in her intentions towards her friends by having persons forct upon her by those whose services would not bear a denial and that merit in such cases was out of the question. That for her own part people were deceived as to her interest at Court, that she had never been able to do much for herself or her friends, and hinted as if others had made a very large purse, by means she was ignorant of or would not take. She is a very understanding and I feel a Lady of great Honour, Religion and Integrity. If there was a greater No of these it could not be worse in any point for the Mistress. Those that serve her with other views and upon bad principles would all forsake her at the Day of Tryal which I pray God long avert. Nothing seems to be more dangerous to the King than going abroad. There is some talk of it this year but I hope without any foundation. It will foment disturbances which are hardly laid since the last Journey. Came home to dinner. Mr Rivington dined with me.

SUNDAY 5. *Trinity Sunday*. At Newington Church.

Thursday 9. Went in the morning to Bell Bar to the Master of the Rolls. Dined there. Came home in the evening. He told me that my Lord Chancellor would certainly think of me for a Living.

SUNDAY 12. Preached at the Rolls Chappell for Mr Terrick. Dined with Mr Sergeant Skinner in Chancery Lane, his brother, Mr Peters brother to the Dr. and another gentleman. Preached in the afternoon at St. Poule's for Dr Lavington. Came home in the afternoon a Horse Back.

Monday 13. At home. At London. Dined with Mr Rivington.

Called upon Dr. Bamber and Mr Halsey, Cheesemonger in Thames Street.

Tuesday 14. My wife much out of order. Took tincture of Roses with the acids.

Wednesday 15. My wife, I thank God, much better. Is to take physick to morrow. Mr Ziegenhagen [246] and another German Minister made me a visit in the afternoon.

Thursday 16. Much alarmed by an itching between my fingers. Took a dose of Physick. I hope 'tis only heat in my blood.

Friday 17. Sent for by Mr Griffen, clerk to my Lord Chamberlain, acquainting me that I was nominated one of His Majesty's Chaplains in Ordinary.

Saturday 18. I went to the office and received my warrant bearing date this day and am appointed for the month of June.

SUNDAY 19. At home.

Monday 20. I was sworn in Chaplain at Court by Sir Charles Dalton Gent. Usher of the Black Rodd.
Fees.

To the Lord Chamberlain.	3.	3.	0.
To Mr Griffen.	1.	1.	0.
Door Keeper.		5.	0.
Gent. Usher's fee.	3.	3.	0.
Door Keeper.		5.	0.
Servants at the Chaplain's Room.		10.	0.

[Break in the Diary until August 1737.]

AUGUST 1737

Thursday 25. Went with Mr Oglethorpe to Hampton Court. Called upon Capt. Trench at Chelsea. A very good sort of man. Waited upon the Duke of Newcastle. He told me that Mr Hunne, Tutor to the E. of Lincoln many years had no preferment and he should be glad he had Topplesfield in Essex. And accordingly he had wrote to the Master of the Rolls about it. I had no great inclination for that Living but desired that I might be assured of the next which his Grace solemnly assured me of and Mr Stone

[246] Chaplain to George II at Kensington.

further told me that upon the next vacancy the Duke himself would apply for me. Dined with Mrs Titchbourn and Mrs Purcell. Came home in the evening. The whole town alarmed by a report of the death of the Queen occasioned by a Highwayman, who being afraid of being stopt at the Turn Pikes cryed out that he was an Express going with the news of the Queen's death. Abundance of Tradesmen made contract for black cloth, Mourning Shoos etc. are likely to be losers. Lay at Mr. Rivington's. Letter from the Master of the Rolls inviting me to Bell Bar.

Friday 26. Dined at home.

Saturday 27. Set out for Bell Bar. The Master dined at Mr Sambroke's. Came home in the evening and received me with his usual good nature and friendship. Shewed me a long letter he had from the Duke of Newcastle in which he assured the Master that I should be the next and only one in his thoughts for a Living in the King's Gift. He answered it and laid in for a Prebend.

SUNDAY 28. Preached at North Mimms. General Wade dined with the Master. Shewed us a most scandalous and treasonable pamphlet called A Memorial to the People of Scotland reflecting grossly upon the Act of Parliament ordered to be read in the churches concerning the murder to Capt. Porteous, in which the King and the Parliament are grossly abused and the People of Scotland excited to shake off the Yoke; in one place they are told that they are under the Paw of The German Eagle. Mr Pulteney told the General the other day that he had a letter from a good hand that if the General should be sent down at this time to Scotland there was a formed resolution to show him some Indignity, which his officers in all probability resenting Disturbances would insue. The clergy there he says are a very odd sort of people are far from being Ministers of Peace. This pamphlet is very much in the style of 1640. All Scripture Language perverted to the worst purpose in the world, raising a Rebellion.

At the death of Queen Anne the General carried a letter from the hated general to King George 1st. who did not seem at all elated, nor indeed any of the Court. Speaking of the Present King being at that time invited to take his seat in Parliament he said his father, knowing his temper, would not suffer it, which had occasioned a coolness between them and they had not dined together for 6 months. When Secretary Craggs brought in the Proclamation to the late King he said he thought it all a Chimera. He never imagined he would come in, or at least not without great confusion, which he was resolved not to have hazarded. The General told the Master that his nephew the Lord Chancellor had laboured in vain to reconcile the King and the Prince. That the King insisted upon his asking pardon for what happened last winter in the Houses of Parliament which the Prince will not do for in so doing he gives up his friends that have won great riches from him and have already hazarded if not lost the King's favour. Mr Littleton and Mr Pitt are the Prince's Chief Consellors. Very young men and the former Rash and Hott. There is no liklyhood of an Accommodation unless the Present Ministry should be greatly distressed and should take the Princes Friends in full share in the Administration of what happened so in the late King's reign. The General is amazed at the Memorial of Geraldino demanding for the King of Spain Carolina and Georgia, which he thinks is preparation to a demand of Gibraltar and Port Mahon. He wishes the former was given to them on Advantageous Terms without which they will never be at peace with us. They would willingly give us quiet possession of Port Mahon for ever or a large sum of money and there is a port there for an Fleet of Men of War. Gibraltar cost us an immense sum of money every year. The Master would come in to this. The General told us that he was the occasion of our taking Minorca having with a glass discovered the Spaniards asleep in their Trenches in the Day time, made a vigorous and sudden attack and gained the Outward Works, upon which they capitulated and when they went out they were greater nos. than the Beseigers. The Master told me that some years ago there was an Excellent Memorial given in by the Board of Trade to the Ministry in which amongst many other good things a Frontier was proposed as absolutely necessary for both North and South Carolina and this before Georgia was ever thought of, which is now in some measure done by the Trustees and shew the importance of it in this Kingdom and indeed the Spaniards demanding of it is a very good reason for us taking more care of putting it into a good Posture and Defence. Sir John Barnard when the Petition of the Trustees was first delivered into Parliament said it was of the utmost importance to our Trade.

Monday 29. At Bell Bar. The Master told me that the Prince had now a fine part to act. To retire as a Private Gentleman. Contract all his unnecessary expenses and declare himself an enemy to Corruption in all shapes. He told me that Sir R. W. makes as free with the King as anyone. Said one day "I am just come from the Captain. He has been upon his Prancer but I have taken him down."

Tuesday 30. Dined at Bell Bar. The Master sent me home in his chaise. Found everything well, thank God for it.

Wednesday 31. At home.

SEPTEMBER 1737

Thursday 1. Went with Mr Oglethorpe to Hampton Court. Saw Mr Hone who assured me of the Duke of Newcastle would certainly be my friend for the next Living in the King's Gift. Told me of the Living of Sutterton being supposed to be vacant very soon, bid me enquire about it. I hear that the Difference between the King and the Prince is wider every day. That the Day his Highness having wrote to the King he asked the Lord that brought it whether he had any more to say, being told in the negative he bid him tell the Prince that he need write no more, that he would receive no more messages. God only knows what will be the consequences of this Quarrell. Came home by myself in Mr Oglethorpe's chariot. Lay at Mr Rivington's.

Friday 2. Went home. The Princess baptised by the Name of Augusta in private by the Archbishop.

SUNDAY 4. At home.

Thursday 8. Went again with Mr Oglethorpe to Hampton Court. Dined with the chaplains. Came home by water. Lay at Mr Rivington's.

Friday 9. Wrote to the Master of the Rolls. Sent him Limbourgh's [247] *Amica Collation cum Eruditio Judaeo.* This day the Duke of Grafton brought a long letter from the King to the Prince setting forth the reasons of his being angry at him, amongst which, they say, his hurrying the Princess away when she was in labour to the great hazarding of her life and the life of the Heir Presumptive to the Crown is chiefly insisted upon. Upon the whole his Grace told him that his Majesty could no longer suffer him to stay in the Royal palace etc. I am apt to think this sudden order arose from all the news papers saying that the Princess of Wales was to see Company a Monday Tuesday and Wednesday following etc. which popularity I presume the King did not like. However the Prince obeys and all things are taking down in the greatest hurry.

SUNDAY 11. At home.

Monday 12. In town.

Tuesday 13. A message from town that Dr. Watson was supposed to be dead carried me in some hurry to London. Found that he had been very ill but not dead. Spent the evening with Mr Rivington at the Coffee House and lay there.

Thursday 14. Father Patten's Birth Day. 69 years old. Molly and I dined with him. Came home in the evening.

Friday 15. In town.

Saturday 16. At home.

SUNDAY 17. Walked to Tottenham. Dined with Mr Husbands the Minister. Drank tea there with my wife and came home.

Wednesday 20. In town. Saw Mr Oglethorpe who told me that the Master of the Rolls said the kindest things of me, that my Lord Chancellor stood firm for St. Stephen's Walbrook.

Saturday 23. N.B. In town this morning. The evening Mr Hayward told my wife and I that some things had been said or done of late that he had not liked at all, that he must have a man which was not agreeable to us and that upon the whole it was much better to part, which I willingly agreed to, and next Lady Day is fixed for us leaving this house, much to my satisfaction. My wife not very well at night.

[247] See entry for 30th following.

SUNDAY 24. My wife not well. Staid at home. The following letter was handed about town in relation to the Misunderstanding between the King and the Prince.

TO THE PRINCE.

The Professions you have made in your letters, of your particular regard to me, are so contradictory to your actions that I cannot suffer myself to be imposed upon by you. You know very well you did not give the least Intimation to me, or to the Queen, that the Princess was with Child, until within a month of the Birth of the Young Princess.

You removed the Princess twice in the week immediately preceding the Day of her Delivery from the Place of my Residence in Expectation (as you voluntarily declared) of her Labour, as both times upon the return you industriously concealed from the knowledge of me and the Queen, every circumstance relating to this important affair. And you, at least, without giving notice to me or to the Queen, precipitately hurried the Princess from Hampton Court in a condition not to be received. After having thus, in Execution of your own determined Measures exposed both the Princess and your Child to the greatest perils, you now plead surprise and Tenderness for the Princess, as the only motives that occasioned these repeated Indignities offered to me and to the Queen your mother.

This extravagant and undutyful behaviour, in so essential a point, as the Birth of an Heir to my Crown, is such an evidence of your Premeditated Defiance of me, and such a contempt of my authority, and of the Natural Right belonging to your Parents, as cannot be excused by the pretended innocence of your intentions nor disguised by specious words only; but the whole Tenor of your Conduct for a Considerable Time, has been so entirely void of all real duty to me, that I have long had reason to be highly offended with you. And until you withdraw your regard and confidence from those by whose instigation and advice you are directed and encouraged in this unwarrantable behaviour to me and to the Queen and until you return to your duty *You shall not reside in my Palace*, which I will not suffer to be made the resort of those who, under the appearance of an attachment to you, foment the Division you have made in my Family and thereby weakened the Common Interest of the whole.

In this situation I will receive no reply but when your actions manifest a just sense of your duty and submission that may induce me to pardon what at present I most justly resent.

In the meantime it is my pleasure that you leave St. James's with all your family when it can be done without Prejudice or Inconvenience to the Princess.

I shall for the present leave to the Princess the care of my grand daughter until a proper time calls upon me to consider of her education.

G. REX.

Monday 25. Went to town. Dined at the Globe Tavern in Hatton Garden. Dr. Houseman of the Street came to me, told me that Dr. Watson was very ill, not likely to recover. Saw Mr Biscowe who told me the same, that the Dropsy was coming upwards. Came home at night. My wife, I thank God, recovered from her late indisposition. I see the newspapers take notice of a design of the Spaniards upon Georgia, which I now question because I believe we are entering upon a Treaty between Spain, Denmark, Sweden, Portugal and the States of Holland to curb the exorbitant powers of France and the Emperor which joyned at present with the Zarinas move the Ballance of Europe.

Tuesday 27. At home.

Wednesday 28. This day I received a letter from Medlicott. Went to his house in Bolton Street, Pickadilly. Sat with him till near 9. It was to tell me that Mr Lamplugh, lecturer of his Chappell in Conduit street was dying,[248] that the nomination lies in the Rector of St. Martin's and St. George's Hanover Square and that the last time they left the nomination to him, and that he believed they would do so now and therefore offered me his assistance, which I heartily thanked him for and he promising immediately to mention the thing to Mr Trebeck and jointly to nominate me to Dr. Pearce. It is £40 paid by Dr. Pearce and will be mightily convenient if I have a city living. Walked home much fategued and lay at Mr. Rivington's. My wife better.

Thursday 29. Came home to dinner. It rained prodigiously from 11 to 12 at night.

Friday 30. At home. A letter from the Master of the Rolls that it was needless to write in my case to my Lord Chancellor till a vacancy when he would immediately do it. Admires Limborgh's *Amica Collation cum Eruditio Judaeo.* In great anxiety at Georgia and hopes care will be taken of its defence. Indeed I am afraid the Ministry have too long neglected the repeated information they have received from Mr Oglethorpe of the Spaniards design upon the Colony. He only desired 2 20 Gun Ships and 600 Men to

[248] See note for 2 Oct. following.

defend this and Carolina, but has been put off from day to day. The English Nation do not at present apprehend the Consequence of this Colony. It will see and feel it whenever it is gone. The very demand the Spaniards and running the risk of a thorough breach with us shews the advantage of such a Frontier. If it is lost for want of care Wo! upon those thro' whose negligence it has happened this next sessions of Parliament.

OCTOBER 1737

Saturday 1. At home. Went to town this evening in order to preach for Mr Medlicott tomorrow morning at Trinity Chappell Conduit Street near Hanover Square. Saw Mr Oglethorpe. Told me that the King had given him a Commission to raise a Regiment for Georgia. That they had been so dilatory that he was afraid it was already lost. That it would still be some time before he could get it ready, and even after that he could not go 'till he had orders. In short I find by him that he thinks they are not in earnest and are afraid of breaking with Spain. I am apt to think if it is lost the Prime Minister will go so near to be called to account if it has happened thro' his neglect, for tho' the English Nation have not the regard for so important a Colony now, they will be very angry when it is lost, especially to the Spaniards whose late depridations have made our Merchants very angry. Lay at Mr Rivington's.

SUNDAY 2. Preached at the Trinity Chappell in Conduit Street for Mr. Medlicott. Dined with his lady and daughter and one Miss Pagenham a very beautiful young lady. Very good sense. Staid all the afternoon. Mr Medlicott returned from Court. Told me that Mr Lamplugh was not dead yet [249] but was dangerously ill of an Ulcer in his Kidney. That upon his death he did not doubt but to bring me into the Lecture which I shall like very well. Came to Mr Rivington's. Lay there. Rained hard for 8 days and does so still. The floods very much out.

[249] But Mr Lamplugh did not die until 1776, becoming a prebendary of Ripon in 1746 and vicar of Dewsbury in 1761.

Monday 3. Dined at the 3 Crowns. I find abundance of people are taken suddenly ill in their heads and some go quite out of their senses. Mr Newey's nephew at Cambridge this week was Melancholly and starved himself to death as I hear. Rained all night. At home.

Tuesday 4. The wind northerly and the rain abated. I hope we shall have better weather.

Saturday 8. I paid the Bishop of Durham a visit in Grosvenor Square and thanked him for the favour he did me in the Chaplainship which I believe was wholly to his Grace the Duke of Grafton. He advised me not to speak of any interest I had with my Lord Chancellor, because if the Court heard of it I should be entirely turned over to him. Speaking of the Bishop of Salisbury succeeding the Bishop of London as Premier Ecclesiast. he believed he hardly would because he was too enterprising a man, rather imagined the Archbishop would be trusted with the Lesser Preferments and sometimes advised with in the Greater. That Sarum was to have York and Hereford Sarum. That the Bishop of London last sessions in the Scotch affairs mistook the Court, run warmly into their Schemes without being acquainted with them, contradicted himself, recanted his own sentiments, and then at last ran out of town. Bishop of Chichester aiming at being in power. Speaking about Whiston the Bishop told me he had advised him when Bishop of Litchfield to retire and come no more to Court. The Bishop told him that was what the enemies of the Church wanted. That they might have a pretence to take away their seates in Parliament and afterwards, when they were of no use, their revenues. Perhaps says the Bishop "Will. Whiston you have a mind I should be as poor as you are, but I am resolved not to be so." The Queen once told the Bishop that Whiston [250] was a very impertinent man though she had never talked to him about her sentiments in Religion. If so I say Whiston is a very false man for he has often asserted the contrary in publick. His Imprudence

[250] William Whiston (1667–1752), chiefly remarkable for his translation of Josephus. Professor of Mathematics at Cambridge but expelled from the University in 1710 for his Arian views. Joined the General Baptists in 1747.

indeed may not be excuseable. Came home pretty late in the evening.

Tuesday 17. Went to town. In the evening at the Cock Pitt White Hall. The London Merchants having the week before presented a petition to his Majesty complaining of the depridations of the Spaniards his Majesty referred the consideration of it to a Committee of the Privy Council, which met this night at 7. Present: Lord Archbishop, Lord President, Lord Chancellor, Duke of Newcastle, Richmond, Grafton, Lord Harrington, Pembroke, Sir Robert Walpole, Sir Ch. Wager. About 150 Merchants were present in the Council Chamber and Mr Sharp, their Agent, opened their complaint very fully and proved Captures on the High Seas 25 Leagues from the Spanish Coast, upon no pretence whatever. A ship condemned at the Havanna for having Loggwood abroad which grew upon the Isle of Providence, that the Governor of Porto Rico said he would take all English Ships that he could master, disputed our right to the Island of Providence. No reparation made, tho' promised by the Court of Spain for 8 Ships taken in 1734. The Council told them that they might be assured of his Majesty's readiness to protect the Trade of his subjects and that in the mean time Mr Sharp should get all the other Proofs from Bristol etc. and lay them before the Council. Returned about half hour after ten. Lay at Mr Hayward's lodgings in Barge Yard Bucklersbury. Mr Parr's.

Wednesday 18. Upon seeing in the Gazette that Mr Chandler was dead I went to the Bishop of Durham and found it was a mistake, he being in very good health. Returned home to dinner.

Tuesday 24. I went to town. Visited the Master of the Rolls who came this day to the Rolls for the winter. Appointed to dine tomorrow. Spent the evening at the Rumour Tavern. Mr Trench Mr Yerbery, Dr. Watts the Physition. Mr Bird formerly member for Coventry, now Commissioner of the Stamp Office. He spoke very much against the Merchants for not waiting first upon Sir R. W. before they petitioned the King. For arguments' sake I took the side of the Merchants with a good deal of Modesty. Whether he is not fool enough to make a Merit of this at my expense to Sir R. W. I can't say. If he does he is a mean man, because I told him that I argued only to keep up and improvise a Debate for the entertainment of the Company. Lay this night at Mr Rivington's lodgings in Barge Yard.

Wednesday 25. Dined with his Honr. at the Rolls. Mr Idle, Counsellor Clerk, Mr Jekyl, Mr Terrick. Some course must be taken to punish the rioters about Gin which increases every day to the scandal of the Government. In a little time they will suffer no law to be executed but what suites their Vitiated taste. Licentiousness as Evil as well as Religious is the Disgrace of the Present Generation.

SUNDAY 29. At home.

NOVEMBER 1737

Tuesday 1. Went to town. Dined with Mr Newey.

Friday 4. In town at the Guild Hall Coffee House. Mr Newey.

Saturday 5. At home. Went this evening at the great hazard of my life to town to see for Master Hayward, his mother being in a good deal of concern about him.

SUNDAY 6. Preached for Mr Husbands (out of order) at Tottenham. Dined at home. Mr Robert and Billy here. I hope he will mend for the future.

Monday 7. In town. Dined with Mr Medlicott in Bolton Street. Lay at Barge Yard.

Tuesday 8. At home.

Thursday 10. This day the Queen was taken ill as they say of the Gout in the Stomach. Lets blood twice. A very bad night.

Friday 11. The Queen much worse. Thought to be in a dangerous way.

Saturday 12. I was alarmed with an account of the Master's illness. Only a slight illness. Went to town. Found him feavorish. The Queen very ill. The King discovered to the Physitians for the first time that her Majesty had a Rupture for the last 6 years a little above her Navle, which at this time has disordered her intestines. This night about 12 she was cut by Mr Shipton and the Gut reduced as it is thought she has had no through passage these 4 or 5 dayes. It is a dangerous operation and very like from the grossness of her body it will mortify.

SUNDAY 13. I preached for Mr Medlicott at Trinity Chappell Conduit Street. The Queen rested pretty well and they hope she is better. The Master of the Rolls better. I supped at Mr Newey's Stck Market. Lay at Barge Yard.

Monday 14. At home.

Tuesday 15. In town.

Wednesday 16. At home.

Thursday 17. At the Society in the Mews. Afterwards at Court. Yesterday the Archbishop administered the Sacrament to the Queen. She behaved with great composure and recommended her children to take the advice of the Archbishop as she had done. At Mr Oglethorpe's. He told me that a few days ago the Queen told the King that she had brought him a great many children and now she would bring him another, meaning the Prince. The King understood but would not seem to do so, upon which her Majesty told him that she had never willingly offended him and would not do so now, but heartily recommended it to him to receive the Prince whenever he would return to his Duty. By which I guess the Queen would have been very much pleased to have had a Reconciliation before she had died, and Nos. of well wishers to their Family would have rejoiced should an happy incident might have been attached also to the loss of the Queen. Met Dr. Bundy at Court. He took notice that it was very late before anything of Religion was mentioned, that this day was the first in which Prayers were ordered in the Churches about the Palace. That it was a very indecent thing to have Plays acted during her Majesty's illness. That she too much favoured those who were inclined to Arianism. Told me of the dispute there is like to be between the Archbishop of Canterbury and Mr Watts Preacher of Lincolns Inn, which is like to make a good deal of noise. Mr W. applied to the Archbishop for a Dispensation to hold two Livings. The Arch Bishop did not approve of his answers —being given in the Words of Scripture an old Trick of the Arians. Upon the second exam. he gave a very Orthodox Account of his Faith now filed at large and the Archbishop passed his Dispensation. After this he wrote to the Archbishop a long letter complaining of all the delays, the attendance upon his Grace and his chaplains etc. and intending to go to the Press. We shall hear more of this soon.

Friday 18. The Queen in the same way. No through passage. Dr. Sands gave her a Turpentine Glister which gave her present relief. She is in great pain and yet behaves with great chearfulness and composedness of Temper. The Archbishop prays twice a day by her.

Saturday 19. This day orders from the King were sent to the Bishop of London to all the Chappels and Churches in the town to pray for the health of her Majesty. The Gazette this evening said this evening that the Queen was much better and upon the mending hand but it was only lighting before death.

SUNDAY 20. At 4 a clock this morning Her Majesty alarmed the whole Court with Pangs of Death. The King abandoned himself to all the Weakness and Transport of uncontrollable affliction and his loss in some measure justified his Grieff. The Duke and the Princesses were afflicted in the most sensible degree having in her lost their chief support, their great instructor, their best friend. She recommended them all very tenderly to their father, forgave the Prince who they now say never did desire to see her Majesty, that if he had the King was so softened that he would certainly have forgiven and taken him into his favour. How true it is I can't say. The Queen was heard to say to the King "Take care of Amelia, Caroline will soon follow me." They say she is in a dangerous way with swelling in her knee. Her Majesty continued in the Agonies of Death till between 11 and 12 when she resigned her soul into the Hands of her Maker, to the inexpressible grieff of the whole Court and no doubt will be so to the whole Nation. She told the King she had never during her life given him any uneasiness. I shall know more in time of her behaviour in her last illness which, they say, was wonderful, great and becoming her first station, Virtue and Religion.

Monday 21. Being appointed 3 weeks ago by the Bishop of London to preach before my Lord Mayor at St. Paules so I think it is my Duty to call the Honr. I am able to the Memory of so excellent a Princess.

Saturday 26. Went to town. Dined with Mr Rogers. Supped at the Swan and Hoop with Mr Moseley in Finch Lane. Lay at Barge Yard.

SUNDAY 27. I preached this morning upon the Queen's death at St. Paules. Sir Jo. Barnard, Lord Mayor and 4 Aldermen there. Dined with the Lord Mayor at Grocers Hall.

Thursday 31. A messenger this morning brought me word that Dr. Watson [251] died last night. I went to town. Waited upon the Master of the Rolls who sent immediately to the Lord Chancellor which gave me good hopes I shall succeed.

DECEMBER 1737

Friday 1. Waited upon Mr Idle, Secretary to the Presentations, who mentioned my request to the Lord Chancellor who told him that I should be Rector of St. Stephen's Walbrook and accordingly the papers should be drawn up.

Monday 4. I this day received the Fiat for the Great Seal for which I paid Mr Idle 15 Guineas and tomorrow I am to have the Great Seal.

Tuesday 5. This day I received my Presentation for the Living of St. Stephen's Walbrook and St. Benet's Sherehogg and carried it to the Bishop of London. Fees of the Great Seal £18. 10. 0. Waited in the evening upon my Lord Chancellor who received me with a great deal of goodness and told me he was very well pleased that he had done it for me. Gave his gentleman £2. 8. 0.

---

[251] Joseph Watson, D.D., B.N.C. Oxon. Lecturer at St Botolph, Bishopsgate 1711 and rector of St Stephen's Walbrook and St Benet Sherehogg from 1719 until his death in 1737. Died in Hatton Garden and buried in St Stephen's Walbrook.

Porter £1. 1. 0. 4 Footmen £1. 0. 0. To the Master of the Rolls'
servants £1. 1. 0. Coach Hire for 5 days £2. 2. 0.

Wednesday 6. At home.

Thursday 7. In town.

Friday 8. This day I was instituted by the Bishop of London at
White Hall. His secretary £6. 6. 0. His officers in the Common.
£5. 15. 0. Servants 5s. Dined at Court. Came home with Mr
Venn. Left my papers at the Archdeacon of London's office for
his Mandate of Induction.

Friday 15. Dr. Watson buried.

Saturday 16. I walked at the Queen's funeral. It was not
managed with that Decency one would have wished. A great
deal of confusion in marshalling the procession. It began at 6 and
was over at a quarter after 9. The Princess Amelia walked as Chief
Mourner assisted by the Dutchess of Mountague and the Dutchess
of St. Albans held up her train and she was supported by the Duke
of Grafton and the Duke of Dorset. I came to Barge Yard about
12.

SUNDAY 17. Dined with Sergt. Skinner in Chancery Lane.
Came home in the evening.

Monday 18. Went to town. Spent the evening with Dr.
Anderson at a Coffee House corner of Fleet Ditch. Lay at Barge
Yard.

Tuesday 20. This day (my father's Birth Day) I was inducted
to the Rectory of St. Stephen Walbrook by the Revd. Mr Bis-
cowe, Rector of St. Martin's Outwich, a good No. of the
Principal of both Parishes being by. Afterwards I treated upon a
General Invitation above 50 of my Parishioners of both parishes
at Dinner at the Fountain Tavern in Bucklersbury. A very good
Entertainment of 17 Dishes of Meat. Cost, wine and all, near £15.
The Archdeacon of London's Fee for a Mandate £1. 5. 0. Lay at
Barge Yard.

Wednesday 21. St. Thos. Day. I read prayers at my church for
the first time. Dined at home.

Thursday 22. At home.

Friday 23. At St. Stephen's. Dined with the Master of the

Rolls. His Honr. is of the opinion that there is no putting an end to the pernicious custom of drinking Gin etc. without laying such a Duty upon the Still Head as will prevent its being retailed unless at an excessive price. Ordered me to desire Mr Vernon and the Commissioners of Excise to think of proposing a Method for the better suppressing it and that I might assure him that Sir R. W. and the Parliament would willingly come into any scheme to suppress it. Mem. to wait upon Mr Vernon at the Excise Office next Thursday with the message. The Master told me that the King desired Dr. Butler, Clerk of the Closet to the late Queen, might preach before him in the Princess Amelia's Apartments. He preached upon the subject of being bettered by afflictions which affected his Majesty so much that he desired the sermon and assured him that he would do something very good for him. The Master desired this might be known publickly. It was told him by the Bishop of Oxford. The Master seemed mightily pleased and was in hopes it would be of great service to the Publick as well as his Private Family, which will be a pleasure to everybody and make even the death of her Majesty (so great a seeming loss) of Advantage to the Nation. Sat at Grigsby's Coffee House with Mr Christian and lay at Barge Yard.

Saturday 24. Came home.

Christmas Day 25. I preached for the first time as Rector of St. Stephen's Walbrook and afterwards administered the Sacrament to a little above 30 seemingly serious people. Collected £1. 13. 2.

St. Stephen. At home.

St. John. Mr Clements dined with me at Newington.

Innocents Day. I read prayers at my own church.

Thursday 29. I had the large house overagainst the Church belonging to me as Rector surveyed by Mr Dance,[252] Clerk of the

[252] George Dance, Clerk of the City Works from 1735 until shortly before his death in 1768. Designed the Mansion House, St Leonard's Shoreditch, St Matthew's Bethnal Green, St Botolph's, Aldgate, the Fleet Market, Surgeon's Hall, the Corn Exchange Mark Lane, and was associated with Sir Robert Taylor in alterations to London Bridge 1756–60 (Colvin, *Dictionary of British Architects,* pp. 164–5).

City Works, in order to sue for Dilapidations. He found it in a ruinous condition and the necessary repairs before it could be tenanted come to £120. Lay at Barge Yard.

Friday 30. Came home.

Saturday 31. Went to town. Desired Mr Prime to wait upon the Executors of Dr. Watson's Will which he will do a Monday. Sat this evening with Whittridge at the 3 Tunns Cornhill till 10 a clock.

Thomas Wilson's Diary
1750

JANUARY

1. We met at the King's Arms about the Fish Market. I find Sir Richard Lloyd is for pleasing some of the great men, that are Commissioners, and to give up several things that are by the last resolution of the House. To that I find this will turn out into a sort of Jobb in the end, for which reason I shall soon leave them. Private interest governs all ranks and orders of men. My wife out of order with cold in her head and bones and looks very thin. I am all over Cholick, pains and Toothe Ache.

2. The Bishop of Peterborough,[1] Mr Lewis and Mr Lloyd came to see me. Jenny went away and gave her 17s. 6d. A very fine day tho' I am mightily out of order.

6. Mr Halsal called upon me and dined. I showed him the Tombs etc. and got so violent a cold that at night I was seised with great Cholicky Pains [2] all over me and did not sleep all night. Last Wednesday the India Company met and by a Ballot it was carried against the Directors who were for complying with the late act for reducing interest by a majority of 87. Mr Pelham, Lord

---

[1] John Thomas, Bishop of Peterborough 1747. Translated to Winchester 1757.

[2] Dr Wilson's Cure for Cholick:

"2 oz. of Senna pluckt from the large stalks. 1 oz of the best Rheubarb sliced thin. 3 oz. of Turkey Figgs slit. A Lb. and an ½ of Raisins stoned. 2 oz. of stick liquorice sliced. Two handfulls of Red Field Poppy Leaves, with the black taken off. Put them all into 3 qrts. of the best Anniseed water (half double and half singles) and let them stand in a wide mouthed glass or glazed pott in the sun or by the fire tyed down close for about a week. Shake often. Then strain thro' a coarse cloth and when settled bottle it for use. In common cases take 3 spoonfulls going to bed and 3 next morning. In extream cases you may take 4 or 5 or even 6 spoonfulls at once. It is best to make this Medicine when the Poppies are in season."

222

Anson, Duke of Bedford etc. were to ballot and influence all they could. This was reckoned very mean and I think they will lose their credit in the city and if there should be a war will never be able to raise money. What step they will take next I cannot tell, but they have not given up their scheme.

7. Not having slept all night and being in great pain I took a large dose of Infusion of Senna and of Manna which worked well but did not take away the pain. At night I took a Bolus of Methindate which gave me great ease and I slept well and I hope the fit is abated.

8. Dr. Nicholl [3] came to see me. He tells me that the Bishop of London consults often with Beavercroft and that he is to have £100 a year added to his own salary to do the Society's and the Bishop's business and rarely it will be done. Surely there never was such weakness as this. A creature that can scarcely write a sentence of English. Last wednesday Lord Pembroke met Mr Smith, one of our Trustees for the Fish Market, and insulted him in a most opprobrious manner at Horace Walpole's and afterwards followed him in the street cursing and abusing him and swearing he would have his blood. Under such direction no body will wonder that the bridge [4] had miscarried and indeed I shall be

[3] Dr Nicholl, Prebendary of Westminster and Headmaster of Westminster School.

[4] In 1738 Charles Labelye was appointed by the River Commissioners engineer for a New Westminster Bridge, his commission being to provide stone piers on which either a stone or a timber superstructure could be erected. Labelye, a Swiss, was a protégé of the Earl of Pembroke and his appointment gave great offence to British architects. Pembroke laid the foundation stone on 29 January 1738/9 and in the building of the piers caissons were used for the first time in England. Unfortunately a subsidence took place as the work was nearing completion and it was not until Nov. 1750 that the bridge was open to the public. This disaster and the consequent delay occasioned vigorous attacks on Lord Pembroke, Labelye and the Commissioners. Batty Langley publishing in 1748 *A Survey of Westminster Bridge as 'tis Sinking into Ruin* violently attacking the Commissioners for employing "an insolvent, ignorant arrogating Swiss". Labelye was, however, provided with an honorarium of £2000 by the Commissioners "for his great fidelity and extraordinary labour and attendance, skill and diligence". He became a naturalized British subject in 1746 but after the completion of the Bridge returned to France. The Bridge was replaced by the present Westminster Bridge in 1861 (Colvin, *Dictionary of British Architects*, pp. 351–2).

surprised if it ever be finished. Nobody of sense will come to the Board and he has driven most of them away, so that for 7 months there were no meetings at all.

9. This morning we had a meeting about the Fish Market and the Commissioners of the Bridge conveyed to us ground for a temporary one. Neither can we have the whole. Lord Pembroke did it very unwillingly and some days before with great execration declared we should not have it and wished all evil to himself if we had an Inch at present and yet after he did it he went home and was taken ill suddenly and died [5] in the night. A very remarkable thing. But there has been a little madness in the family for an age past.

10. I went into the city and ordered the sale of my 4 per cents which brought £2369 [6] which I gave into the hands of Mr Dangerfield to make the best interest he could of it. Nobody believes that the scheme for reducing interest of money will take place, tho' people are spoke to about it as if the Ministry were to get themselves something by it.

13. This evening the late order of Council relating to the

[5] "Lord Pembroke died last night. He had been at the Bridge Committee in the morning, where, according to custom, he fell into an outrageous passion; as my Lord Chesterfield told him, that ever since the pier sunk he has constantly been *damning* and *sinking*. The watermen say today, that now the great *pier* (peer) is quite gone" (Horace Walpole to Mann, 10 January 1750).

[6] Note at the beginning of Diary.
"Cash. Jan. 10. 1749.

"Sold my 2300 Bank Annuities and left Produce to be laid out by Mr Dangerfield a Broker in the City, in Exchange Alley, and he promises to make me 6s per cent. and to have Government security for it by lending for month. And I intend to see the India Bonds and to put them in the same way. He has given me a note for the £2300. They sold for £2369.
"Jan. 13th.

"Left with Mr Dangerfield 6 India Bonds which he is accountable to me for and is to be laid out with the rest to bring in interest by the Month. He gave me his note. Jan. 16. Lent out at 6 per cent.

"Dr Wilson seems to have been very comfortably off, for in the front fly leaf of his diary for 1750 he gave a list of his 'estates and Cash 1749–50'. Together with the above holdings, his estates in Cheshire, Bedford, and the Isle of Man, the value of his house in Dean's Yard together with furniture and plate and his wife's property, made them both worth about £16,000."

cattle was revised. How weak is this. Not to forsee what mischief it was likely to do and no good could follow from it. Lord Chancellor orders the Accountant General to subscribe the money of Minors, Ideots etc. unless before the 12 of next month they should declare their Dissent to it.

14. There being a Charity sermon at our church I preached at the Somerset Chappell and afterwards dined with Mr Murrell. Called upon the Bishop of London. Brought Dr. Bruce home with me. Talked about Wynne's affair.

15. This Fish Market opened this morning at 7 and vast Quantityes of Cod etc. was brought up and there being vast Nos. of Byers the price was very high, 'til towards afternoon. The Fishmongers came down and did all they could to damp the affair, but I think it will not be in their Power, if no Jobbs are made by some of our own people. Something appears already. I will oppose it in every shape and if I can't carry it I will withdraw from the trust which we are at liberty to do by the Act.

16. Dangerfield sold my 6 India Bonds [7] and put the money out with the rest. I have taken his receipt for them and his Promise of doing properly by me.

17. Went out this night at the Sun Tavern and settled the Comptrollers Duty and Mr Moore to be his clerk and to take care of everything relating to the market and he was called in and told so. Long Debates on the Mutiny Bill, which I suppose will be altered by the Ministry to make it go down better. Doddington [8] spoke against the Mutiny Bill in times of peace, the civil magistrates being sufficient.

18, 19, 20. Complains haveing been made of the Fishmongers and combining against the Market we met again and are to apply for a new Bill to make the last stronger and to destroy entirely the Well Boates and Store Boates etc.

23. Great Debates about the Mutiny Bill. The Speaker and all the Lawyers were for amending it in relation to the Oath of

[7] See note for 10 Jan.

[8] George Bubb Doddington (1691–1762), Lord Melcombe. From 1722–54 M.P. for Bridgwater and from 1755–7 for Weymouth.

Secrecy, by making it then amenable and oblige them to a discovery if called upon by a Court of Law which is certainly right.

26. Mrs Clayton from Liverpool and Miss Case dined with us. She is a sensible shrewd woman and has restored the broken fortunes of several of her relations. This day we agreed in Chapter with Mr Combes and Mr Goodman to apply to Parliament for the Erecting of a New Fish Market upon the scite of ground where the Quakers Tavern stood. Dr. Taylor [9] was the only person that opposed it and in a very unprecedented manner endeavoured to break up the Chapter. How the Dean may resent it I cannot tell. I am sure I should in another sort of manner. Mr. West agreed for a fine of £350 and Mr Verney's Lease was sealed for Otford. Mr Ingram and Mr Davis spent the evening with us.

27. This day came to Malancholly Account of the Loss of 3 Men of Warr and several India Men at Fort St. David's and some 1000s. drowned. Boscawen was ashore.

28. I preached this day for Dr. Kerrich at St. Margaret's, he being ill. Visited Mr Lane in the evening.

[9] Dr John Taylor, Dr Johnson's friend and schoolfellow, was admitted prebendary in place of Dr Laurence Broderick on 11 July 1746.

Chapter Minutes 25 January 1749–50. "Resolved that Mr Richard Combe assignee of the house granted to Mr John Read for 40 years of the late Market House or the Round Woolstaple and of the office of Keeper and Sweeper of the Market be at liberty to present to Parliament a Petition in the Name of the Dean and Chapter and the said Richard Combes or of the Dean and Chapter only and to proceed therein in order to obtain an Act to pass, or a proper clause or clauses in some other Bill, to enable the Dean and Chapter to revive and restore the said market to the Public Use and the exercise of the said office in some other convenient place and to lay out the money arising from the sale of the said woolstaple in the purchase of such ground or premises as are held of the Dean and Chapter by lease, or, if it conveniently may be, on a Free hold; the expense of which Bill or Clauses the said Richard Combe, together with Joseph Goodman Esq., hath agreed to bear and pay. And in consideration thereof and the said Richard Combe surrendering the remainder of the said term in the said office, that a like lease of 40 years of such new place, when purchased, shall be given to the said Richard Combe and Joseph Goodman and of the said office of Keeper and Sweeper of the market there and the annual market rent of £40 a year, and such further rent as may have been annually reserved on such premises to be purchased if the same are leasehold, as covenant for them or their assigns to build the necessary shops and conveniences for holding the said market and any other building as may be agreed upon and the plan approved by the Dean and Chapter."

30. I read prayers at St. Margaret's and Dr. Bentham [10] preached an excellent sermon and the Bishop of Norwich [11] a very good one at the Abbey. A very great storm at south west.

31. A General Court at the Bank held at Merchant Taylors Hall. Mr Gideon, Mr Tomkins, Mr Bruce all against agreeing to the proposal for lessening the Interest. Mr Walpole and Sir Richard Lloyd etc for it. Upon holding up hands there was at least 5 to one against the proposal, so that the matter is dropt and I think the Ministry could have met with a complete defeat and I am glad of it for they bear us no good. When I came home I met with a Melancholly Letter from my father, not syned by him, that he has the gout all over him without pain and I am sadly afraid it is the breaking up of his constitution. God forbid. I am afraid he has got cold by doing some Imprudent Thing. I shall write to him and several other friends in the Island tomorrow.

FEBRUARY

1, 2, 3. The greatest storms of wind and rain. Wind W. and S.W. and S. I almost ever knew in my life. The Petition for the Fish Market delivered to the House of Commons by Sir T. Warren and committed for Tuesday next. Saw the Speaker yesterday who says baiting the acrimonious Dr. Middleton Sherlock a very Ingenious Treatise. Spoke much about the want of Publick Spirit and sad way of the great spending of time and money. Last night Dr. Taylor talked of filing a Bill against the Broadway, for which he appears to be a very great fool, as well as a knave, and this day exposed himself about his reasons for not agreeing with Mr Combes which was founded upon misrepresentation as well as untruths. And the Dean spoke to him with great and proper resentment and I think none of our body will ever have any more regard for him. They talk of a new scheme

[10] Edward Bentham, D.D., Fellow of Oriel 1731, Vice-Principal of Magdalen Hall 1730, canon of Christ Church 1754 and Regius Professor of Divinity 1763–7. Brother of James Bentham, canon of Ely and historian of Ely Cathedral.

[11] Thomas Hayter, Bishop of Norwich 1749. Translated to London in 1761. As Archdeacon of York he has appeared before in the Diary.

for raising money to pay off the India Company and a Lottery but their weakness has been already too much shewn for the City to come into a new one. Mr Ingram tells me that the Ministry are jealous of one another and that the Duke of Bedford went to get N. out to be Premier, for which he is an unfit as any other. The King has fixed his going for the 1st May, tho' I think the Business will not be over so soon, but go he will and his father went for the last time at just the same age!

5, 6, 7. Very windy and rainy. Great Ship Wrecks and more Melancholly Accounts to be expected. Captain Littler luckily not sailed from Liverpool.

8. Very windy thus morning. Wind S.W. and warm. At 45 minutes after 12 the Two Cityes of London and Westminster were alarmed with a violent shock of an *Earthquake*.[12] It affected People and Houses very differently. Some thought it was a prodigious weight thrown upon the roof, others that the side of the house was blown down. Others felt it more below stairs. There was first a trembling and then a Report like thunder and then a Shake. The Bank, East India and S.S. House were mostly alarmed as were the Treasury and Westminster Hall here. Most people thought it was the blowing up of Powder Milns, but this vanished in the evening. This tremendous shock did not hinder 12 or 1300 people from going to the Masquerade this evening and I believe they would have gone if 1000 Houses had sunk into the earth.

[12] Horace Walpole to Mann, 25 February 1750. "You know we have had an earthquake. Mr Chute's Francesco says that a few evenings before it there was a bright cloud, which the mob called *The Bloody Cloud*; that he had been told there never were earthquakes in England, or else he should have known by that symptom that there would be one within a week. I was told that Sir Isaac Newton foretold a great alteration in the climate in the year '50 and that he wished he could live to see it. Jupiter, I think, has jogged us three degrees nearer the sun; but I don't tell you this for Gospel, though I talk as bad astronomy as if I were inspired."

At the beginning of the Diary for 1750 Dr Wilson began to make notes on "Remarkable Events During the Year": "Jan 23. A Red and Bloody Canopy encompassed the sky. A most remarkable one at 9 a clock Feb. 16 a few nights before the earthquake. Also notes on the earthquake at Constantinople on Oct. 6th–9th."

9. Dr. Kerrich and Mr Ingram and Mr Gall spent the evening with me.

10. I preached at Walbrook. I don't find people are much affected with the shock as one would have imagined; but they are grown callous and regard nothing but their pleasures.

11. At the Society, Called a General Meeting for Tuesday next to consider of subscribing their Annuities into the New Scheme which they say here will take. Indeed for these 2 dayes people are come in owing to a very fallacious pamphlet published yesterday by Sir Jo. Barnard, which was cooked up last week by him and Mr Pelham. In which they are cajoled and threatened and wheedled out of their senses. I apprehend they have got Gideon over tho' he does not appear publickly for fear of offending the people in the Abbey. Colebrooke is a mighty advocate. These Decoy Ducks must be well taken care of to come into a scheme apparently to their disadvantage.

12. Went to see the Bishop's Improvements at Fulham, which are very great ones. The Great New Room 36 by 24. The Gardens will be better.

20. At the Society. Came to a Resolution to subscribe our money into the New Scheme.[13] Against Archdeacon Denne's opinion absolutely, but the whole town is run Madd; and are as fond of a loss of what they are worth as in the year '20 they were crazy with Imaginery Estates. Anything would do with the English Nation. A Pannick brought the Pretender to Derby and this stroke on Publick Credit may bring him to London if we have any Disturbances abroad, and sure no one can be so sanguine as to think we shall be easy 7 years to come. Dined this day with Mr Godfrey in Crutched Friars. Wrote a Letter to the Corresponding Society in Dublin about a school soon to be erected in Galway. People subscribe fast so I think they will carry their point at last. Very hot weather.

[13] S.P.C.K. Minutes. "The Society taking the Minute of the 13th inst. relating to the subscription of their Annuities, under consideration, came to the following resolution. Viz. That Mr Archdeacon Denne be desired to subscribe the New Joint Stock of the Society's South Sea Annuities standing in his name on the terms proposed by the Honble. House of Commons 29 Nov. 1749."

21, 22. Remarkably warm. Preached at Walbrook.

26. The South Sea Company met again to reconsider the Reduction Scheme, but determined not to come into it as they think they have not time to be paid off as other people are.

27. The Bank met to reconsider and Colebrooke moved for consenting to it and was seconded by Gideon with a Declamation about the following the great example of the head of the Law so famous for his Judgment and Equity and telling them that Bank Stock would rise upon coming to a resolution of subscribing. But this was owing to the Terrors artfully thrown out by the government. That they would be distressed, if they did not. I observed this time no Questions were asked at the Door and the Hall filled with people that they could depend on (not half Proprietory) and that before 11 a clock. So that upon holding up of hands there was a considerable majority for subscribing, without giving any other reason than following example. So fickle are the people of England and so easily governed by two or three leading men who have got the plunder of this poor undone nation which is capable of becoming a prey to France, whenever she thinks it has interest to quarrel with us. And in less than 7 years we shall want to raise new money and who will lend it us or what security will there be. In all probability the Forreigners will draw out and leave the Ballance of Paper on our hands and then we shall be in a pretty condition.

28. They are all crowding to subscribe, who shall have first advantage of losing a quarter of what they are worth 7 years next. A hard frost last night and today very cold but it will not last long. Mr Combes and Mr Gall spent the evening with me. Letter from Mr Eyre of Galway and Sandforth with Bills for £76. 3. 6. from Macklin.

MARCH

1. Rain and warm day. Great lights in the east and N. last night about 9 a clock.

2, 3. So warm and close that many fear another shock of an earthquake.

6. An Opinion of Counsel was sent us that we had as Prebendaries a Right to vote at this Election of Middlesex and I find they intend to go for Honeywood.

8. This morning at 25 minutes after 5 we were alarmed with a much severer shock of an Earth Q. than the last.[14] It began with shaking the whole house and every thing in the room and then a Loud Report much louder than thunder. How far this has been felt cannot yet be told. But certainly it was much severer than the last and we may expect more. I pray God fit us for whatever His Providence shall think fit. I went this morning to Brentford to poll for Mr Coke with Mr Vernon, Mr Phillips and Mr Steadman. He carried it against Honeywood by a majority of 416. There was a great deal of corruption on the other side which was the reason of my voting at all. We dined at an Ale House at Kensington Gravell Pitts. Very warm day.

10. Hott and so on 11th. This evening there was in the south a surprising Phemenemon in the air and a Ball of Fire was seen to shoot thro' the air and fall as it were beyond Buckingham House.

[14] Horace Walpole to Mann, 11 March 1750:
"Portents and Prodigies are grown so frequent
That they have lost their Name.
My text is not literally true; but as far as earthquakes go towards lowering the price of wonderful commodities, to be sure we are overstocked. We have had a second, much more violent than the first; and you must not be surprised if by the next post you hear of a burning mountain sprung up in Smithfield. In the night between Wednesday and Thursday last (exactly a month after the former shock) the earth had a shivering fit between one and two; but so slight that if no more had followed, I don't believe it would have been noticed. . . . I had been awake and scarce dozed again . . . on a sudden I felt my bolster lift up my head. I thought somebody was getting from under my bed, but soon found it was a strong earthquake, but lasted near half a minute, with a violent vibration and loud roaring. I rang my bell; my servant came in frightened out of his senses; in an instant we heard all the windows in the neighbourhood going up. I got up and found people running into the streets, but saw no mischief done: there has been some; two old houses flung down, several chimneys and much china ware. The bells rang in several houses. Admiral Knowles, who has lived in Jamaica, and felt seven there, says this was more violent than any of them. Francesco prefers it to the dreadful one at Leghorn. The wise say that if we have not rain soon, we shall certainly have more. Several people are going out of town, for it has nowhere reached above ten miles from London: they say they are not frightened, but that it is such fine weather. Lord! One cannot help going."

From the air it looked too likely as if we should have another Shock.

12. I preached this morning at my own church on the subject of the Mortality amongst the Cattle and the Earth Quakes to a very attentive congregation. Very warm day. I was taken this evening with a shivering fitt and a sickness in my stomack. Could eat nothing. Mr Murrey of Chester dined with me.

13. Very much out of order. Eat a little pudding and took Rheubarb and Senna at night.

14. At home. A little better but did not go out. Weather very warm and wind S.S.W.

15. Took an airing and came home better.

16. Our Annual Meeting of Georgia. Mr Franklin preached and we dined at the Horn Tavern. Much cooler. The wind in the north which I am glad of. A great many families running out of town for fear of the next shock of an E. Quake which they are apprehensive of April 15th. The Bishop of Oxford preached an excellent sermon on the occasion at St. James's last Sunday as did the Bishop of Exeter at the Chappell before the King. And the Bishop of Salisbury is printing a letter to his clergy on the same subject.[15]

18. I preached an old sermon on the same subject and people in general very attentive and serious. How long it will continue I cannot tell. People of Quality flying out of town for fear of another shock and prophaning the Sabbath by travelling of a

[15] "Showers of sermons and exhortations. Secker, the Jesuitical Bishop of Oxford began the mode. He heard the women were all going out of town to avoid the next earthquake, and so for fear of losing the Easter Offerings he set . . . to advise them to await God's good pleasure. . . . But what is more astounding Sherlock (Sarum) who has much better sense, and much less of the Popish Confessor, has been running a race with him for the old ladies and has written a Pastoral Letter, of which 10,000 were sold in two days. You never read so imprudent, so absurd a piece. The earthquake which has done no hurt, in a country where no earthquakes ever did any, is sent, according to the Bishop, to punish bawdy prints, bawdy books (in one of which Mr. Pilkington drew his Lordship's picture), gaming, drinking etc. (No, I admit drinking and avarice, those orthodox vices, are omitted) and all other sins, natural or not, which he makes a principal ingredient to the composition of an earthquake" (Horace Walpole to Mann, 2 April 1750).

Sunday. Strange inconsistencies. But there is no accounting for a General Pannick.[16] The Bishop of Salisbury's letter came out and sells prodigiously. He has not taken notice of the Vices of the Great and tender enough in other cases. We are to meet the Welsh Bishops next Tuesday to consider of a new Impression of Bibles.

22. At the Royal Society they had accounts from the Isle of Wight, Portsmouth, and Bath of a shock of an earthquake last Sunday at six in the afternoon and they say there was one felt in some parts of Kent. Where will these timorous people fly to, to be safe as they call it.

[16] "I told you the women talked of going out of town. Several families are already gone, and many are going today and tomorrow; for what adds to the absurdity is that the second shock having happened exactly a month after the first, it prevails that there will be a third on Thursday next, another month which is to swallow up London. I am almost ready to learn my lesson, but you think I am laughing at you; but it is so true, what Arthur of White's told me last night, that he should put off the last ridotto, which was to be on Thursday, because he learns nobody would come to it. I have advised several who are going to keep their next earthquake in the country to take the bark for it as it is so periodic. Dick Leveson and Mr Rigby, who has supped and stayed late at Bedford House the other night, knocked at several doors, and in a watchman's voice cried 'Past four a clock and a dreadful earthquake'." (Horace Walpole to Mann.)

The general panic is reflected in the notes Dr Wilson made on the flyleaf of his diary for 1750 on the subject of earthquakes. "We do not read", he says, "of any earthquakes before in the Island of Jamaica since it was in the English power, nor before while under the Spaniard. But have had several instances of earthquakes formerly in England and other parts of Europe, tho' more seldom than the rest, therefore it is not unreasonable for us to expect and fear the like. 'Tis true those countries which are very hot or very cold, are least subject to earthquakes and therefore it hath been a matter of wonder in Egypt or Scythia to have the earth tremble. Great Britain and Ireland have been the least liable to earthquakes yet historians mention several." He then mentions the principal earthquakes recorded in England, Europe and other parts from 1081 to 1688 and five examples from the East between the years 344 and 740. On 1 November, 1755 was the terrible earthquake at Lisbon which entirely destroyed the city, the effects of which were felt all over Europe. "There is a most dreadful account of an earthquake at Lisbon," wrote Horace Walpole to George Montagu on 25 November 1755, "but several people will not believe it.... There have been lately such earthquakes and water quakes and rocks rent and other strange phenomena that one would have thought the world very much out of repair. I am not prophet enough to believe that such convulsions relate solely to the struggle between Mr Pitt and Mr Fox, or even portend any between the Georges and the Jameses." See also *The Lisbon Earthquake*, by Sir Thomas Kendrick (1956).

23. Went to visit Mr Richardson at North End. Called on Lady Annandale and Mrs Rogers at Hammersmith. Dined with Mr Richardson, Miss Collier, a sister of the Dr. of the Commons and Miss Highmore, the Limner's daughter.[17] Two very ingenious ladies.

25. Preached my own turn at the Abbey. The same sermon I preached at my own church to a very attentive congregation of midling sort of people. It rained all day and has cooled the air finely. They talk of an earthquake at Liege that has thrown down 200 houses. Mr Boleme and Mr Clements dined with me.

26. A great storm and rained a good deal in the night.

28. I preached the same sermon at Court with a great many alterations and spoke strongly against Masquerades, Playing at Cards of Sundays etc. The Princess Amelia not at Church. She has not been on Fridays all this Lent because it hinders her from dressing to go to the Drawing Room! All decency gone. I dined at Court. Mr Shaub, Dr. Head, Mr. Molesworth.

30. I preached the same sermon at St. Sepulchre's to a large audience and a very attentive one. People seem to be mightily affected. God grant they may continue so. Abundance of persons are running out of town for fear of a return of the earthquake and many foolish persons hawked about sheets full of enthusiasm and madness which will be of very ill effect if nothing should happen on the period.

31. By letters we hear that a pretty violent shock has been felt last Sunday evening in the Isle of White and at Portsmouth.

APRIL

1. Preached at my own church and had the largest number of people I ever remember at the Sacrament and people very serious.

2. We met the Welsh Bishops who came to a Resolution to

[17] Joseph Highmore (1692–1780). His daughter Susanna married in 1761 the Rev. John Duncombe of Canterbury and in 1762 Highmore retired from business as a portrait painter, sold his collection of pictures and went to live with them at Canterbury. Buried in Canterbury Cathedral.

print another impression of Bibles. of 15000 on the same letter and paper but leaving out the form of Ordination, the Apocrypha and Psalter.

3. At the Society. Confirmed the former resolution and I ordered 1000 of Mr Bacon's sermons to himself and many others.

4. My wife being terryfyed with thoughts of another shock I consented, though much against my Judgment and Inclination, to go to Mr Richardson's and lay there.

5. At a Chapter and nobody asking for Alconbury it was given to the Dean to dispose of. People so alarmed that many 100ds are going out of town. Lay at North End.

6. Preached my own turn at the Abbey and returned to North End and came back with my wife home. Some 100ds of people lay last night in the fields about town and many sat up in Coaches in Hyde Park all night but God be thanked nothing happened.

7. Letters in town that they have had a shock at Liverpool and Chester last Thursday night at $\frac{1}{2}$ an hour after ten, which they say affected all the neighbourhood 5 miles around.

8. Dr. Delany preached a Charity Sermon at my Church. I think not at all judicious to this congregation against Luxurious Eating etc. and computed that a penny a day out of every meal would keep all the Charity Scholars in England! Strange Calculation.

9. At the Society. 4 Welch Bishops.[18] The Bishop of Llandaff did not seem to care whether any Bibles ever came into his diocese. Wants to destroy the Language which it will never be in any body's power to do. Mr Jones having shown the Inconveniences of doing it.

10. At the Society. Agreed with Mr Baskett to print 15000 Bibles at £13 13s. a sheet and with Mr Caston for a Fount of Types at 3s. 6d. a pound to be ready next August and Mr Baskett agrees to deliver the Bibles collected in one year and 3 quarters after he has received the types.

12. The King went to the House to put an end to the Sessions.

[18] Dr Zachary Pearce (Bangor), Hon. Robert Hay Drummond (St Asaph), Richard Trevor (St David's), Edward Cressett (Llandaff).

The Speaker made a very long speech extolling the Reduction of Interest and the Flourishing State of the Publick Credit tho' many other good bills pased this sessions and told them in the end that Luxury etc. would destroy us. Dined with Mr Combes, Goodman etc. at the Horn Tavern on Account of the passing of the Flesh Market act. Went to see poor Mrs Conner who has been a dying for 4 dayes and found her very ill. Violent inflammation on her lungs and a fever.

13. Preached at my own church. Mrs Conner a little better.

14. Report as if the Zarina had begin hostilityes against Sweden. The King talks of being against the aggressor but this will not do. He had better sit still and do nothing lest he brings us into a General Warr.

15. Preached at our Church.

16. Preached at my own church last night. The advertisements stuck up against Masquerades in all publick places about these two cities, but they will I fear have little effect. They were sent to all the Great People.

17. Preached at the Abbey. Went to St. Paules. Heard the Bishop of Worcester [19] against the Idleness of the Poor and their drinking of gin. An admirable sermon. Dined at Dolleys.

18. I hear the Prince of Wales declares he will not himself nor suffer any of his servants to go to the next Masquerade. However they have published for next wednesday certain.

19. Put to the Press a little pamphlet against it. To come out a Saturday but nothing I fear will do to prevent it.

20. Paid £10 to Mr Davies for the money awarded for the Broadway Chappell which he has no right to but I did it to avoid a Law suit with him.

23. Preached at my own church yesterday. My little Touch about the Masquerades was printed and published which I believe will put the Sheriff Janssen and the Justices of Westminster upon something to stop it.

24. Took leave of several people in order to go to Tunbridge tomorrow. It is very cold N.E. Wind. Letter from my father.

[19] Dr Isaac Maddox.

25. Set out thro' the citty to the Wells. Breakfasted at Farnborough and dined at 7 Oakes.

26. Rained a little. Capt. Smith, Mr Dowding here.

27. I visited Capt. Smith, Mr Dowding, Mr Murrey. A fine day.

28. Foggy morning and cold.

MAY

4. Set out for London.[20]

6. Preached at my own church.

8. Bishop of London's Visitation. Dined at Sion College.

9. Read a Lecture at the Abbey. Dined with Dr. Johnson. Set out with him and lay at Farnborough.

10. Returned to Tunbridge.

13. Preached for Mr Dowding and read prayers in the afternoon.

14. Set out [21] at 4 this morning. Very raw and cold. Dined with Mr Gell. Very ill of the Cholick. Lay at the Coffee House. A very bad night.

[20] For this journey to London Dr Wilson gives a shopping list in the fly-leaf of his Diary.

Mem. for London May 5th.

"A hoop for my wife—in the press up two pairs of stairs.

"6 pds. of Jar Raisins from Wilson.

"2 papers and ½ pd. of Jordan Almonds.

"My clothes to be made at Mr Dawes.

"To bring my soap to shave with and to bye a brush.

"To enquire for Capt. Gibson at the New England Coffee House or of Chancellor Johnson White Hall.

"To enquire when the Society for Promoting Christian Knowledge meets.

"A pint of Orange Flower water from Mrs Temple.

½ lb. of snuff."

[21] *Mem. May 13th.*

"4 pd. of Jar Raisins. The coachman's coat, salt, the surtains, lampreys at Mrs Dawes'

"To send my wife 4 pd. more of Jar Raisins and the Hams from New England.

"Mem. Wheeler, Tunbridge Wells carrier sets out from the Old King's Head in Southwark Tuesdays and Fridays at Noon and comes to the Wells Wednesdays and Saturdays in the afternoon."

15. The Messiah was performed the second time at the Foundling Hospital. About 800 Persons. I was there but much out of order and had an indifferent night.

16. Read a Lecture at the Abbey and set out for Farnborough. A little better.

17. Came home, shewed my wife my father's letter and she consents that I should go in Whitsun week for the Isle of Man.[22]

[22] At the back of his diary for 1750 Dr Wilson sets out his expenses at Tunbridge and on his journey to the Isle of Man.

1750. Expenses at Tunbridge.

April 24. Farnborough and 7 Oakes.		19.	6.
To Williams 6 months at 5s a month.	1.	10.	0.
To himself and boy.		3.	6.
A Load of Wood.		14.	6.
Musick Subscription.		10.	0.
Turnpikes.		4.	3.
To pocket money.	1.	1.	0.
Hollonby for spinning.		12.	0.
For a mattress.		13.	0.
Neats Foot Oil.		1.	2.
Pocket Money to London.	2.	2.	0.
Grocery, Snuff etc.		10.	6.
My horses keeping.	2.	5.	6.
Making of clothes. 2 pair of servants' sheets.	1.	8.	6.
Carriage of Goods.			
M. W. House Expenses.	6.	6.	0.
Expenses to London.	3.	12.	0.
Making of clothes.	2.	3.	9.
2 Loads of Wood.	1.	8.	0.
Oates.		4.	0.
1 load of Wood.		14.	0.
Subscriptions and Play.		15.	0.
M. W. House expenses June 5th.	20.	0.	0.
Expenses on the Road to the Isle of Man. Sea and Land.	8	10.	0.
In the Isle of Man.	5.	5.	0.
A piece of cloth. Repaid by my father.		19.	6.
To Mr Lane. Expenses on the road.	2.	2.	0.
To Mr Lane. Horse Hire and to himself.	6.	16.	0.
My own expenses back.	7.	18	0.
Carriage of goods there and back again.	2.	12.	0.
Expenses in the Isle. Servants etc.	7.	7.	0.
Carriage of Goods to Tunbridge.		15.	0.
Expenses to London on the road	1.	15.	0.
Pocket money.	2.	2.	0.

18. Much out of order. Took soap pills.

28. Visited Mr Perry at Penshurst and dined with Sir Thos. Jansen. A very cold windy day.

29. Dined with the Skinners Company. Came home. Not well.

30. A very bad night.

31. A sore throat and head ache.

JUNE

1. Lat night very restless. Sore throat so that I could not go to town [23] as I purposed. Rained gently most part of last night and today.

On the previous page further notes of "My wife's expenses in my absence besides the £20 I left with her."

To Dr. Johnson.	4.	4.	0.
Mr Dowding.	1.	1.	0.
The Taylor.		12.	5.
House Expenses.	3.	16.	0.
Sept. 2nd. House expenses.	6.	6.	0.
1 doz. of Port.	1.	0.	0.
1 doz. of Mountain.	1.	0.	0.
Maids' Mourning.	3.	3.	0.
Hire of Horses in my absence.		18.	6.
1 doz. of China Plates.	1.	1.	0.
Sept. 15. Dr Johnson.	1.	1.	0.
Oct. 3. ½ doz of Port.		10.	0.

[23] "*Mem. June 2nd.*

"Soap in the drawer in the Physick Closet Passage Room to carry with me and take one oz. a day on the Journey.

"To bye an 8vo. book 'God's Judgment Upon the Gentile Apostasized Church against the Modern Hypothesis of Some Eminent Apocalyptical Writers. Lond. 1713.' To recommend it to Mr Eyre."

"*Mem. for the Isle of Man.*

"To carry my father Spring Temple Spectacles 3 pair 75 to 90. To carry him the Book on the Sacrament in my study and some of Mr Bacon's sermons. To ask Mr Blydistone for a pint of Juniper Water and to take a Bottle of Friars Balsam along with me.

"My wine comes on Whit Monday early in the morning. Clear one of the Bins.

"To bye at Blakinston 6pd. of Jar Raisins and 4pd. of dry sixpenny.

To desire Dr Johnson to speak to Mr Pomeroy for Fry the Butcher and Hollanby.

"*Tincture for the Cholick.* Mr Payne in Beaufort Buildings. 10s. a quart. A glass over night.

4. Set out for London and lay at Farnborough 7s. 6d.

5. Came to London. Dined with Mr Davis and lay at the Coffee House. Mr Moseley spent the evening. 5s.

6. Set out at ten. Called at Ricks End and lay at the White Hart at St. Albans' An excellent and reasonable Inn. Visited Mr G. Pembroke, an Attorney, and receiver general of the Land Tax. A very sensible worthy man. Left my Portmantua Trunk and Hatt Box at the Crown to be put into the Warrington or Liverpool waggon a friday morning.

7. Set out for Harpenden. Manor of Shires 5 miles off. A beautiful common. Kept Court at the Red Lyon and dined at the Bull on the Common. Treated by Whitearmiger Esq., who lives at Rothampstead and ought to renew near 9 years gone. Warm hot weather. Set out at 3 and went thro' Woburn to Newport Pagnell (fine road) except a mile of Sands which we avoided by going thro' the woods the 2nd. turning after you set out from Woburn on the right hand. Got to Newport at 9, They had put up a New Ring of Bells and all the people drunk and noisy. In great pain with the cholick. Took Turpentine which eased me for a few hours.

8. Took another dose of Turpentine and was perfectly easy. Set out in the coach cross the country, excessive bad roads 10. miles. To Stoke Bruern. Mr Leigh gone to Northampton. Went on to Fosters Brook. Dined there and sent back the coach to Mr Davis and went to the Dun Cow at Dunchurch 16 miles. Expenses of a Guide, dining, servants etc. 12s. 6d. Gave Mr. Lane 1. 1. 0. for Horses and Turn pikes. Rained a little. Enught to lay the dust. Much better today.

9, Set out from Dunchurch at 6. Rode thro' Coventry [24] to

"*Mem.* There is a pint of Orange Flower Water at St Margarett's Coffee House from Mrs Temple.

"To send Mr. Heywood some greene silk for a nightgown.

"To give Mrs Mills an answer to her letter about leaving my Rectory House."

[24] "*Mem.* To enquire for Blanketts for my father at Coventry. Midling size. To send Miss Stevenson 2 bottles of Strasborg's Liquid. Put in my father's Box. Sent it.

"*Mem. for Liverpool.* To visit Mrs Clayton. To subscribe to the Infirmary 2 gns. To see Crebbin.

"*Isle of Man.* Garter Blue Perdusa or White Damask or blue for a nightgown for myself. Linnen for shirts."

Meridon 17 miles To breakfast. Very hott. Set out at 11 and went to Moxam 16 miles to dinner. Set out at 4 and went to Wolseyes Bridge 14 miles. Lay there (not a good inn). Expenses last night and this day. 18s.

10. Set out at 6 and came to the Crown at Stone (an Excellent Inn) 12 miles. Went to the Church. Part of which fallen down last Christmas occasioned by digging a grave too near a pillar. The whole in so ruinous a condition that it is dangerous I think to meet there. Set out at 5 to the old Row Buck 9 miles. Expenses 13s. Rained a little tonight. Most of the people wear White Roses. Stone a miserable poor town. Newcastle a fine well built street and handsome Market House and stands charmingly; and plenty of everything in this country. This a mighty civil good Inn. The roads without mighty good though in some places stony and rough for a coach and worse for post chaises.

11. Set out at 5. Baited at Holmes Chappel 2 Hours and came to cousin Dalton at Warrington for dinner.

12. Drunk some bottled beer and all night found the ill effects of it for I had a pain in my stomach.

13. In great pain all day.

14. This morning early I took a dose of physick. The Rheubarb I took the night before not working. Easier at night.

15. Set out this morning and dined at the Talbot in the afternoon went to Crosby. Not well. Took sack whey and hartshorne and slept tolerably.

16. Pretty well today. The cruiser Capt. Dow came yesterday. The wind contrary.

17. At Crosby.

18. The wind contrary. Went over to Wirral with Mr Halsal. Lookt over all the estate at Londican. The New barn, stable house and necessary house at Stanleys very well done. Cost above £14. New paved Lorrens House. New paved Hostes house with good stone. Intend to build a new house next summer for Peace which will cost with outhouses £150 and when that is done I hope everything will be in order for ten years to come. Lookt over [gap in text]. Things very much out of repair, a new house but slight upon one of the farms. Dined at Stanleys. Gave away 8s. Other expenses 6s. Lay at Mr Whalley's.

19. Dined at Mr Gosforth's. Mr Colquest and Capt Dew. Lay at Mr Whalley's.

20. Wind contrary. Dined at Mr Colquest's. Lay at Mr Whalley's.

21. This morning at 10 a clock weighed anchor at the town side with a fair wind. Got beyond the banks at $\frac{1}{2}$ hour after eleven and landed safe in Douglas harbour, God be praised, at 12 a clock this night. Lay at Mr William Murrey's.

22. At 9 a clock got a horseback and came to Bishopscourt at 12 and found my father much better than I could have expected. Very hearty but feeble in his leggs. Swell much of a night.

23. I was not well all day and slept ill.

24. At Bishopscourt.

25. This morning I drank $\frac{1}{2}$ pint of sea water. Purged me gently. But not well all day. Ill pains in my side and stomach.

27. Dr. Pocock from Dublin came here and presented my father with his Travells.

28. I went with the Dr. to Ramsey. Found the cruiser in the Bay and 10 of his hands ashore under arrest and he one man and a boy left on board. He fired Gunns of Distress but nobody went out to him. The cause is, as I hear it, is this. 2 nights before a Wherry from Ireland came along the Cruiser in Douglas harbour and ill language being given the Cruiser's men boarded the Wherry in search for money and took from them 25 Gns. The next day a large Dogger coming into Douglas Bay the Cruiser's boat went off to search them. In the interim a Mob arose and assaulted the Capt. of the Cruiser, threw stones and wounded him. His men returned to rescue their captain. In the meantime the Dogger made sail. The Cruiser at last was forct to cut away and chasing the Dogger she ran ashore on Ramsea Beach. The Cruiser's men put off in order to board her. Capt. Matt. Christian at the head of 200 men came armed to defend the shipp seized all the cruiser's men in pretence of the Douglas affair and then unloaded the Dogger and put a very rich cargo consisting of

Pepper. Teas etc. from Holland and pretending to be bound for Drontheim, but actually conveyed to our Merchants. They kept them in close confinement till they had unloaded the Dogger and then told them they might have the liberty of the town. In the meantime the Cruiser got some Ramsea men a board and sailed directly for Whitehaven. What will come of this affair I can't tell, but I think the Government of England will hardly bear the insult.

29. The Dr. went to Peel. I rested so ill last night that I was not able to go with him. About 1 Capt. Matt. Christian and the 10 Cruiser's men called here on their way to Castletown. The Irish Wherry having taken an action for 25 Gns. against the men, tho' there were but 2 or 3 concerned and this by the Captain's orders which they were obliged to fulfill. They intend to give Bail, to stand the determination of the Chancery Court which they not caring to do I suppose are all sent to jail. Taking this whole affair together it has been very imprudently managed and may be attended with bad consequences to this poor country. If the Promoters and Carriers of this Iniquitous Trade were to be the only sufferers it would be no great matter but suppose they were to take off the Drawback upon Salt they would ruin us effectually. I have taken down this affair just as I heard it from both sides in order to relate it truly on the other side of the water if called upon.

JULY

1. Went to Ramsea. Preached there. A letter from Capt. Dow desiring I would apply to the governor that some of his men might be sent him to navigate his shipp to Liverpool. He complaining that they detain the Kings Arms and the Tender.

2. I wrote to Mr Taubman to desire that some of the Captain's men might be sent him and he assured me that they were detained for debt and could not be discharged.

3. Sent an answer to Capt. Dow by Mr Lane. Lawyer Christian. Capt. Murphy, Mr Lewhall and James Christian at Guisby's Coffee House here. The Mate and five of the Cruiser's men called here this evening. The Governor thinking better of it,

Sent them to Capt. Dow. They detain the rest to answer at the Chancery Court a Thursday. I believe the Government are sick of the whole affair but they may be called to account for it in London yet.

4. The Deemster Aylmer and Receiver Christian called here and would have me write to Capt. Dow to deliver up the 25 Gns and no more should be heard of the matter. I told him I could not do this because I am not certain whether he was in the right or no in seising it and therefore could not take upon me to advise the giving up the King's money. I find they are all sick of the matter and know not well how to act in the affair, nor do I care how much they blunder.

5. Fine rain all this day an like to continue. Letter from my wife. A malignant disorder in Normandy. Liege in Brabant almost destroyed by an earthquake.

7. I went to Douglas. Lay at Mr Murrey's.

8. Preached at the Chappell. Dined at Mr M. Spent the evening with Capt. Heywood. He is rebuilding the old house a very good one it will be.

9. Came home. Expenses 12s. 6d.

14. Set out for Castletown. A very windy day. Lay at Bally-dool.

15. Preached at Kirk Marlew. Dined with Mr Quayle. Spent the evening at Deemster Taubman's.

16. Went to the Calf which is one of the most delightful Romantick Scenes I ever saw. Returned to Ballydool.

17. Rained all day. Dined with Capt. Heywood. Mr Murrey the Comptroller etc. at Mrs Watkins at Castletown. Lay at Bally-dool.

18. Returned home. Rained all the evening. Expenses 1. 1. 0.

19. 2 letters from my wife by way of Whitehaven. Answered the same day. Wrote to Mr Leland, Mr Kean, Mr Moseley.

26. Miss Steavenson came home.

27. Mr Murrey here.

28. Went and dined with Capt. Murphy of La Zayce and made a visit to Major Christian who has lately been at Dunkeld

to see the Duke of Atholl and brings word that his Grace is very angry about Dow's seising the money and has directed the Solictor General to make complaint to the Commissioners of the Customs against the high infringement of his prerogative. I think this is not so prudent, since it may open such a scare as may bring in the dreadful resentment of the Legislature. They ought to keep things as snugg as possible. A large shipp loaded with Tobacco consigned about 10 days ago to Mr Reeves which to be sure has had the Debenture. This is a scandalous and iniquitous practice. The occasion of infinite perjuries and is a direct robbing of the Treasury. I believe the Running Trade from this Island has doubled since I was here last and all the shipps and wherrys employed by the government do not catch 1 in 50 as a Merchant of this place assured me himself. The Tobacco is now sent to Holland receives the Debenture and then sent here and run from hence. Monstrous quantities of tea. The Tobacco sometimes comes from Glasgow in Dutch Bottoms. Another Large Shipp loaded with Teas and Tobacco etc. from Holland or at least in a Dutch Bottom. This will sure never be allowed. Capt. Dow shewed me the opinion of the present Lord Chancellor when Attorney General. viz. That any Body might seize and condemn any goods from the East Indes without the Company's Leave and landed in England, Ireland or the Isle of Man and ought to be condemned in the Courts there. Q. How is this to be done?

29. Preached at Kirk Michael.

30. Rained and blew excessively.

31. Rained and blowed.

AUGUST

1. At Peel saw the roof put upon the New School. Dined at Mrs Parr's. Mr Carter, Miss Stevenson. Went in the evening to Douglas and lay at Mrs Murrey's.

2. Came home. Letter from my wife of the 17 July. Rained hard. Mr Murrey and Mr Moore here.

3. Rained and blew.

4. In the evening blew hard and about 3 a clock in the morning a Rank Storm. Went aboard Capt. Dow in Ramsea Road. He has wrote to all his friends about the usage he met with at Douglas and Ramsea.

6. A letter from Dow. The Capt. Matt. Christian has threatened that he should not cast off his morrings nor go out of harbour. What is the meaning of this new Insult I can't apprehend. Sure the Court of England will never admit of this behaviour to pass with impunity. I am getting ready to leave the Island tomorrow and to go with the first Shipp, if he can't carry me. My father gave me a silver Branch Candlestick for my wife which he bought some years ago from Dublin, which cost above £20. Put it up in my Portmantua Trunk directed with the Box to Mr Moseley.[25] Wind S.W. blows hard. The Deputy Governor, Receiver etc. gone down to Ramsea. They say to give orders for seizing Dow. If they do he will make resistance and bloodshed may ensue, which I pray God may not happen if he does no hasty imprudent things. I think he must get the better of them in the end. What they want is to provoke him, that they may make reprisals. The Iniquitous Trade now carrying on against the interests of Great Britain can never be permitted to go on with impunity, nor the King's Shipps insulted or maltreated. Perhaps it will give the D. more uneasiness than his offisers imagine. All I fear is any uneasiness it may give my dear father when I am gone by nonsensical lyes. For my own part I shall, as I have done, do everything to shew that I am ever the True Friend of His Majesty and his Government and do all I can to support and encourage the fair Trades. I hear that Capt. Dow went out of harbour when the tide came in with colours flying and is gone to Douglas where I shall follow him tomorrow. The Government here I find would give no orders for arresting or stopping him which they were wise in. Whatever imprudences he may have been guilty of the Courts

[25] "*In a Deal Box sent to Mr Moseley.* 5 Pieces of Linnen. Wares History of England 2 Vol. Strype's History of the Reformation 3 Vol. Folio. 12 small bottles of Hungary Water. 1 Pint of Cologne Geneva. My Thick Cloth Coat and Thin waistcoat. About 2pd. of Soap for the Gravel. A Pair of Stirrup Stockings."

of England are the Judges and the D's Rights will now be determined.

9. I took leave of my dear Father with little hope of ever seeing him again in this world. Pray God we may meet in another. Came to Douglas. Very bad windy weather. S.E.

11. Went to take leave at Ballydool and Castletown. Rained hard. Lay there this night. Came to Douglas, Had a letter from Capt. Dow that he was driven from his anchor from Ramsea Bay and was at Whitehaven. Supped at Mr Forbes. Capt. Heywood, Mr Murrey, Mr Moore. Agreed to go with Capt. Oliver aboard ship bound for Liverpool and he had the best Pilot of the place aboard and a good ship.

12. Preached at Douglas Chappell. At 5 a clock set sail with the wind N.W. a fine gale but dropt and came contrary at 12. Made little way and was not a Monday 6 Leagues from land. In the afternoon wind contrary but got to the Bay about 7 and came to an anchor and rode safe and well. At 9 made sail contrary to common sense and in about ½ hour stuck upon the Point of Barber Sands where we struck and beat for 2 hours. By the Blessing of God it did not blow hard or else we must have gone to pieces and would have been all lost, but by the advise of an Old Guinea Capt, Mr Clay, we cast anchor which held her and the tide coming in and the wind rising we were in the utmost danger of being lost, but she held till 4 a clock in the morning high water and the wind coming fair we providentially landed at the Town side at 6 a Tuesday morning.

14. I went immediately to bed at the Talbot and slept well till 12. Got up and visited Mr Sandforth. Mr Macklin supped with me and I went to bed tolerably well. I was not two hours in bed (having just received a letter from my poor wife that her son dyed the 8th) but I was seized with a violent fit of the cholick. The pain greater than ever. I sent in the morning early for Mr Parr an Apothecary who gave me a dose of Rheubarb but it came up immediately.

16. The pains increasing with violent reaching he gave me a large dose of Philonsum Romanum and a second in 3 hours which gave me some ease and about 4 a clock I took another dose of physick which had its effect and gave me some ease tho' I did not sleep above 2 hours.

17. Very weak and full of pain tho' I slept this night 4 hours. Very unfit for it but anxious and uneasy to the last degree about my wife I got, or rather was helped, a horseback and rode to Warrington very uneasy and full of paines. Got there about 4 and took a little Rheubarb and went to bed and slept tolerably well and though Cousin Patten and all my friends would have had me staid and sent to my wife I was determined not to put her, in her weak way to such difficultyes that must attend so fatigueing a journey. I therefore set out.

18. Dined at Stockport and went to Buxton. Lay at a Private House very ill. Took my father's Anodyne as was.

19. Much better. Bathed in the Warm Baths which I thought relieved me much.

20. Set out at about 10 and came to Ashbourne. The Talbot. A good Inn. Was taken very ill with the stiches all over me. Went to bed. Took a large draught of Spermacetea Mixture and harts-horn dropps and slept a little.

21. Set out about 10. Much relieved and easier tho' a good deal sore outwardly. Dined at Derby and went to Loughborough. The Post House. A good Inn. A poor Ill Built town.

22. A good deal better. Went to Leicester. A fine old town. Excellent Market famous for a coarse kind of stockings they say returns 100,000 a year in the manufacture there. Dined at the 3 Crowns. An excellent Inn. Took a large dose of Sack Whey, Rheubarb every morning which helps me much.

23. Went to Northampton. To the Angel. Visited Dr. Stonehouse to whom I am to send my father's Parochialia. Lay there.

24. My Birth Day. Went to Stoke Bruern and dined there tolerably well. To Hockley and lay there but indifferently at the White Hart. The Inn being full.

25. Set out and dined at the Bull at St. Alban's and went to Ricks End and lay there much fategued.

26. Staid at Ricks End and in the evening met Mr Moseley and I heard that my poor wife had been under the greatest affliction upon my letters from Warrington and had been herself much out of order.

27. Came, God be thanked, safe to London where I bought many things for my poor father and supped and slept at St. Margaret's Coffee House and wrote to my wife by Mr Moseley who promised to put it into the post. Rested tolerably well.

28. Settled with all the people about mourning and sent my things to Tunbridge. Wrote again to my wife.

29. Sent all my father's things [26] in a box to Liverpool. Set

[26] "*Mem for my father.*
"300 Catechism Books with Short Questions.
Dr Stonehouse's Letter to a Patient. 30.
Watts' Hymns for Children. 100.
Pemberton's Trans. of Dispensatory.
Dr Short on Tea, Sugar and Tobacco.
To send my father Ophiomaches. 20 of the 2nd. Edition for the Clergy, $\frac{1}{2}$ lb. of Red Sealing Wax.
A pair of the lightest and finest small blanketts.
To send my father the Receipt for Gooseberry Vinegar.
12 or 14 Yards of Worsted Cambric for cassocks. Thin and soft.
Philo's Transactions. 3. Vol.
To get my father a pair of spectacles made after that manner. To speak to Mr Freake about it. Athenian Oracle. Vol. I.
Spectacles. To send my father No. 8, 9, 10. In those I sent last he reads better with No. 10. In a black leather case with spring at top. No. 11, 12, 13 in leather case.
Great Importance of a Religious Life. 50.
Christian Monitor. 50.
50 on the Sacrament plus Mr Sketches Devotions by our printer Bartholomew Crew.
Delany on Tithes. Mr Richardson.
25 of each of Mr Bacon's Tracts.
A sett of Jones' Welch Piety.
"*Mem of my father.*
"4 oz of Rheubarb. 3 oz. of Henna. Mr Skeat's Devotions.
Cinnamen. 1 lb.
Nitmeggs. 2 lb.
Mace $\frac{1}{2}$ lb.
Cloves $\frac{1}{2}$ lb.
Pepper 4 lb.

out about 2 and got, God be praised, safe and well to Farn-borough where I lay this night. God be praised for all His mercies.

30. Met my dear wife at Tunbridge Town. Breakfasted there. Rested very ill. Feaverish etc.

31. Eat heartily and was immediately with a vomiting. Drank warm water. Stomack very foul. Much easier and rested by the help of a Sleepy draught.

SEPTEMBER

1. Wrote to Mrs Mills, Mr Gell, Mr Davies and Mr Wood enclosed to Mr Moseley. Looks as if it would rain which will do great good now the harvest is come in well.

2. Was at Church. Very hott and sultry.

3. Wrote to Dr. Hales, Mr Cole and Mr Eyre.

15. My wife was taken this morning with a shivering fit, went to Chappell which was very imprudent, came home ill and went to bed and had a hot fit then sweat naturally. Sent for Dr. J. who found her in a pretty high fever and full of stiches. Gave her Nervous Draughts with Senna Treacle. She sweat freely in the afternoon.

16. My wife had a very restless night and this morning had a blister which did very well and I hope she is better.

18. My wife rested well and the fever being gone she is much better tho' will feel very weak for some time.

20. Great Meeting yesterday of the British Fishery when they nominated to the King Proper Persons to be Governors etc.

"Ginger 2 lb.
Millet 6 lb.
Jordan Almonds 2 lb.
All Spice 1 lb.
Lowth on the Profitable Reading of the Holy Scripture as a present.
A Strait Knee Cap for a swelling to be laced tight.
A Box of Soap for shaving.
2 yds and a $\frac{1}{2}$ of Black Shagg from N. Newey.
Supplement to the Bishop of London's Letter with the Prayers.
A Truss for a Rupture in the left groin. A small swelling and painful at times.
  Kept up with a warm hand."

Some people think it will not do because they can't transfer their Stocks nor can ever sell so cheap as the Dutch. My wife better.

22. My wife took an airing and is upon the whole better. A letter from the Bishop of London. Wrote yesterday to my father, Mr W. Murrey, Mr Sandforth and to Dunhill Macklin etc.

26. A letter from Macklin that the Distemper had got amongst my tenants' cattle. That Worral and Lester had lost 3 and that hardly one in 30 recovered. Wrote to him upon this Melancholly Occasion. To act as the rest of the Landlords do in Wirral. They will suffer greatly and God knows what may be the consequences of it.

OCTOBER

4. Set out with Dr. Johnson for London. Lay at Farnborough.

5. Called upon the Bishop at Bromley.[27] Dined at the King's Head at the Park Gate, a good Inn. Saw the Yachts sail for the King. Spent the evening at St. Margaret's Coffee House. Fine day.

6. In the City. Dined at the Chop House Spring Garden.

7. Preached at Walbrook. Wind and rain. Came home to St. Margaret's.

8. Met the Subscribers to the Fish Market. Agreed for 2 Cod vessels and 2 or 3 Trawlers to come nowhere but the supply of our Market. Raw cold and misling rain.

9. Exceedingly wet and cold. Dined with Mr Gell and one Dr. Wall of Dublin and spent the evening at Dr. Johnson's.

10. Saw Mr Combes who promises to set about the Fish Market as soon as possible. Set out and lay at Farnborough.

11. Came home to dinner. Found my wife pretty well. Very cold.

12. Bad day.

13. Very fine.

[27] Bromley was the residence of the Bishop of Rochester, who so often at this period held the deanery of Westminster *in commendam*.

14. Cold and rainy in the evening.

15. Had 13 gallons of Port Wine from Mr Dowding.

17. Wrote 2 letters to my father about his medling in the clergy's affair tho' he had contrary to my opinion lent them £100 more. Enclosed to Mr Sandforth.

18. Mr Dowding dined with us and Dr. Morley.

19. Wrote to Mr Eyre, Mr Davies.

21. A fine frosty day. Glas falls for rain or snow.

22. Snowed all day very hard. Paid everybody at Tunbridge and sent some things by Hall [28] to the Queen's Head. They will be there on Wednesday 3 a clock afternoon.

23. Set out for Westminster. Letter last week from Macklin that Hanley had lost 4 or 5 and that 3 or 4 were ill. Worral promises to pay his arrears and rent and goes away. Pears intends to take his with ours if I will agree to his leasing some part and marling and building which will cost me £150. But then the whole will be done for 10 or 12 years. A letter from Capt. Fowler at Old Tunns Coffee House that Nat. Wilson behaved very well during the whole voyage and has made many curious observations. Snow 4 inches thick. Set out this morning (fine day). Dined at Farnborough. Came to the New Bridge just before 5. Came over it in chairs and safe at home. God be thanked.

24. Very cold. A letter from my father.

26. Wrote to my father.

28. Preached at my own church. Mr Wilson and Mr Moseley dined with me. Cold.

29. Another letter from my father by one Walker who is come about Col. Stephenson's affair.

30. Mr Wilson brought several things for my wife. He and Mr Davies and Mr Rogers dined here.

31. A fine day. Sent my horse to grass at Hutchinson's this day for the winter.

[28] "Sent by Hall the carrier 23 Oct. 1750. 3 Portmantua Trunks. 5 Deal Boxes. A Hamper."

NOVEMBER

1. Went [29] into residence at Westminster. Dined at Court. Foggy weather.

2. Chapter at Westminster. Dr. Phil. Yonge installed in the room of Dr. Manningham. Dividend £51. 6. 5. Sealing fees 15s. 6d. My very good friend Mr Eyre dyed the 18 Sept. A great loss to his Private Friends as well as to the Publick. Nat. Wilson dined here and brought some more curiosities. Talks of mortgaging his estate and going to try his fortune at Bengal or some other of the Indian Settlements.

4. In Residence at the Abbey. Dr. Yonge, [30] the new prebendary, Mrs Connor and Mrs Blyvers dined with me. The King landed this morning at Harwich at ½ hour after eleven. The messenger brought an account of it at 7 and the King was at St. James's at ½ hour after Ten in good health. Dined with Mr Blydestine.

5. Visited Mr Chauncey in behalf of Mr Wilson who promised to do him all the service in his power and directs him to wait at 12 next wednesday at the India House when I shall be with him. I am to carry him a plan of my Ch. and a coppy of the Grant etc. A letter from Mr Sandforth that Gouldbourn had paid £20 and that the other 10 would be paid in a week owing to a proper letter written to him by Mr Brownel. Mr Sandforth wrote me word that the Distemper amongst the cattle rages violently in those parts especially at Walton etc. Hardly a farmer free. That it returns so often and that it will be a great disadvantage to the Landlords. Mr Chauncey gave me leave to recommend

[29] "*Mem for London.*
"Nov. 1750. To leave all the keys with Mr Catlin. To send to the Brewer to bring 2 barrels of beer, not so harsh as formerly. To leave out coales for all fires. To send my Cocks and Henns from Farnborough by the waggon next week. To bye a Nett to cover the Henns Yard. To bring the curtains out of the drawing room. A Pound of Snuff from Wilson. To send Mr Bingham my nightgown to dye black."

[30] *Dr Philip Yonge*, Master of Jesus College, Cambridge. Bishop of Bristol 1758, Norwich 1761–83.

a chaplain to him for St. Helena and I can procure 2 or 3 Livings for any body of character at Jamaica. All in the gift of the Government.

11. I preached at my own church. Very cold.

14. The King kept his Birth Day. No Ode nor Te Deum nor Speech from the Archbishop. All this by the express orders of the King. A very full Court. Ladies I think too fine.

15. About 8 days ago all the horses almost in the kingdom were seized in one day with a violent cough and running at the nose which took away their stomach and made them so weak that they were hardly able to do any work. We gave ours hot maches and morning and evening a head of Garlick boiled in a quart of milk sweetened with a little honey which has I think done them a great deal of good. If it should be such a distemper as is amongst the cattle we should be a miserable people and we deserve greater punishments for we have not regarded the threatenings of the Almighty. The distemper amongst the cattle increases and spreads now about town. Owing very much to the Jobbers and Drovers driving Scotch cattle thro' the infected countries, all up the south and so carry it as they go along. If they cannot be prevented we shall in all probability never get rid of it.

18. This day (a very improper one) [31] the new Bridge at Westminster was opened. The greatest concourse of people that ever was known on the occasion, being a very fine day. It made it a very idle and drunken one.

19. The Princess of Wales' Birth Day. A very full Court. She entered her 32 year. The gentlemen of this part of Westminster met at the King's Head and dined together and had a large bonfire and Rejoicings on account of the opening of the Bridge. And this day arrived the first fish caught purposely for our Market and sold dear. Some rogueish trick in this which must be prevented.

20. Very cold and hard frost. I called upon Mr Chauncey who had promised what I desire for Nat. Wilson. Mr James the secretary was very civil to me. I wrote tonight and sent a mem-

---

[31] I.e. a Sunday (according to the old Style Calendar).

orial to Mr Gough in Winchester Street which I dare say will be read and signed for him tomorrow.

25. I preached in the morning at St. James's Chappel and read prayers and preached before the Princess at Noon. Fine day. Generally freezes a little every night.

26, 27. At the Society. Agreed about printing a new impression of the Welch Bibles and are to meet again to talk next Tuesday about Mr Baskett's correction, for a great deal will depend upon this the last edition being very incorrect.

28. Terence's Adelphi acted by the King's Scholars [32] for the first time.

30. It began to blow hard this morning and about 12 was a hurricane. A great deal of mischief I fear at sea. The Gravesend Tilt Boat lost 23 men and women. This day I ended my waiting at Court and at Westminster and went thro' it better than I could have imagined.

DECEMBER

2. Met at the Sub Dean's and agreed with Mr Combes and Goodman about the Plan and Buildings for the new Flesh Market and a very compleat thing it will be and pretty near finished I hope by next Michaelmas. They preserve all the old lower vaults and intend to have a new Tavern and Coffee House in the centre. The vaults are themselves worth £40 a year. We have increased our income near £20 a year by this Scheme and they are to pay Rent for the Market from next Michaelmas. Blew hard tonight and looks as if it would rain soon. My wife got cold and feaverish.

3. Preached at Walbrook. Called upon Mr Blydestine, who has failed lately by great losses at sea and in the West Indes where we have crowded the marketts so full, to procure a false credit, that our woollen goods sell cheaper at Jamaica than they cost us at home. He says that if the truth was known it was as bad with many Merchants who look high and live at a great rate which he has never done, baring the expense of a Coach which was his

[32] Westminster Scholars.

wife's fault. In all other respects he had behaved well. Been industrious and saving. But times were never so bad. Money in few hands who make others pay for it. I comforted him as well as I could. My wife a little better with her fever gone off.

4. Rained very hard all last night. Blown a storm at Westminster.

5. Great damage in the Thames. Gravesend Tilt Boat gone down. 23 people drowned.

8. Married Mr Dangerfield to Mrs Eliz. Maynard widow of Rumford. She will be a very good fortune to him and he a sober industrious young fellow. A Broker in Change Alley.

9. At my own Church. Nat. Wilson dined here and would have me bound with him for his good behaviour in £1000 which I declined upon a Promise I made to my father never to be bound to anybody and tho' this may be called a matter of Meer Form yet I cannot take it in this light and many people may be glad to plague a clergyman. Mr Moseley will do it I believe.

10. Audit at Westminster. Dividend £20. We agreed to make one Parson [33] a barber near St. Margaret's Church our Beadle with a salary of £5 instead of £1. 5. 0. the usual salary on condition he will keep the Abbey and Cloysters and Dean's Yard free from vagrants and Beggars with which we are horribly pestered. They forgave Taylor his month upon a Quirk which none else could have found in our late Act at Residence. But we are threatened with a Law Suite if he had not. A great misfortune to any Society to have such a troublesome person in it. The college debt near £1000 which we ought to find some method of paying or else we shall be doubly imposed upon by our Workmen and Tradesmen. We continued the same Treasurer and Taylor steward which will be the last office he will ever be in and can do us no mischief. They continued me Term Lecturer. Dr. Pocock called upon me and promises to see me some evening soon.

11. Called at the Society. The Welch Bibles put to the Press

[33] "10. Dec. 1750. Ordered that the Salary of Mr Richard Parsons the Beadle be augmented to £5 a year and to continue during pleasure" (Chapter Minutes).

and will be printed I hope two years and bound in 2 years and a $\frac{1}{2}$.

12. Our Audit Dinner. Dividend £27. 13. 6.

13. In the Citty. At Justice Fieldings.

14. The darkest and foggiest day I ever saw and must be extreamly unwholesome. Paid my subscription to the Irish Schooles. Last night I talked over the affair of Vice and Immorality with Justice Fielding. The 3 great sources of our present Enormities about this citty are Gin, Gaming and the Infinite Number of Places of Diversion which ruin the Midling Tradesmen. As for Gin the government will never, 'tis feared, prohibit it in earnest while it brings in so prodigious a Revenue, upwards of £200,000 a year. The other two something may be done. But all will not do till the poor are in earnest set to work all over the Kingdom. And if this could be brought about in earnest there would not be time to get drunk and follow wicked diversions which Lord Chief Justice Hales and Sir Josiah Child just hinted at. He thinks he has brought into a system. and when it is called for by our Great Men will be ready for them. In the meantime he will publish a little pamphlet to introduce it. I wrote an account of the conversation to the Bishop of Worcester at Hartlebury who is going to print his excellent Spittal Sermon preached last year at St. Bride's with an appendix relating to Gin etc. Dr. Hales, Myself and Mr Tucker of Bristoll to be assisting in this. We must do what we can and leave the event to God. He, Mr F., divides the poor into 3 classes. 1. Those that by accident or sickness are prevented from working are now happily provided for by the Hospitals and Infirmarys. 2. Those that are able and willing and have not proper employment. 3. Those that are able but not willing who should be obliged by correction to become usefull members of the Common Wealth. And this can never be done by single workhouses. So that very few from 5 years old to 70 but what may give a livlyhood. The consequence would be saving half a Million a year to the Poor Rate and the saving of 100ds. of souls and Bodies. Preventing a great many executions for the lesser crimes and clearing our streets of beggars and being able to undersell to our neighbours in those Manufactures for which we are remarkably deficient. It would lower workmen's wages and make them labour 6 days in the week when they now hardly work 3. Something of this kind must be done or else we shall be undone in a few years. The new Manufacture of Herring Netts would emply 200,000 Men, Women and Children. The Charity Schooles as well as the Parish Poor may all be enclosed in this scheme. Whether our Great Men are disposed yet to attend to such satisfactory fiscal schemes God only knows. We must do our duty and leave the Issue to the Great Governor of the World.

15. Dr. Ayscough and Dr. Brisconden visited me and I went with them to the Play of the Adelphi which was extreamly well acted by the Westminster Ladds. Duchess of Bedford, Portland and People of Great Rank being present. Commissioners of the Bridge agreed yesterday that we should have full possession of the ground for the Fish Market 2 months hence, which is a vast inconvenience to us for we should have it immediately for our erections. But they were never our friends. This day a little better than yesterday. The glass high but extreamly foggy. Visited Sir Jno. Cross. Not at home.

19. Visited Sir James Lowther in Queens Square. He is surprisingly well, especially to have a legg cut off at over 80 owing to his great temperance. The old gentlemen is strongly of the opinion that we are undone as a Nation, or shall be in a few years under the heels of France thanks to the excess of Gaming and Diversions of all kinds. Seems to be glad that he has a little longer of life allowed him [34] to do more good in, and I hope he will be extreamly charitable. He has many virtues but a little too near. I think he intends extream kind things for Col. Stephenson who constantly attends him and really deserves all he will leave him. Very bad foggy weather for this last week but now I believe set in for a hard frost.

20. A fine frosty morning and I think likely to continue. I buried this evening Mrs Jennings, daughter to Sir Samuel Mayer, in my chancel. She has left the bulk of her fortune to her niece

[34] Sir James Lowther, Bt. Died in January 1755, his estates passing to James Lowther, Earl of Lonsdale.

Lady Harcourt. This is my dear father's Birth Day when he enters his 88th. year. May he live long to do much good and be a blessing and comfort to his friends.

21. The Ballot for a Physitian at the Infirmary in James Street. Dr. Cox [35] carried it against Pringle [36] by a majority of 58. The greatest contest for a thing of this nature I have heard of. Duke of Newcastle, Mr Pelham, Princess Amelia for Dr. Cox and Duke of Cumberland, Bedford etc. for Pringle who was Physitian to the Army. People threatened for not voting on one side that they shoud lose the Duke of C's business. Strange way of treating mankind. Our Church and dependants all voted I believe for Dr. Cox who is a man of good sense and religion.

22. Mr Cossart here and a gentleman from Boston about building the King's Chappel there which will cost £5000 sterling. Dr. Pocock [37] called upon me and tells me that there is one Dr. Parsons [38] a Physitian writing a very ingenious book upon the Immortality of the Soules of Brutes which he thinks may be of use. I question it much. The weather foggy. People in general ill of colds.

23. At Walbrook. Dined with Mr Chauncey, who wishes that the government had kept 4s. in the pound for 7 years and applied the whole Sinking Fund towards paying off some of the most burdensome taxes that affect Trade and the Poor. Thinks it will be but 2 next year and yet says they are far from being clear of the expenses of the War and incurring new ones every day. One thing the landed gentlemen are greatly assisted by the government and as in generally attended to and that is in the Bounty

[35] Dr William Coxe, physician to the Royal Household. His son, Archdeacon Coxe (1747–1828) was the historian of the period in *The Memoirs of Sir Robt. Walpole* (1798).

[36] Sir John Pringle (1707–82) was physician to the King and to other members of the Royal Family; F.R.S. 1772. Chiefly famous for his reforms of military medicine and sanitation. His *Observations on the Diseases of the Army* (1752) having a European reputation.

[37] Richard Pocock, D.C.L., Bishop of Ossory 1756, Meath 1765.

[38] James Parsons (1705–70), F.R.S., F.S.A. Possibly the book referred to was *Philosophical Observations on the Analogy Between the Propagation of Animals and that of Vegetables* (*with remarks on the Polypus*), 1752.

upon the Exportation of the Grain, without which they could not support themselves, as it is considering the Distemper of the cattle has ruined so many farmers which will fall in the end upon the Landlords. If our Government do not take care of the Industry and Sobriety of the Common People we shall soon be ruined without any forreign enemies. Gaming and Luxury and Extravagance amongst the great being never at a higher nor more shameful height. No government upon earth but ours would suffer such a place as White's Chocolate House in the sight of the Court. All Nations besides our own if we are informed right are putting a stop to Rioting and Gaming and are making a Proclamation of £100 Reward for apprehending the Notorious Street Robbers that infest our town. It is high time indeed but what then? They won't strike at the Root—Gin and Gaming.

CHRISTMAS DAY. At my own Church. A large regular congregation.

26. Dined at Mrs Blyvers. Mr and Mrs Blomfield. A very warm, unwholesome foggy day with Misling Rain.

27. Mrs Levett tells me that her husband was brother to the Duchess of Kendal in the year 20 and that by her being let into the secret she and some Germans got immense sums even to the last moment in that Knavish Year. It was all done in other people's names.

28. This day I had a letter from Mr Joynes of Gravesend desiring I would stand God father to his son, who he intends to call Thomas Wilson Joynes and which I have consented to and wrote to him accordingly. His father in law Mr Leigh of Itham is to be the other. A fine warm day. Wind S.W. Rained in the night.

Select Index of Names and Places

Only the more important persons mentioned in the Diary are included in this index and for them only the more significant references; similarly only the places of particular significance in the life and career of Dr Thomas Wilson are included.

261

INDEX

Tomo Chichi, 117
Trebeck, Andrew, 115
Tubb, Mr, 72
Tullibardine, Marquis of, 42
Tunbridge Wells, 12, 26, 28, 160-8, 237, 250
Twells, Leonard, 57
Tyrwhit, Dr, 92

Upton, John, 75

Vesey, William, 54

Wade, General, 108, 206
Wade, Mr, 93
Wake, Dr William, Archbishop of Canterbury, 189, 190
Walker, Dr John, 123
Walpole, Sir Edward, 110
Walpole, Horace, 17, 28
Walpole, Horatio, 110
Walpole, Sir Robert, 110, 114, 125, 134, 162, 163, 164, 199, 200, 203
Walton, 37
Warrington, Lord, 35
Waterland, Dr Daniel, 53, 57, 76
Watson, Dr Joseph, 201, 209, 211, 218, 219

Watts, Isaac, 27, 139, 145, 155, 175
Watts, Mr, 152, 216
Wesley, Charles, 72
Wesley, John, 25, 26, 72, 135, 146
Westminster, 11, 12
Whiston, William, 213
Wilbraham, Henry, 54
Wildair, John, 25, 50, 63
Wilkes, John, 15, 18
Willis, Browne, 71
Willis, Richard, Bishop of Winchester, 59, 87, 118, 130
Wilson, Joseph, 33
Wilson, Mary (wife of Dr Wilson), 25, 44, 102, 103, 104, 113, 114, 121, 122, 123, 147
Wilson, Mary (wife of Bishop Wilson), 2, 7
Wilson, Thomas, Bishop, *passim*
Wilson, Thomas (son of Dr Wilson), 121, 152, 153
Winwick, 2, 34
Woodforde, James, 27, 28
Woolston, Thomas, 92

Yonge, Dr Philip, 253

Ziegenhagen, Mr, 205